FRESH FRUIT AND VINTAGE WINE

Fresh Fruit
&
Vintage Wine

*The Ethics and Wisdom
of the Aggada*

Yitzchak Blau

KTAV Publishing House, Inc.
In Association With
OU Press and Yeshivat Har Etzion

Library of Congress Cataloging-in-Publication Data

Blau, Yitzchak.
Fresh fruit and vintage wine: the ethics and wisdom of the Aggada /
Yitzchak Blau.
    p. cm.
Includes bibliographical references and index.
ISBN 978-1-60280-008-3 (alk. paper)
1. Aggada – History and criticism. 2. Jewish ethics. I. Title.
    BM516.5.B59 2009
    296.1'27606 – dc22

2009024837

Published by
Ktav Publishing House, Inc.
930 Newark Avenue, Jersey City, NJ 07306
orders@ktav.com · www.ktav.com
(201) 963-9524 · Fax (201) 963-0102

ISBN 978-1-60280-008-3

Typeset in Minion Pro by KPS

Support me with wine; comfort me with apples, for I am sick with love.

– Shir haShirim 2:5

R. Yizhak Napha opened his discourse as follows: "Support me with wine. This refers to halakhot that strengthen. Comfort me with apples. This refers to aggadot which have a sweet smell like apples."

– Soferim 16: 4

CONTENTS

🌳 Chapter 3: Festivals

🌳 Chapter 4: Learning

🌳 Chapter 5: Education

🌳 **Chapter 6: Interpersonal Obligations**

🌳 **Chapter 7: Character Traits**

🌳 **Chapter 8: Speech**

🌳 **Chapter 9: Halakhic Observance**

🌳 Chapter 10: Jewish Philosophy

🌳 Chapter 11: A Balanced Religious Life

🌳 Chapter 12: The Goal of Life

🌳 **Chapter 13: Modernity**

🌳 **Chapter 14: Leadership**

🌳 **Chapter 15: Conclusion**

PREFACE

Halakha and *Aggada* are often mistakenly considered to be two separate realms. However, in truth, each informs the other, and it is for this reason that both are integrated into the discussion and discourse of the Talmud. An authentic Jewish philosophy must be rooted, Rabbi Soloveitchik believed, in both the *Halakha* and the *Aggada*. Indeed, the Rav said that the *Aggada* is the *Halakha* of Jewish thought. This new volume, *Fresh Fruit and Vintage Wine*, gives us an opportunity to delve deeper into the meaning of the *Aggada* and thereby to be inspired by its lessons and guided by its teachings.

OU Press is committed to serving as a platform for young, distinguished scholars. Rabbi Yitzchak Blau is a rising star in the world of Jewish scholarship and education. His book is an important contribution toward increasing interest in the crucial area of *Aggada*. Rabbi Blau not only gives readers a clear and concise overview of the spiritual insights of the Sages, he shows how these ideas are relevant to the struggles we all face in contemporary life. This is a book about the timeless wisdom of Torah and how to apply its messages in all ages and circumstances.

Knowing Rabbi Blau's substantial talents, I am confident that we will continue to encounter his scholarship and insights in the years to come, and that this book – the first fruits of his labors – will guide students and scholars toward a deeper understanding of the words of the Sages.

Menachem Genack
General Editor of ou Press
10 Av 5769 / July 31, 2009

AUTHOR'S PREFACE

I n what way are the principles of Jewish law similar to wine, whereas the issues of theology and ethics found in aggadot resemble apples? R. Barukh Epstein offers an interesting explanation in his *Tosefet Berakha*. Wine gets better with age, but fruit is at its best when fresh. In the same way, Halakha speaks with an ongoing consistency, and the older the halakhic source, the more legally authoritative. Although new historical situations generate novel halakhic questions and formulations, a remarkable consistency exists in the legal realm. Questions such as what to do when a drop of milk falls into the cholent or who is eligible to serve as a *shohet* have not changed in the last fifteen hundred years. Halakha resembles wine with regard to the primacy of older material. Aggada, on the other hand, always must speak in the idiom of the age. Only a Jewish thought that successfully relates to the cultural currents of the day can address our community's most pressing issues and influence the multitudes. Therefore, we search for freshness in aggadot, just as we do when choosing apples.

R. Epstein's analysis sounds an authentic chord. Indeed, the sermons of R. Nissim of Gerondi and R. Moshe Sofer differ far more than their halakhic discussions. This reflects the vastly different intellectual currents these two luminaries contended with in their sermons. The intellectual challenges of fourteenth-century Spain were not the same as those of nineteenth-century Hungary. The different ideologies and personalities of the rabbis also played a role. As R. Avraham Bloch noted, aggadic discussion often relates to the individual's personality and ideology more profoundly than halakhic issues do (see *Torah u'Madda Journal* 1, p. 2). The personal quality of aggadic issues can also affect how a rabbi responds to individuals asking him questions. For example, a rabbi might give the same answer to anyone who asked him how to serve hot tea on Shabbat. However, he might not offer the same answer to two questioners asking about the balance between human initiative and divine activity.

Of course the distinction must not be drawn too sharply. Halakhic discussions and rulings also reveal something about the personalities of their authors. Nor has talmudic methodology remained static over the last thousand years of Jewish history. Like Aggada, Halakha also allows for individual expression and partakes of freshness and novelty. Conversely, the Aggada also incorporates consistency and objectivity. Intellectual trends may change, but certain underlying Jewish beliefs and ideals remain constant. Our tradition includes a consistent core of fundamental beliefs and moral ideals, even though terminology and subsidiary values change. We may no longer be able to envision the cosmos in terms of Aristotelian separate intellects, as Rambam did, but Rambam's writings on ethics and the reasons for the commandments continue to instruct and inspire. Thus, Aggada must be thought of as both a well-aged wine and a juicy fruit just plucked from the tree.

This work attempts to study Aggada with an eye to the needs of both tradition and novelty. The novelty is dual. Some of the aggadic readings in this volume address specific intellectual and social challenges of the modern world. As mentioned above, works of Jewish thought usually confront some of the challenges of the day.

In addition, the very focus on Aggada represents something of a novelty. The world of contemporary yeshivot tends to emphasize study of the halakhic sections of Talmud. Indeed, when the class reaches an aggadic section, many *rabbeim* choose to either skip the section entirely or to read it through quickly and perfunctorily in order to get back to the meat and potatoes of Jewish legal study. Nor is the bias in favor of halakhic sections a recent phenomenon. Many of the great medieval and modern commentators focused their interpretive energies almost exclusively on the legal sections. A brief glance at the standard Vilna *Shas* confirms this point. Aggadic pages contain many more words than halakhic pages because the scholars of the Tosafot school, whose comments on halakhic sections take up significant room on the talmudic page, said little about aggadic passages, thereby leaving more room for talmudic text.

If focusing on Aggada and confronting contemporary issues reveals freshness, other aspects of this book draw upon the wisdom of the old. In fact, the central methodological claim of this book is that the history of traditional aggadic interpretation proves tremendously helpful both for understanding the aggadic sections and for attaining wisdom relevant to our own time. Many students of Aggada fail to appreciate this point. Some very fine interpretations of Aggada appear in the writings of contemporary academics like Yonah Frankel and Jeffrey Rubenstein. Their approach employs various literary and historical techniques in a productive fashion. They also tend to approach the talmudic text mostly unaided by the wisdom embodied in the last fifteen hundred years of rabbinic writing. I contend that readers of aggadic texts who fail to utilize the history of rabbinic commentary are ignoring a treasure trove of profound insight. Despite the gaps in time and the changes in intellectual and cultural life, these insights of our luminaries speak tellingly to the issues that confront us today. A sharp insight from a medieval source still satisfies like good Bordeaux.

In fact, the study of Aggada is not fully novel. Aggada may not have received the same kind of attention as the legal sections, but some of the best Jewish minds have devoted considerable attention to it. The commentaries of R. Shemuel Edels (Maharsha), R. Yehuda Loewe (Maharal), R. Yosef Hayyim (*Ben Yehoyada*), and the collection of commentaries in the *Ein Yaakov* come immediately to mind. R. Avraham Yizhak haKohen Kook wrote an extremely helpful commentary on the aggadot of *Berakhot* and *Shabbat*. As we shall see, good commentary can be found in some less obvious places as well. Thus, the current interest in Aggada reflects an older tradition as well as new emphases.

Rabbis and scholars sometimes overlook this material because they do not know where to find it. With regard to halakhic texts, the classic medieval and modern commentaries are quite well known in the yeshiva world. Nor is it their fame alone that makes them accessible. They tend to be running commentaries on the tractate and can therefore be located quite easily by checking the commentary on a specific page of Talmud. With regard to Aggada, the yeshiva world does not have a storehouse of traditional material, so that finding the excellent material that does exist proves far more difficult. The classic *rishonim* are frequently silent. My impression is that certain *aharonim*, including R. Yehuda Leib of Gur (*Sefat Emet*), R. Yizhak of Karlin (*Keren Ora*), R. Arye Leib Gunzberg (*Turei Even* and *Gevurat Ari*), R. Yaakov Ettlinger (*Arukh laNer*), R. Moshe Sofer (*Hatam Sofer*), R. Yehoshua Falk (*Pnei Yehoshua*), and R. Yehezkel Landau (*Ziyyun leNefesh Hayah*), devote much more space to aggadic passages than do their medieval counterparts (see my "Aggada and *Aharonim*" for some examples). As many serious Talmudists do not always check these works, they miss out on invaluable resources for understanding Aggada.

Furthermore, much significant discussion does not appear in page-by-page talmudic commentaries, but in philosophic or theological works, collections of sermons, Hasidic homilies, works of Mussar, commentaries on the Torah, and the like. Clearly, finding such material demands a much greater effort and a far more wide-ranging search. I hope that this book will help convince the reader that the effort is well worth it. The collected writings of R. Meir Simha haKohen of Dvinsk, R. Yosef Dov Soloveitchik, R. Yizhak Hutner, R. Zadok haKohen of Lublin, and R. Yehiel Yaakov Weinberg, among others, will prove extremely helpful even if they did not include their insights in commentaries on the talmudic page.

Our wider scope will also extend to the best works of Western literature. The wisdom of Søren Kierkegaard, C.S. Lewis, and others helps illuminate our path toward an understanding of the Aggada. R. Joseph B. Soloveitchik and, *yibadlu le'hayyim*, R. Aharon Lichtenstein and R. Shalom Carmy, have shown how much the Torah learning community has to gain from an exposure to a broader education. Indeed, we should appreciate the help that those outside of the Jewish tradition can offer when thinking about matters of the soul and the religious personality. While the wine of our rabbinic luminaries is our main focus, it will be served with fruit sometimes plucked from the trees of Western literature.

Focusing on aggadot plays an important role in meeting some contemporary challenges in Jewish education. Many students have difficulty finding religious meaning in the talmudic debates about the finer points of Jewish law. They feel that religious experience gets lost in the minutiae of technical details. Introducing more Aggada into Gemara study will help our students realize that the sages of the Talmud also grappled with the perennial ethical and theological conundrums. The same rabbis who tried to determine when various vessels are considered finished products for the purposes of ritual purity also discussed the proper balance between truth and peace and debated the conundrum of the problem of evil. Exposing our students to this material will enhance their respect for Gemara and have a helpful trickle-down impact on their study of halakhic material.

Elsewhere (see my "Redeeming the Aggadah in Yeshivah Education" in *Wisdom from All My Teachers*), I have highlighted some of the educational issues pertaining to a renewed commitment to Aggada in our curriculum, so I will not rehash them here. Permit me to add one more argument for including Aggada in any Gemara class, be it in elementary school, high school, or a yeshiva for older students. This inclusion hearkens back to the bold decision of the *amoraim* to incorporate the aggadic material in the Talmud. Ravina, Rav Ashi, and other talmudic redactors could easily have chosen to compile a totally separate aggadic work. Instead, they decided to integrate aggadic and halakhic material within the same work. Thus, the student studying a tractate devoted to the laws of *eruvin* suddenly encounters a discussion about the relationship between conflicting legal opinions and halakhic truth and a debate regarding whether or not it was better for man to have been created (*Eruvin* 13b). Apparently, our sages wanted Talmud students not only to encounter both types of material but also to see them as jointly forming an integrated whole. Our community will benefit greatly from following their model.

Perhaps somewhat arbitrarily, I have limited this volume to aggadot found in the Babylonian Talmud. The limitation does not reflect any position on the relative status of these aggadot in comparison to those found in the Yerushalmi or in various midrashim. A simple educational perspective dictated the decision. Our educational institutions dedicate great time and energy to the Bavli, and I want to encourage the equal application of energy to the aggadic materials in the very same volumes. Those studying the different categories of tort law should turn a few pages (to fol. 17a) and confront *Bava Kuma*'s perspective on different routes to piety. Aggadic material found in other works certainly merits careful study as well.

Most of the translations of talmudic passages are my own although I did occasionally consult with the Soncino and Schottenstein editions.

I hope that my readers will not object to the didactic tone of the essays. From my perspective, the wisdom that matters most is the wisdom that teaches us how to live religiously and morally better lives. The authors of these texts composed them with such edification in mind. Of course, offering guidance need not entail exhortations on the obvious. My readings attempt to extract guidance while avoiding the pitfall of excessive preaching.

The quest for religious insight also guided the interpretations. If an individual commentary said something profound and instructive, that was reason for inclusion even if the interpretation might not reflect the simplest reading of the Gemara's words. In our tradition, the thought of rabbinic luminaries has value in its own right that justifies incorporating their intelligence and insight when possible. However, I did avoid more fanciful interpretations, such as those found in the works of R. Nahman of Breslav, which totally ignore the basic meaning of the Aggada's language.

I organized the work topically rather than based on location in the Talmud. Those interested in aggadot from a given tractate can avail themselves of the talmudic index at the end of this volume. As most of the categorical divisions designated by the chapter headings are self-explanatory, I will here mention only those that require elucidation. "Learning" refers to issues that emerge from the encounter with the traditional texts per se, while "Education" addresses questions specific to a yeshiva or school setting. "Halakhic Observance" confronts broader themes in the religious Jew's commitment to an extensive system of law. "A Balanced Religious Life" deals with conflicting impulses and ideals. "The Goal of Life" takes on questions relating to our conception of human flourishing. Finally, "Modernity" addresses problems that modernity has highlighted.

"If you want to recognize the One who spoke and the world came into being, learn Aggada" (*Sifrei, Devarim* 49). This work attempts to serve that goal by expanding the recommended method to achieve it. "If you want to comprehend the wisdom of our tradition on such issues as the nature of religious leadership, educational philosophy, the purpose of prayer, the dangers of arrogance, the balancing of competing values, and on making difficult decisions, then study the Aggada with the best of rabbinic commentary." I hope that this work will prod our educational institutions and our community toward renewed and enriched interest in the treasures of Aggada.

I have been truly blessed with regard to family, friends, teachers, colleagues, and students. My parents, Rabbi Yosef and Dr. Rivkah Blau, are both world-renowned educators and extremely loving parents. I heard a great deal of insight into Jewish education while sitting at the dining room table or on the living room couch. My father is one of the most courageous and morally sensitive voices of contemporary Orthodoxy. My mother combines aristocratic dignity with tremendous human warmth.

My two brothers, Rabbis Binyamin and Yaakov Blau, fabulously successful educators in their own right, have always been wonderful sources of support, encouragement, and wisdom. They are like best friends as well as brothers. I thank their wives, Faith and Sara, for adding much happiness and compassion to our family. I also thank my in-laws, Aryeh and Sura Jeselsohn, both for their support and for their bringing Noa into this world. Thanks to them and to Natan, Tova, Adam, and Adina for creating a warm and caring family atmosphere.

At the Mesivta of Long Beach and at Toras Moshe, I learned about the immense value of time and the need to not waste it. When I came to Yeshivat Har Etzion, R. Aharon Lichtenstein had a profound effect on my intellectual and religious growth. R. Lichtenstein's *shiurim* awakened my intellectual yearning, while his *sihot* inspired my religious passions. I consider myself fortunate to have heard so many hours of Torah from such a profoundly special person.

At Yeshiva University, R. Michael Rosensweig and Dr. David Berger were important sources of my ongoing education. The two figures who had the greatest impact were Rabbi Shalom Carmy and Dr. Will Lee (see my essay "Two Outstanding Educators" in *My Yeshiva College*). Both taught excellent classes, and both cared far more about student development than about publishing and academic politics. I actually took the two of them for a joint total of fourteen courses. Rabbi Carmy continues to be one of my main sources of friendship and wisdom. I thank both of them for commenting on the manuscript, and I emphasize that Dr. Lee's comments improved the writing of nearly every chapter.

In this context, I would also like to mention the fine copy editing provided by KTAV's Robert Milch. In general, KTAV and Mr. Bernie Scharfstein were a pleasure to work with. I would also like to thank the OU Press for their participation in the publication of this book.

My social and intellectual companions over the years have been of the finest quality. They all encouraged my writing. I thank David Glatt, Eli Razin, Avi Shmidman and Rabbis Josh Amaru, David Brofsky, David Debow, Seth Farber, Zvi Hirshfield, Robert Klapper, and Chanoch Waxman. Two friends deserve special thanks for a more direct role in the creation of this book. Rabbi Jeffrey Saks edited *Wisdom from All My Teachers*, which included my first published essay on Aggada. Rabbi Ronnie Ziegler arranged for me to write an Aggada *shiur* for the Har Etzion Virtual Beit Midrash which provided the raw material for this book. In this context, I also thank the VBM administration and ATID for permission to reuse the material. The VBM's editors and the comments of its readers greatly aided my efforts.

I thank the editors of *Tradition* and the *Torah U-Madda Journal* for providing me with a forum for publishing articles on Jewish thought. Dr. David Shatz, editor of the latter, has been a wonderful source of encouragement, advice, and humor. The many serious, thoughtful, and morally sensitive people in Alon Shevut, especially those who live on our block, provide a different kind of forum for my thinking about Torah.

I have now spent more than fourteen years of my teaching career in two excellent institutions. My colleagues at the Yeshivah of Flatbush High School thought seriously about educational issues and generated a pleasant work environment. Rabbi David Eliach was a supportive principal, and Dr. Joel Wolowelsky provided insightful advice. Yeshivat Hamivtar also enabled participation in a sterling staff. Rabbi Chaim Brovender was a *rosh yeshiva* who enabled his rabbinic staff to flourish. Lunch table discussions with Rabbis Dovid Ebner and Menachem Schrader were enjoyable and educational. Both are sensitive readers of Aggada who should publish their own interpretations.

Almost all of the material in this book was taught at Yeshivat Hamivtar over the years. Although I thank every Hamivtar student from the last decade, I will only mention by name those with whom I had an Aggada-related *chavruta*. Learning with Yaakov Cohen, Ira Dounn, Eddie Farbenblum, Aaron Finkelstein, Etai Lahav, Steve Nadel, Yoel Oz, Yedidya Rausman, Benyamin Ron, Josh Rosenbloom, Michael Rosenfeld, Josh Rosenthal, Dovid Ruderman, Moshe Sasson, Zev Stender, Yonatan Udren, David Wolkenfeld, Ben Wahlhaus, and Shmuly Yanklowitz helped invaluably in producing this book. Marc Herman, David Perkel, and Brahm Weinberg also provided good feedback. I particularly thank Rabbi Gabe Pransky for years of intelligent comments on the *divrei Torah* I delivered at the yeshiva.

Having saved the best for last, I now thank my family. Zecharya, Mordechai, Zadok, and Tehilla teach me new things every day in a great variety of ways. Zecharya and Mordechai have already joined the Aggada conversation. Whether at the Shabbat table or on the long drive to the Basketball Hall of Fame, their interpretations of talmudic stories give me great joy. I look forward to many years of learning with all of my children.

Finally, I express my deepest gratitude to my wonderful wife, Noa, and I dedicate this book to her. She is a terrific life partner for all endeavors, be they intellectual or social, religious or recreational, communal or domestic, sublime or mundane. "Her mouth opens with wisdom, and the Torah of compassion is on her tongue."

CHAPTER 1

Aggada

Halakha and Aggada

R. Ami and R. Assi were sitting before R. Yizhak Napha. One
said to him: "Let the master teach Halakha"; the other said to
him: "Let the master teach Aggada." He started to teach Aggada,
and one student did not let him proceed; he started to teach
Halakha, and the other student did not let him proceed.

He said to them: "I will give you a parable for comparison
to this matter: A man had two wives, one older and one
younger. Since the younger wife plucked out his white hairs,
and the older wife plucked out his black hairs, the two of them
made him bald.

"That being the case, I will teach something that will
please both of you. *If a fire goes out and finds thorns* (*Shemot*
22:6) – even though the fire goes out on its own, the person
who kindled the fire must nevertheless pay. So the Holy One,
blessed be He, says: 'I must pay for the fire that I kindled. I lit a
fire in Zion, as it says: *He kindled a fire in Zion and it consumed
the foundations* (*Eikha* 4:11); I will, in the future, rebuild it with

1

fire as it says: *And I will be for her…a surrounding wall of fire, and I will be the glory in her midst (Zekharya 2:9)*. The halakhic part is as follows: Scripture begins with damages caused by a person's property and then concludes with damages caused by the person himself. This teaches that one's fire is considered like one's arrow."

(Bava Kama 6ob)

The teacher, R. Yizhak Napha, is stymied by a voting deadlock: one student insists on hearing Halakha, matters of Jewish law; the other student demands Aggada, stories and maxims of a nonlegal nature. After stating his parable, R. Yizhak offers as a compromise a verse that incorporates both halakhic and aggadic material. Let us focus on the parable: Is it just a striking image to lightly chide his students, or is there a deeper correspondence between the *mashal* (parable) and the *nimshal* (moral)?

R. Yehiel Yaakov Weinberg offers a remarkable reading of this story in his *LiFrakim* (p. 333). He begins by contrasting the qualities of Halakha and Aggada. The former represents tradition and consistency: we Jews today practice the same daily rituals that our ancestors observed for centuries; these rituals provide the bedrock of stability upon which to build our Jewish lives. Aggada, on the other hand, represents freshness and fiery enthusiasm; while Judaism relies on a set of concrete, unchanging beliefs, its philosophical expression often employs the idiom of the time to convey its ideals. Thus, Aggada will frequently allow for novelty in a way that Halakha does not. Furthermore, aggadic discussions often inspire youthful enthusiasm in a way that Halakha does not.

The older woman in the parable represents Halakha. She insists on the consistency and stability of tradition, the white hairs. The younger woman represents Aggada. She champions the black hairs – the freshness and vitality of new insights as well as the inner soul of observance. R. Yizhak explains to his students that each of them has too narrow a view of Torah. Without Halakha, one will not have a solid foundation upon which to build a Jewish life, for the grand ideas of Aggada cannot easily be translated into concrete practice. Conversely, Halakha bereft of Aggada would be dry, soulless, and flaccid.

The closing verse of R. Yizhak Napha's parable emphasizes the need for integration. God speaks of a "wall of fire": the protective wall of Halakha and the burning flames of Aggada jointly provide the framework for a Jewish life that combines tradition with novelty and stability with enthusiasm.

Cheap Trinkets, Expensive Stones, and the Aggada

> R. Abbahu and R. Hiyya bar Abba arrived in a certain town [and there gave public lectures]. R. Abbahu taught Aggada, and R. Hiyya bar Abba taught Halakha. Everyone left R. Hiyya bar Abba and went to R. Abbahu. [R. Hiyya] became depressed.
>
> [R. Abbahu] said to him: "I will give you a parable to compare to this matter. There were two merchants, one who sold precious stones and the other who sold notions [inexpensive items, such as needles]. Whom did people jump on [i.e., buy from]? Was it not the one who sold notions?"
>
> Every day, R. Hiyya bar Abba would accompany R. Abbahu back to his lodgings to honor the house of the emperor. [R. Abbahu was a favorite of the royal family.] On that day, R. Abbahu was the one to accompany R. Hiyya back to his lodgings, but even so, [the latter] was not appeased.
>
> (*Sota* 40a)

R. Abbahu tries valiantly but unsuccessfully to appease R. Hiyya after the latter finds an empty shul, in sharp contrast to the packed hall awaiting R. Abbahu. He walks R. Hiyya home and employs a parable to encourage his colleague to feel better. *Ein Yaakov* cites a different version of the text in which the phrase *amar la'hem* ("he said to them") precedes the parable. In our version, R. Abbahu offers this parable only to his friend. According to the *Ein Yaakov*,

R. Abbahu says it to the townspeople during his discourse as a form of subtle chiding.

What is R. Abbahu's parable meant to convey? As R. Hanokh Zundel of Salant points out in his *Ez Yosef*, R. Abbahu presumably does not intend to denigrate the study of Aggada; after all, he himself is teaching this very subject. When he says that Aggada resembles the cheap items, he means this only in the sense that they are more easily acquired, not because they are light in value. In other words, people choose the Aggada *shiur* because they prefer a light story to the intricacies of Jewish law. However, popular choice may not reflect authentic worth.

Two important principles emerge from this parable. First, in all areas of education, we should take care not to think that the best teacher is the one who is the most popular. All things being equal, it is certainly a good thing for a teacher to be liked. However, popularity can be achieved in all kinds of educationally dubious ways. A teacher can achieve popularity by being too easy on the students, telling them inappropriate jokes, always siding with them against the administration, or encouraging them to adopt the arrogant attitude that only in his classroom is the truth being taught. All of these methods ultimately harm the educational process. Popularity and quality teaching are quite different things.

We should also be wary of popularity in the narrower realm of Aggada. If we treat Aggada as light stories for easy entertainment, then we do not do them justice. If, on the contrary, we truly sweat to plumb the depths of the Aggada, we may lose some students, but we will gain in understanding. Our interest in Aggada must rest upon the realization that appreciating stories also demands hard work. In this anecdote, a deeper appreciation of the meaning should motivate us to find the subtleties of each and every talmudic narrative.

CHAPTER 2

Prayer

The Purpose of Prayer

> And God said to Moshe: *Why do you cry out to me? Speak to the children of Israel, and they will go forward* (*Shemot* 14:15).
>
> At that moment [when the Jews seemed trapped between the Egyptians and the sea], Moshe was prolonging his prayer. The Holy One, blessed be He, said to Moshe: "My beloved ones are drowning in the sea, and you are prolonging your prayer before Me?"
>
> Moshe said: "Master of the Universe, what is in my power to do?"
>
> He said to him: *Speak to the children of Israel, and they will go forward.*
>
> (*Sota* 37a)

Before commenting on this gemara, we should note that not every commentator agrees that Moshe was engaged in supplication. R. Avraham Ibn Ezra points out that Hashem had already informed

Moshe that Pharaoh would pursue them (see *Shemot* 14:4), so the pursuit should not have caused Moshe any concern. He argues that the people had cried out to God, and God speaks to Moshe as their representative.

Ramban raises the same objection as Ibn Ezra, but offers a different solution. Moshe knew that Pharaoh would pursue them, but he did not know what he was supposed to do when this happened. He cries out to Hashem in order to find out what action to take. Hashem answers that Moshe should have simply asked the question; there was no need to cry out.

An important point emerges from Ramban's analysis. A person who is given a prophetic promise does not know exactly how that promise will play itself out. Thus, drama, suspense, and difficulties remain part of the process, even if the process reflects the realization of a larger prophetic vision. Were this not so, those engaged in helping to actualize a prophecy would not be exhibiting any heroism. Ramban's view, on the other hand, leaves individuals working with prophetic knowledge the leeway to express their courage and wisdom.

Rashi paraphrases a midrash (*Mekhilta* 3) quite similar to the gemara in *Sota*. According to Rashi, Hashem says: "This is not the time for a lengthy prayer, because Israel is in dire straits." This approach differs from that of our other commentators. According to Ibn Ezra, Moshe did not pray at all; Ramban maintains that Moshe did indeed pray, but should simply have asked God what to do. Rashi, following *Hazal*, understands that the problem lies in the duration of Moshe's prayer in the given circumstances.

This raises the question: what is wrong with a protracted prayer? A simple explanation might be that dangerous situations call for an active response, and long entreaties delay taking the necessary actions. If so, this gemara might relate to the need for people to solve problems using human initiative and working within the natural order. The religious individual responds to danger with both prayer and human deeds. Hashem tells Moshe that in such a situation, the need for action mandates a shortened prayer.

R. Yizhak Hutner (*Pahad Yizhak, Pesah* 14) discovers another approach in the commentary of Maharal (*Gur Aryeh, Shemot* 14:15). Maharal contends that God will not save the Jewish people while Moshe is praying; Hashem therefore tells Moshe to stop so that He will be free to save them. For Maharal, the problem with a prolonged supplication is not that it gets in the way of human action, but that it holds back divine action.

Why should this be so? If God wants to save the Jewish people, what prevents Him from doing just that, even if a great prophet has not yet completed his prayer? Rav Hutner answers by citing a midrash in which *Hazal* compare the relationship between Hashem and the Jewish people to that between a king and a princess he would like to marry. If the princess only turns to the king in times of distress, the king may actually invite some misfortune in order to make the princess turn to him for succor. In the same way, God sometimes brings about a difficult situation so that the Jewish people will turn to Him in prayer.

This parable completely shifts our perspective. We normally think that prayer is offered only because of distress; now we can claim that the misfortune comes to motivate the prayer. If so, Maharal's insight makes sense. Had the sole purpose of the prayer been to rescue Israel from distress, God could have done so without waiting for Moshe to finish. However, as the perilous situation was meant to generate prayer, God would not remove the jeopardy as long as the prayer continues. Thus, God asks Moshe to stop so that He can save the people.

A profound idea about prayer emerges from R. Hutner's approach. Let us examine R. Hutner's reading of one more biblical passage to clarify the significance of his idea. *"I love God because He has heard the sound of my supplication. For He has inclined His ear to me"* (*Tehillim* 116:1–2). R. Hutner asserts that "heard the sound" refers to fulfilling what was requested. He then observes that the sequence seems to be backwards: surely a listener inclines his ear toward the speaker before hearing and fulfilling a request?

Resolving this dilemma depends upon a deeper understanding

of the purpose of prayer. We could think of prayer solely as a means for obtaining our needs from God. Alternatively, we could view the very act of turning to God as good in its own right, irrespective of whether or not we receive a favorable response. There is something important about a child turning to a parent in times of difficulty even when the parent is unable to alleviate that distress. According to the second approach, even in a case where our entreaties fail to produce results, the endeavor maintains its value. Of course, we also hope for an affirmative answer to our requests.

R. Hutner suggests that we are sometimes happy that God fulfills our request simply because this indicates that He is indeed listening and close to us. If so, we need to make a remarkable reversal: most people think that we want God to incline His ear to us so that He will fulfill our requests; the reality is that we want God to fulfill our requests so that it will become clear that an authentic relationship exists between our Maker and ourselves. The sequence in *Tehillim* 116 makes sense because God's hearkening to our voice indicates that He has inclined His ear, the true end of prayer.

Many religious thinkers have addressed the question of the purpose of prayer. In his commentary on *Bereishit* 20:7, R. Shimshon Raphael Hirsch describes prayer as a form of introspection. R. Yosef Dov Soloveitchik (in "Prayer, Redemption and Talmud Torah") writes about how we become aware of our genuine needs. Employing the child-parent analogy, I have made brief reference to another possibility above. The common denominator of these approaches is that the success or failure of a given prayer cannot be measured solely by the degree to which God accedes to our appeal. While we hope to receive a positive response, the mere act of turning to the *Ribbono shel Olam* with a request represents a great religious value in its own right.

Praying in Ruins and Praying on the Way

> R. Yossi said: I was once traveling on a road, and I stopped in
> one of the ruins of Jerusalem to pray. Eliyahu *zakhur li'tov* came
> and guarded the door until I completed my prayers.
>
> When I finished…he said to me: "My child, why did you
> go into a ruin?"
>
> I said: "To pray."
>
> He said: "You should have prayed on the road."
>
> I said: "I was afraid that the passersby would interrupt my
> prayers." He said: "You should have davened a shorter prayer."…
>
> He said: "What sound did you hear in the ruin?"
>
> I answered: "I heard a heavenly voice that cooed longingly
> like a dove and said: 'Woe to the children whose sins caused
> Me to destroy My Temple…and exile them among the nations.'"
>
> He said: "By your life, not only now does it say this but
> three times daily, and not only then, but every time Jews enter
> a shul or *beit medrash* and answer 'May God's great name be
> blessed' [we say this in *Kaddish*], God shakes His head and says:
> 'Fortunate is the king who is praised like this in His house. Woe
> to the father who exiled his children and woe to the children
> who were exiled from their father's table.'"
>
> (*Berakhot* 3a)

Rav Kook, in his *Ein Aya*, understands this gemara as emphasizing the dwindling stature and influence of the Jewish people now
that they have been driven into exile. According to his reading, the
gemara expresses this in ascending order. First, great figures like R.
Yossi have seen their influence become limited. Thus, his presence
in the ruin inspires a heavenly voice of sadness. Second, service of
God, as manifested in prayer and sacrifice, has been diminished
by the absence of the Temple. Therefore, the voice of longing can
be heard three times a day, corresponding to the three daily *tefillot*.
Finally, all of religious life has been negatively affected. Indeed, every
performance of *mizvot* brings forth a voice that mourns the exile.

Yonah Frankel offers a beautiful alternative understanding in his *Sippur haAggada – Ahdut shel Tohen veZurah* (pp. 147–156). He explains that R. Yossi and Eliyahu represent two contrasting religious approaches. Following the destruction of the Second Temple, R. Yossi sees religious life as now predominantly about mourning the past. That is why he prays in the ruins of Jerusalem and hears a voice that is only woe. Eliyahu comes to remind him that mourning the past is crucial, but building for the future is even more important. This is symbolized in his preferring a prayer on the way, on a road going somewhere. Eliyahu then refers to a prayer in the future tense for God's name to be made great because he is directing R. Yossi toward the future. The last heavenly voice mentioned includes a dual focus on the positive and the negative, the accomplishments of the here-and-now and the losses of the past.

Frankel's reading has special resonance for me and perhaps for every Jew since the *Shoah*. In his eulogy for my grandfather, R. Pinchas Teitz, R. Berel Wein recalled his own experience as a yeshiva student in the 1950s. He said that all the other European *rabbonim* spoke of the world that was, but only Rabbi Teitz spoke of the world that could be. Without denying the significance of memory and mourning, the bulk of our energy must always be directed to anticipation and building.

The Integration of Study and Prayer

> Abbaye taught: I used to learn in my house and pray in the synagogue. Having heard that R. Hiyya bar Ami taught in the name of Ulla, "From the day that the Temple was destroyed, God only has in this world the four cubits of Halakha," I now pray only in the place where I learn.
>
> (*Berakhot* 8a)

> Abbaye said: I used to learn at home and pray at the synagogue. Having heard what David said, *Hashem, I loved the abode of your home* (*Tehillim* 26:8), I now learn in the synagogue.
>
> (*Megilla* 29a)

Several commentators note the contradiction between Abbaye's two statements – one calls for moving prayer to the study hall, the other advocates moving learning to the synagogue. They suggest various resolutions. Some differentiate between the scholar, for whom the study hall is a full-time spiritual home, and the ordinary Jew, for whom the synagogue is the central religious venue (see *Arukh haShulhan, Orah Hayim* 90:22). *Turei Even* understands the two statements as reflecting two opposing traditions that need not be reconciled. Whatever approach one takes to the contradiction, these two statements clearly share a certain value. They both assert the need for praying and learning to be integrated, not bifurcated. What do study and prayer represent, and what is accomplished in the union of the two?

R. Zadok haKohen of Lublin understands the combination in an interesting way (*Zidkat haZaddik* 211). For R. Zadok, prayer represents human dependency. Religious people turn to God in prayer to express their needs, and are thereby reminded of human frailty and dependence on the divine. Torah, on the other hand, reflects human self-sufficiency. The learned can utilize the Torah as a guide to life without making explicit reference to God. Indeed, the human role in interpreting Torah can lead to a feeling of assertive independence not balanced by a healthy sense of submission to the divine.

Each of these two factors requires the balance provided by the other. A sense of independence devoid of submission lacks a basic element of religious life. Even if we do not accept Schleiermacher's claim that the fundamental religious experience is one of dependence, we can still assert that dependence reflects a crucial component of the religious experience. The truly devout express gratitude to God for creating and sustaining us, accepting His authority as He teaches us the road to a noble existence. At the same time, a dominant feeling of dependence can undermine the human activity and initiative necessary for religious success. Those who engage in prayer must also try human, naturalistic methods to relieve their distress, and they are religiously irresponsible if they fail to do so. Thus, R. Zadok offers an intriguing view on the integration of prayer and study.

A more obvious approach might understand Abbaye as calling for intellect and emotion to be in balance. While prayer certainly involves some cognitive understanding, and study can be a powerful emotional experience, it still seems reasonable to identify the essence of prayer as residing in the affective aspect of life, and the essence of learning in the cognitive process. If so, we must analyze the need for this type of integration.

As mentioned, each activity depends to some extent on the coming together of intellect and emotion. A prayer devoid of serious thought will inevitably incorporate problematic conceptions of God or a shallow view of religious life. For example, the praying individual might come to conceive of God as a capricious tyrant who responds well to flattery. Only a prayer purified by the intellectual element will allow for the emotional component to exert a powerful influence in a purified form. Conversely, study devoid of emotion becomes a dry intellectual endeavor that fails to foster a sense of connection with divinity. Furthermore, the study itself may generate erroneous conclusions when it does not take place in a context of awe and love for the divine word.

Beyond the issue of the optimum performance of prayer and study, the successful combination of intellect and emotion prevents religious extremism. This is obvious in the case of an emotion untouched by intellect. The powerful passion of religion can lead to immoral behavior when left unchecked. Pagan child sacrifice represents a prime example of this possibility. Recent history unfortunately provides multiple instances of violence fueled by religious passion. For an example closer to home, we might think of those whose love of tradition leads them to react too harshly to their less knowledgeable or less observant Jewish brethren.

Less obvious is the possibility that intellect devoid of emotion can also engender extreme behavior. In a talk delivered in 1974, R. Yosef Dov Soloveitchik articulated just such a possibility. It is well known that the Rav evaluated himself as far more successful in teaching students how to learn than in teaching them the depths of religious experience (see, for example, his comments in "*Al Ahavat haTorah uGeulat Nefesh haDor*"). In the 1974 talk, he reiterated this idea and linked it with the extremism of his students.

> I will tell you frankly, the American *ben Torah* or good yeshiva student has achieved great heights on an intellectual level. However, experientially, he is simply immature. When it comes to Jewish religious experience, people of thirty and even forty years of age are immature. They act like children and experience religion like children. As a result, Jewish youth is inclined and very disposed to accept extremist views. They do this to such an extent that my own students examine my *zizit* to see whether they are long enough. The youth is very pious but also very inconsiderate. Sometimes they drive matters to an absurdity. Why? Because they have no experience.
> (Rakeffet-Rothkoff, *The Rav*, vol. 2, pp. 238–239)

For an illustration of what the Rav meant, imagine a young student who chooses to spend Rosh Hashana afternoon listening to every type of *shofar* blast imaginable in order to ensure fulfillment of the *mizva*. From an intellectual standpoint, his position can easily be justified. After all, hearing (or blowing) the *shofar* is a biblical *mizva*, while eating lunch with one's family or learning Torah are *mizvot* that can be minimized on this day, if not pushed off for another time altogether. It is only a healthy sense of the emotional and experiential components of Rosh Hashana that prevents this conclusion. The totality of the day's experience requires festivity and awe, seclusion and sociability, and cannot be achieved by sole dedication to a particular *mizva*, however significant.

The extremism generated by pure logic is encapsulated in Samuel Butler's comment that "Extremes are alone logical, but they are always absurd" (*Erewhon*, "The Colleges of Unreason," p. 187). It is easy to be logically consistent when we adopt the same answer to every question and the same approach to every problem. Of course, this logical consistency comes at the expense of ignoring subtlety, nuance, context, and the balance of opposing values. A robust emotional life prevents an obsession with a narrow, logical line of thought.

Thus, in these two brief talmudic statements, Abbaye imparts an important message about the need to integrate prayer and study, humility and independence, and intellect and emotion.

The Synagogue as Home and Temple

> R. Helbo taught in the name of R. Huna: "A person who leaves the synagogue should not take big steps [as when running]." Abbaye said: "This was only said with regard to leaving. But with regard to coming to the synagogue, it is a *mizva* to run, as it says, *Then we shall know, we shall chase after knowing God* (*Hoshea* 6:3)."
>
> (*Berakhot* 6b)

On the surface, this gemara is advocating enthusiasm on coming to shul and reluctance to leave. R. Yehiel Yaakov Weinberg adds a deeper level of analysis (in his *LiFrakim*, p. 362) that takes on added meaning in the context of his own biography. R. Weinberg learned in the Slobodka yeshiva in Lithuania and pursued academic Jewish studies in Berlin. He understood the tension between the ways of the East European Orthodox and those of their brethren in the West, and he lived out that tension in his own life. With this introduction, we can now turn to his commentary.

R. Weinberg points out that royal courts place much emphasis on ceremony and etiquette. People's clothing and movements must demonstrate exacting precision. In the same way, Western Jews have made the synagogue into a temple in which aesthetics and order are paramount. They come to shul once a year and make sure to correctly follow all the rules of procedure. They look down on their Eastern brothers, who lack education in manners and etiquette, but the Westerners forget that the East European Jews enter the shul every day. For them, the shul is more like a home than a palace or temple. In one's home there is little need for ordered ceremony.

For R. Weinberg, this gemara in *Berakhot* teaches the ideal balance. A Jew runs to shul with the excitement of a child rushing home to see his parents. While in shul, that Jew encounters the Creator of the universe, becomes purified, and achieves a feeling of nobility. Now, as an aristocrat, the Jew must leave the shul with measured dignity.

May our own shuls strive to achieve this ideal blending of warmth and familiarity with dignity and nobility.

Ashrei: Thanking God for Nature and the Compassion of Justice

> R. Elazar said in the name of Ravina: "Anyone who recites *Tehilla liDovid* (Psalm 145, to which two introductory verses are added in prayer) three times each day can trust that he is worthy of the world-to-come." What is the reason? If it is because that Psalm follows the order of the *aleph bet*, then we should recite *Ashrei Temime Derekh* (Psalm 119), as it has eight verses for each letter of the *aleph bet*. Rather, [it is] because that Psalm (145) contains the verse *You open up Your hand and satisfy the desire of every living thing*. If so, we should recite *Hallel haGadol* (Psalm 136), as it includes the verse *He gives bread to all living creatures*. Rather, the Psalm (145) is special because it has both features.
>
> (*Berakhot* 4b)

According to this gemara, two factors make the prayer we call *Ashrei* special: it contains an alphabetical acrostic, and it incorporates the theme of God sustaining all creatures. One might understand these factors as reflecting two separate points in its favor. Accordingly, it would be the cumulative force of two totally disparate qualities that makes *Ashrei* unique. Some commentators suggest that an acrostic employing the alphabet from beginning to end connotes the exhaustion of human language in an almost futile attempt to praise God adequately. Among the specific praises we mention is the fact that God provides for each creature's sustenance.

Others see the two themes as complementary but not truly interconnected. Both Maharsha and R. Kook, in their commentaries on *Berakhot*, understand the *aleph bet* as a symbol for the Torah written with those twenty-two letters. According to Maharsha, Psalm 145 highlights Hashem's dual role in sustaining us both physically and spiritually. He provides us with physical food as well as with spiritual nourishment. For Maharsha, these two themes teach related messages, but do not unite in the formation of a specific idea. On the other hand, two significant twentieth-century rabbinic voices insisted on seeing a deeper link between the two themes. In their view, it is the combination of these two factors to emphasize a single idea that makes *Ashrei* unique.

R. Meir Simha haKohen of Dvinsk (*Meshekh Hokhma Vaykira* 26:4) contrasts *Hallel* with *Pesukei d'Zimra*. *Hallel*, recited only on holidays, thanks God for His infrequent but momentous suspensions of the laws of nature on behalf of the Jewish people. For example, He split the sea and took us out of Egypt, and He appeared on a mountaintop to give us the Torah. *Pesukei d'Zimra*, said daily, thanks God for the natural order that sustains human life. A gemara (*Shabbat* 118b) sharply criticizes those who recite *Hallel* daily, on the grounds that doing so is a rejection of the natural order. The desire to always focus on the miraculous implies that one is ungrateful for the regular functioning of the world God created.

Pesukei d'Zimra, on the other hand, clearly should be said every day because it expresses thanks for the regular and the normal. *Ashrei* stands as the centerpiece of *Pesukei d'Zimra* and therefore must refer to the regular rhythms of nature. R. Meir Simha argues that the careful pattern of beginning the verses sequentially with the appropriate letter of the alphabet conveys the theme of nature's regularity. Miracles, by way of contrast, are perceived as sudden interruptions in the normal pattern. The gemara also mentions the verse in *Ashrei* that highlights the natural order's containing the resources to sustain all creatures, a prominent aspect of our appreciation for the natural order. If so, the form and content of Psalm 145 unite to convey our praise for the wonders of the natural order.

R. Yizhak Hutner (*Pahad Yizhak, Pesah* 55) finds a different theme in the combination of these two factors. He cites a midrash that sees *Hallel haGadol* as reflective of the twenty-six generations before the giving of the Torah, when the world was sustained by compassion alone. R. Hutner contends that after the giving of the Torah, God did not stop running the world with compassion, but the nature of His compassion changed. The earlier form of compassion was *hessed-vittur*, a compassion that sustains the recipient without making any demands. When there was no Torah, that was how God ran the world. After *matan Torah*, there was a shift to *hessed-mishpat*. In this model, *Hashem* continues to show compassion, but His giving includes demands made of the recipients and a just, proportional relationship between their actions and His largesse. By analogy, rather than just giving us a handout, *Hashem* finds us a paying job.

According to Rav Hutner, *Ashrei* reflects this second and higher form of functioning. The carefully structured pattern symbolizes the workings of justice, which are steadier than the workings of compassion totally divorced from justice. The two factors combine in an utterance of praise for *Hashem* who runs the world by merging compassion with justice.

Let us recall that the gemara asked why *Ashrei* is superior to *Hallel haGadol*, which also includes a verse about God providing for all. For Rav Hutner, that verse talks of God in His pre-*matan Torah* mode of compassion unmediated by justice. The alphabetic acrostic of *Ashrei* reveals that its verse about divine care-giving refers to the higher level of *hessed-mishpat* that began with the giving of the Torah.

The Connection Between Redemption and Prayer

> The master said: "One should read *Keriat Shema* and then pray [the *Amida*]." This supports R. Yohanan, for R. Yohanan said: "Who will merit the world-to-come (*Olam haBa*)? One who juxtaposes redemption [the blessing of *Ga'al Yisrael*] with the evening prayer."
>
> (*Berakhot* 4b)

> R. Yohanan said: "The *vatikin* [pious people of old; literally, veterans] would finish *Shema* at sunrise in order to juxtapose redemption and prayer and pray when it is day…"
>
> R. Yizhak ben Elyakim testified in the name of the holy community of Jerusalem: "Whoever juxtaposes redemption and prayer will not be harmed for the entire day."
>
> R. Zeira said: "But I juxtaposed and was harmed." He said to him: "How were you harmed? By the fact that you brought a myrtle branch to the king? There too, you must pay a tax to see the face of the king…"
>
> Once, Rav Beruna juxtaposed redemption and prayer, and a smile did not leave his face for the entire day.
>
> (*Berakhot* 9b)

Many commentators explain that R. Yohanan certainly does not mean that those who juxtapose redemption and prayer immediately merit the world-to-come irrespective of the kind of life they have led. No, what he is teaching is that juxtaposing redemption and prayer could make the difference for someone whose portion in *Olam haBa* hangs in the balance. Nevertheless, R. Yohanan was certainly trying to convey the great value of the juxtaposition. Why is this so important?

Presumably R. Yohanan is referring not only to the mere act

of reciting these two texts in succession, but also to actualizing some meaning conveyed by the combination of the two texts. This enables us to understand R. Beruna's smile. After all, why smile at something that most of us do effortless all the time? Rav Beruna said his prayers in the same order every day, but he was once especially successful at internalizing the joint message. What, precisely, is the point here?

Rashi (4b) cites an explanatory parable from the Yerushalmi (*Berakhot* 1:1). In the parable, a close friend of the king knocks at his door but departs before the king answers. Mentioning redemption is apparently the knock at the door; praying would mean encountering the king as he responds to the knock, whereas not praying means leaving before receiving a response. We can further explain the parable as follows. The theme of redemption emphasizes our faith in God as the redeemer. Having asserted such faith, it would seem natural to then turn to God in prayer regarding our own crises. If we do not turn to God, it suggests that our initial blessing of redemption was not truly serious. In other words, it is as if we knocked but did not want to wait for the answer entailed in encountering our Maker in prayer.

The students of Rabbeinu Yona (2b in the Rif's pagination) suggest another interpretation. We link redemption and prayer because prayer, often referred to as *avoda shebalev* (service of the heart), exemplifies service of Hashem. This illustrates the fact that we do not view the exodus from Egypt as a self-sufficient act. No one would deny the joys of freedom, but there remains a question about what we will accomplish with our freedom. Thus the Exodus from Egypt (*Yeziat Mizrayim*) was only complete when the Jewish people accepted the Torah at Sinai (*Matan Torah*). We convey this point each day by following up our prayers about the Exodus with the quintessential *avodat Hashem*.

Those familiar with classical Torah sources will associate this point with the *Sefer haHinukh*'s explanation of the *mizva* of counting the forty-nine days of the *Omer*. The counting links Pesah with Shavuot and helps us to see *Matan Torah* as the crucial culmination of *Yeziat Mizrayim*. Those with a bit of philosophical background may instead associate this idea with a famous distinction drawn by Sir Isaiah Berlin.

In "Two Concepts of Liberty" (included in his *Four Essays on Liberty*) Berlin distinguishes between "negative liberty" and "positive liberty." The former means the ability to act unobstructed by others. It refers to the freedom to do as one chooses. The latter posits an ideal vision of the human being and attempts to remove whatever prevents its actualization. Unlike its negative counterpoint, positive liberty rises from a specific vision of human flourishing.

Berlin presents both sides, but he criticizes a danger inherent to positive liberty. Those who are convinced that they alone know what humanity really needs may set up a totalitarian regime to help bring it about. Governments acting in the name of positive liberty can severely restrict human freedom and choice. Berlin fears that we will "bully, oppress, torture them in the name, and on behalf, of their real selves" (*Four Essays*, p. 133). At the conclusion of the essay, Berlin calls for negative liberty.

The students of Rabbeinu Yona apparently thought differently. Ultimately, freedom is not meaningful without a vision of how to live nobly. Jewish history is significant not because we became free, but because we accepted the divine laws of the Torah. We need to think about how to avoid Berlin's totalitarian nightmare, but throwing out a collective vision of the ideal and the true is not the answer.

R. Yehiel Yaakov Weinberg offers a different perspective in his *LiFrakim* (p. 397). For Rabbi Weinberg, redemption means contemplating the glorious happenings of the past, while prayer symbolizes turning our eyes toward the future. Juxtaposing the two teaches us that a healthy Jewish life demands a combination of past and future.

There have been and still are Jews who see Judaism only in terms of the past. Some of the fathers of the academic study of Judaism saw it as a distinguished historical relic with no contemporary relevance. Moritz Steinschneider famously said that he viewed his bibliographic endeavors as an attempt to give Judaism a decent burial. Some observant Jews may have felt this way after the terrible tragedy of the Holocaust. They viewed themselves as tasked solely to memorialize the world that was destroyed. We can value the need to talk about the glories of our past, but only in tandem with an understanding that our heritage is eternally relevant and currently challenging. (This is not meant as a criticism of anyone who suffered during the war.)

The opposite danger also exists. The constant temptation of radical innovation leads some to imagine that they can restart Judaism without a serious grounding in our centuries of tradition. Arguably, secular Zionism represents such an attempt. For Rabbi Weinberg, such an approach cannot succeed. It is the sense of continuity with the past that both gives us the strength to persevere in difficult times and provides a model for the goals we must fulfill. The power of collective identity in our day depends upon our heritage and tradition.

This point leads R. Weinberg to offer a novel reading of two famous aggadot. One gemara (*Hullin* 91b) suggests that the entire land of Israel was folded up and placed under Yaakov's head during his famous dream. Another well-known gemara (*Sota* 34a) says that Kalev went to the graves of our patriarchs to pray for help in dealing with the challenge of the spies. Rabbi Weinberg argues that each of these sources instructs us that our ability to accomplish Jewish goals depends upon on our being rooted in the past. The concept of the entire land of Israel being folded up under the head of Yaakov is not about a special miracle; rather, it means that our current connection to the land draws its power from the fact that our ancestor Yaakov was connected to this land. Similarly, the story about Kalev conveys much more than the need to find an effective place to pray. It reflects Kalev's understanding that overcoming difficulties requires the vitality that comes from a strong tradition.

Each day's juxtaposition of redemption and prayer allows us

an opportunity to reflect both on our version of positive liberty and on our need to draw from the reservoirs of the past as we look ahead to the future.

The Proper Place for Praying: Of Windows and Valleys

> R. Hiyya bar Abba said in the name of R. Yohanan: "A person should only pray in a house with windows, as it says: *And the windows of his upper chamber were open toward Jerusalem* (*Daniel* 6:11)." Rav Kahana says: "A person who prays in a valley is brazen."
>
> (*Berakhot* 34b)

Although we might think that the preceding statements are purely aggadic, they are both cited in halakhic works. R. Yosef Karo codifies in his *Shulhan Arukh* (*Orah Hayyim* 90:4–5) both that a shul should have windows and that one should not pray in an open place. Of course, this still leaves us with the aggadic question of the theological significance of these two ideas.

Why should one pray in a house with windows? The students of Rabbeinu Yona (24b in the Rif's pagination) maintain that the visual component will enable us to focus our attention toward Jerusalem. Thanks to the windows, Jerusalem is not just an abstract idea, but a concrete entity toward which our eyes can turn. On the other hand, Rashi suggests that looking out at the heavens and seeing the grandeur of the created order subdues the heart to God. Whereas praying in the open can inspire feelings of total freedom and arrogance, the enclosed structure of a building reminds us of the restrictions imposed upon us and our subjection to the divine. According to Rashi, the twin statements reflect an attempt to inspire without losing the sense of subjugation.

R. Kook (*Ein Aya*) offers a different interpretation. Prayer essentially occurs in the heart and mind of the individual praying. In prayer, we stand before the King, affirm basic Jewish beliefs and commitments, sing hymns of praise, and pour out our heart in supplication. All of these aspects can generate a very powerful religious experience. However, that very power also creates the danger that while praying we may lose ourselves in a flight of devotional rapture and forget about the worth and significance of the outside world. Ideally, the inspiration gained through prayer should lead to a renewed commitment to the broader arena of human endeavor. Thus, the windows remind us, as we pray, not to reject the outside world, and they imply that the worth of our *tefilla* will ultimately be determined by its ability to act as a catalyst for sanctifying the totality of human life.

How should we understand the problem of praying in an open valley? Rav Kook takes the analysis in another direction, but I would like to build upon his first point to explain this issue. When we fully internalize the need for windows, the possibility of an opposing danger emerges: we may become so enamored of the broader playing field that we refuse to see any value in withdrawing from that broadness in the interest of seclusion and a narrow focus. Those who pray outside in the wide expanse of the open valley may indeed have arrived at this mistaken conclusion. On the other hand, those inside the structure of a building understand that sometimes we do have to leave the world behind in order to stand alone before our Maker.

This balance between narrowness and broadness extends beyond the question of prayer. I would say that it applies quite powerfully to learning in a yeshiva. Yeshiva life involves a certain intensity of focus on a personal, particular religious goal. This in itself is quite valuable, but it should come with the understanding that the inside of the *beit midrash* must have a positive impact on the outside. The windows of our *batei midrash* remind us that our learning should enable us to bring knowledge, ethical excellence, and sanctity to the workaday world, to our families, and to the entire community.

Chapter 3

Festivals

Shabbat and Continuity

The Rabbis taught: "The *mekoshesh* [the man who gathered sticks in violation of Shabbat, as recorded in *Bemidbar* 15] was Zelofhad. And so it says [introducing the story of the *mekoshesh*], *Benei Yisrael were in the desert* (*Bemidbar* 15:32), and later it says [quoting Zelofhad's daughters], *Our father died in the desert* (*Bemidbar* 27:3). Just as there it is Zelofhad, here, too, it is Zelofhad." These are the words of R. Akiva.

R. Yehuda ben Beteira said to him: "Akiva, either way you will need to answer for your actions. If it is as you say, the Torah concealed it and you are revealing it. If you are wrong, you are slandering a righteous person."

But did he [R. Akiva] not derive it from a *gezeira shava* [an exegetical device, whereby the use of the same word in two different contexts shows a relationship between the two]? He [R. Yehuda] had not learned that *gezeira shava*. But from where [i.e., which sin] was it? It was from *Those that presumed to go up (Bemidbar* 14:44).

(Shabbat 96b–97a)

Before focusing on the central, obvious question that arises from this passage, I would like to touch briefly upon a different issue. There is some debate as to whether a *gezeira shava* must always come from a received tradition or whether it can be suggested by independent human reasoning. The gemarot convey opposing impressions on this matter (contrast *Pesahim* 66a with *Nidda* 22b, and see R. Yaakov Emden's notes on *Nidda*), and there is a range of intermediate positions. If we assume that *every gezeira shava*, in its entirety, reflects a received tradition, it becomes difficult to understand R. Yehuda's objection. After all, R. Akiva simply cited the tradition. On the other hand, if R. Akiva based the argument on his own analysis, R. Yehuda's objection rests on firmer ground.

R. Yehuda objects to R. Akiva's attempt to identify the sin on account of which Zelofhad died. After citing R. Yehuda's objection, the gemara, oddly enough, proceeds to suggest a different sin, that of the *ma'apilim* – the mass of people that charged toward the Holy Land after God condemned the nation to forty years of desert wandering as punishment for the sin of the spies. An obvious question arises: if R. Yehuda so strongly disapproved of attempting to identify Zelofhad's transgression, which the Torah chose to conceal, how does it improve matters to come up with other transgressions to attribute to Zelofhad?

Some commentators distinguish between the two sins on the basis of their severity. Rashi points out that the sin of the *ma'apilim* did not reach the level of Shabbat desecration. R. Kook, in his *Ein Aya*, adds that their sin was motivated by an intrinsically noble intent, a genuine desire to atone for their misdeeds and a yearning to enter into the Land of Israel. The *mekoshesh*, by contrast, was not expressing an authentic religious striving when he gathered wood on Shabbat. Of course, the noble intent of the *ma'apilim* does not alter the fact that their actions were sinful; good intentions

26

do not justify wrongful behavior. But at the same time, it seems reasonable to assess their sin much differently from an act devoid of any redeeming religious qualities.

Sefat Emet provides an alternative explanation, one that does not contrast the levels of the two sins. He observes that the *mekoshesh* was a single individual who violated Shabbat, and the Torah purposefully chose not to mention his name. If the Torah consciously conceals information, we should not attempt to uncover it. In the case of the people who charged toward the Land, the Torah describes a collective endeavor. The absence of specific names may only reflect the equal involvement and responsibility of the many different people, without any single one of them standing out as the prominent player in this episode. Thus, the Torah did not purposely cover up the identity of the sinners, and the Rabbis are therefore entitled to try to identify some of them.

Let us return to R. Akiva's position. If he is not simply repeating a received tradition, we must ask what motivated him to link the story of Zelofhad's daughters with the wood gatherer who violates Shabbat? R. Kook explains that the sanctity of Shabbat constitutes the foundation of the eternity of the Jewish people. Violation of Shabbat brings about lack of continuity. Zelofhad's daughters were struggling to retain ownership of their father's estate. The lack of material continuity mirrors the lack of spiritual continuity brought about by Shabbat desecration. Appropriately, it is the word "in the desert" that links the two episodes. Am Yisrael's sojourn in the desert represents the temporary aspect of Jewish history; the wood gatherer indeed sinned "in the desert," for he chose temporality and eschewed eternity.

Ahad haAm famously quipped, "More so than the Jewish people have kept Shabbat, Shabbat has kept the Jewish people." However, long before Ahad haAm put pen to paper, Jews understood that Shabbat plays a dominant role in enabling Jewish families to successfully pass down their traditions from parents to children. Jews who worked hard all week to support their families often found that Shabbat allows time for more explicit spiritual expressions, such as learning Torah or praying with greater concentration. Parents and children with little time to talk about matters of the spirit during the week found the time on Shabbat. Perhaps most significantly, the warmth and radiance of the Shabbat atmosphere was both a constant memory of tasted sanctity and a spur toward the attempt to spread that sanctity to the broader canvass of human endeavors.

According to R. Kook's insightful reading of this aggada, R. Akiva employed a *gezeira shava* to illustrate this idea nearly two thousand years ago.

The Sabbath, Myrtle Branches, and the Common Man

[This story begins with R. Shimon bar Yohai fleeing a Roman death sentence together with his son R. Eleazar.] So they went and hid in a cave. A miracle occurred, and a carob tree and a water well were created for them. They would remove their garments and sit up to their necks in sand. The whole day they studied. When it was time for prayers, they robed, covered themselves, prayed, and then took off their garments again, so that they would not wear out. Thus they dwelled twelve years in the cave.

Then Eliyahu came and stood at the entrance to the cave and exclaimed: "Who will inform the son of Bar Yohai that the emperor is dead and his decree is annulled?"

So they emerged. Seeing a man plowing and sowing, they exclaimed: "They forsake eternal life and engage in temporal life."

Whatever they looked upon was immediately burned up. Thereupon a heavenly voice came forth and cried out: "Have you emerged to destroy My world. Return to your cave."

They returned and dwelled there for twelve months, saying that the punishment for the wicked in Gehenom is twelve months. A heavenly voice then came forth and said: "Go out from your cave."

Thus they went out. Wherever R. Eleazar wounded, R. Shimon healed.

He said to him: " My son, you and I are sufficient for the entire world." On Friday night just before sunset, they saw an old man holding two myrtle branches.

They asked him: "What are these for?"

He replied: "They are in honor of the Sabbath."

"But is not one enough?"

"One is for *zakhor* and one is for *shamor*."

He said to his son: "See how precious the commandments are to Israel."

Their minds were then set at ease.

(*Shabbat* 33b)

This aggada has many interesting aspects, but we shall focus on the conclusion. After years dedicated to spiritual seclusion, R. Shimon and his son cannot reconcile themselves to the mundane quality of everyday society. They withdraw for an additional year in the cave and achieve reconciliation only upon seeing an old man preparing for the Sabbath. As with any story, the reader should ask whether the details are of crucial symbolic import or just random. Would the ending be the same if they had encountered a Jew holding a *mezuzah* or a *lulav*? Would the story change significantly if the Jew was holding food for the Sabbath rather than myrtle branches? Some thought reveals that the details of preparing for Shabbat and the myrtle branches are highly significant.

Perhaps the same Jew who was running before the Sabbath has been busy all week working in the fields. The two rabbis could not bear the thought of people directing their energies to pursuits with no spiritual import. But those who are justifiably involved in producing sustenance and supporting families need not be spiritually tone deaf. Give them a day free from work responsibilities, and their authentic spiritual yearnings may emerge. Thus, the Sabbath stands as the test case that reveals the truth about those with tools in hand all week. Seeing the old man's passion for the

Sabbath convinced R. Shimon and his son that Jews work in the field for religiously appropriate reasons and not merely to escape the study hall and synagogue.

If so, this story instructs us about Shabbat in particular and about leisure time in general. As *Eruvin* 65b notes, how people spent their free time may reveal more about them than what they do while at work. The many hard-working Jews who utilize Shabbat as their best chance to attend a *shiur*, pray with patience, and devote significant time to their families reveal where their priorities lie. Those who employ the free time of Shabbat to play ball, read vacuous novels, or sleep all day reveal a lack of spiritual striving.

The story also addresses the conflict between scholars and the working class. A natural tendency exists for the former to denigrate the latter, and this story indicates that the scholars must learn to appreciate those who labor in the field. Jeffrey Rubenstein points out (*Talmudic Stories*, p. 337) that this may explain the choice of the myrtle. In the well-known midrash (*Vayikra Rabba* 30:12) that compares the four species of Sukkot with four types of Jews, the myrtle represents those replete with good deeds but devoid of Torah learning. The old man with the myrtle branches symbolizes the genuine piety to be found even among unlearned Jews.

A contemporary example of this phenomenon comes readily to mind. Most of us have encountered zealous yeshiva students just back from learning in Israel who cannot easily acclimate to their old environment. They often feel the need to reject many aspects of their former lives, and this sometimes includes criticizing others who are not engaged in full-time learning. We must respect the ardent idealism of the young firebrands even as we emphasize the need for them to grow beyond the simplistic division between those in the yeshiva and those in the outside world.

Throwing *Etrogim* and the Oral Law

> The Rabbis taught: Once a Sadducee poured the water of the
> libation offering on his feet [instead of on the altar] and the
> people stoned him with their *etrogim*. That day, the corner of
> the altar was damaged and they sealed it up with a fistful of
> salt, not because this renders it fit for service but so that people
> would not see the altar damaged.
>
> (*Sukka* 48b)

Our story takes place on the festival of Sukkot, when, according
to a Sinaitic tradition, we are to enact a libation offering involv-
ing water. The Sadducees, who rejected the oral traditions of the
Rabbis, wanted to sabotage the ritual. A parallel account in Jose-
phus (*Antiquities of the Jews* 13:13:5) informs us that the Sadducee
in question was Alexander Yannai, one of the later Hasmoneans,
but our concern here is more with the religious meaning of the
story than with the historical details. While the image of pelting
someone with *etrogim* is amusing, the story invites the reader to
look for some deeper significance. Rashi assumes that the people
must also have thrown stones, because *etrogim* would not have
dented the altar. If so, we must ask even more strenuously why
the text mentions the throwing of *etrogim*.

A clever answer appears in a collection entitled *Likutei Batar
Likutei*. The Torah describes the *etrog* with the somewhat ambiguous phrase *peri etz hadar* ("a beautiful fruit"). Our ability to
identify the fruit comes from the help offered by the oral tradition.
This issue alludes to one of the classic arguments for the Oral Law.
The written Torah assumes an accompanying oral tradition, for it
does not independently furnish all the information necessary to
implement many rules and practices (see Ibn Ezra's introduction
to his commentary on *Humash* for one version of the argument).
Furthermore, eschewing a tradition that guides our interpretation
of Torah leads to a state of religious anarchy. Thus, although Anan,
the founder of the Karaite sect, preached that his followers should

interpret the Torah for themselves and not rely on his opinions, traditional communal interpretations became the norm even among the Karaites. In light of this, we see that the people pelted the Sadducee with a metaphorical *etrog*. In doing so, they were declaring that the Sadducee rejection of *Torah she'be'al peh* does not work and is ultimately incompatible with the written Torah.

Admitting Wrongs and Long-Term Repentance

> What was the story of Ketiah bar Shalom? There was a Caesar who hated the Jews. He asked the dignitaries of his kingdom: "If a wart [a reference to the Jews] develops on someone's foot, should he cut it off and be healed or leave it and suffer?"
>
> They responded: "He should cut it off and be healed."
>
> Ketiah bar Shalom said to them: "First of all, you will not be able to wipe them out…. Furthermore, you will be called the ruler of a severed kingdom [if you succeed]."
>
> The Caesar said to Ketiah: "You have spoken well. However, whoever prevails against the king [in argument] is thrown into a chamber of dirt."
>
> As the Caesar's men were taking him away, a Roman matron said: "Woe to the ship that goes out without paying its taxes."
>
> Ketiah circumcised himself and said: "I have paid my tax. I shall leave this world and pass into the world-to-come…."
>
> A heavenly voice called out: "Ketiah bar Shalom has a place in the world-to-come."
>
> Rabbi [R. Yehuda haNassi] cried and said: "Some acquire their portion in one moment, and some in many years."
>
> (*Avoda Zara* 10b)

There are many noteworthy aspects to this story (for example, it is not clear why Ketiah circumcised himself, since righteous gentiles merit the world-to-come without a *brit milah*). We will focus on two that are especially relevant to the Days of Awe. The king's comment is striking. He admits that Ketiah is right and offers sound advice but still feels the need to punish Ketiah for besting him in argument. This reflects the difficulty we all have in admitting we are wrong and calls our attention to an additional pitfall. Even when we find the wherewithal to admit that we have erred, we often compensate with aggressive behavior toward the one we confess to. The challenge of Rosh Hashana time is to succeed both at the difficult task of admitting our wrongs to man and God and in not adding a layer of anger because we resent having to acknowledge our shortcomings.

Rabbi's closing comment, which he repeats at the conclusion of two other talmudic stories (*Avoda Zara* 17a, 18a), is also worthy of note. Numerous explanations of why he cried have been offered. Maharsha explains that Rabbi cried because Ketiah merited the *olam haba* born in a moment but not the greater portion of eternal bliss that stems from a lifetime of achievement. Rabbi speaks of two approaches to religious excellence. Some achieve one dramatic moment of heroism, such as martyrdom. Others take the slower and more patient route of steady *mizva* performance. Those who opt for the first approach often undervalue the accumulation of many smaller acts of goodness. Rabbi cries because Ketiah only experienced the grand heroism and did not have the opportunity to live the consistently meaningful life of the observant Jew. Recognizing the worth of steady, quiet daily acts of decency is an integral part of *teshuva*.

The Miracle of Hanukah

> What is Hanukah? The Rabbis taught: On the twenty-fifth of Kislev, there are the eight days of Hanukah, during which we do not eulogize or fast. When the Greeks entered the Temple, they defiled all the oil in the Temple. When the Hasmonean monarchy became strong and overcame them, they searched and could find only one jar of oil stamped with the seal of the

kohen gadol. This jar contained only enough oil to last for one night, but a miracle happened and it lit for eight days. The next year, they established these days as holidays for praise and thanksgiving.

(Shabbat 21b)

One of the many famous questions asked about this gemara is why it emphasizes the miracle of the oil rather than the military victory. After all, many miracles happened in Tanakh without anyone feeling a need to establish a holiday to commemorate them. We might imagine that only an event that changes the historical course of the Jewish people, such as the Hasmoneans throwing off the yoke of the Greek-Syrians, should engender a holiday. The text of the *Al haNissim* prayer that we recite on Hanukah compounds the perplexity, because it stresses the military victory, and does not explicitly mention the miracle of the oil. Are we celebrating the salvation or the miracle of the oil?

R. Yehuda Loew of Prague (Maharal) suggests one answer in his *Hiddushei Aggadot.* Maharal agrees that the military victory and the subsequent reclaiming of Jewish independence were the true reasons for the holiday. Yet any military victory, even one against overwhelming odds, can be explained in accordance with the regular processes of the natural order. The English victory over the much bigger French army at Agincourt in 1415, to cite but one example, is not viewed as a special act of divine providence. A similar claim might be made about the Hasmonean victory. The miracle of the oil comes to clarify God's role in the story. Even though we are celebrating the victory, the gemara focuses our attention on the miracle to make us recall who orchestrated that victory from above.

R. Meir Simha haKohen of Dvinsk suggests a different answer in his *Meshekh Hokhma* (*Shemot* 12:16). According to R. Meir Simha, Judaism shies away from celebrating military triumphs, lest the Jews focus their joy on the suffering of their enemies, which is an improper cause for celebration. This theme

34

reverberates through many of our holidays. We celebrate Purim on the day that we rested after defeating our enemies, rather than on the day of the military triumph. Human suffering is regrettable, but the security, independence, and religious growth that follow in the wake of the victory are worth celebrating. In the same way, the talmudic account of the Hanukah story shifts our attention from the battlefield to the Temple. Additionally, the Torah sanctified the seventh day of Pesah before the drowning of the Egyptians on that very day, so that we would think of the seventh day as sanctified in its own right and not as celebrating the death of the Egyptians.

Thus, the emphasis on the oil either reminds us of God's hand in history or encourages us to celebrate the positive results that emerge from a military victory rather than the death of the enemy. Although both answers are quite important, Maharal's approach helps to explain a another passage on the same page of the Talmud. A different comment by R. Meir Simha will contribute to the analysis.

> R. Kahana said that R. Natan bar Minyomi taught in the name of R. Tanhum: A Hanukah light that is placed higher than twenty *amot* is invalid, like a *sukka* and a cross-beam [over the entrance to an] alley [a case having to do with the laws of *eruvin*].
>
> R. Kahane said that R. Natan bar Minyomi taught in the name of R. Tanhum: What is meant by the verse *and the pit was empty; it contained no water (Bereishit* 37:24)? Once it says that the pit was empty, don't I know that it did not contain water? What does the Torah teach me when it says *it contained no water*? It did not contain water, but it did have snakes and scorpions.
>
> (*Shabbat* 21b–22a)

Much ink has been spilled in attempts to determine what this homily on the Yosef story has to do with Hanukah. It follows a discussion about the proper height of the Hanukah lights and precedes a statement indicating on which side of the doorway we should place the lights. Why interrupt the Hanukah discussion with a seemingly irrelevant piece of *derash*? A surface-level solution would be that the gemara cites this homily simply because it was authored by the same rabbis as the preceding statement – the comments regarding the invalid height and the snakes in the pit both come from R. Kahana quoting R. Natan quoting R. Tanhum. The inquisitive reader cannot help wondering whether there is a more essential connection.

R. Meir Simha (*Meshekh Hokhma, Bereishit* 37:24) offers an explanation that requires a bit of preliminary background. The mishna in *Berakhot* (54a) mentions a blessing to be recited upon seeing a place where God performed a miracle for the Jewish people. Avudraham states (*Hilkhot Berakhot*, beginning of *Sha'ar haShemini*) that this blessing is recited only for a miracle that breaks the bounds of the natural order. If divine providence arranges things within the natural order, no blessing is recited (see *Shulhan Arukh* 218:9 for a debate on this point). We can easily see the logic of the Avudraham's position, for it would be difficult to determine precisely when God works His providence in a miraculous fashion within nature, and we would therefore lack a concrete guideline for when to make the *berakha* if we did not accept his restriction.

The other relevant source is a midrash cited in the name of a R. Tanhuma. According to this midrash (*Bereishit Rabba* 100:9), Yosef, on the way back from burying his father, saw the pit his brothers had tossed him into and recited the appropriate blessing for seeing a place where a miracle occurred. (R. Meir Simha is also utilizing a midrash at the end of *Tanhuma* on *Bereishit*; see the comments of R. Zeev Wolf Einhorn on *Bereishit Rabba* 100:9 in his *Perush Maharzu*.) R. Meir Simha points out that being saved from snakes and scorpions is hardly the essence of the Yosef story – the essence is his moving from near death to the position of second-in-command in Egypt. However, he could not make a blessing on his political ascent, because it occurred without any breaks in nature. Only the pit where he had miraculously survived the company of snakes and scorpions enabled him to recite the *berakha*.

We can now understand the juxtaposition of the Hanukah gemara with the Yosef story. The Hanukah story is about escaping the religious persecution of Antiochus and restoring Jewish sovereignty and religious freedom. Yet this would not call for a *berakha* were it not for the supernatural miracle of the small cruse of oil lasting for eight days. In both instances, the breaking of the laws of nature, be it surviving the snakes or extending the burning power of oil, were not ends in themselves. Rather, they indicated that the broader context of these events reflected the hand of God working within history. We truly bless God for allowing Yosef and the Hasmoneans to achieve the power necessary to better the situation of the Jewish people. The miracle's purpose was to allow us to certify that it was the hand of God that brought about these achievements.

It does not escape R. Meir Simha's notice that the gemara in Shabbat cites R. Tanhum and that the midrash in *Bereishit Rabba* is in the name of Tanhuma. He states that these two names belong to one and the same person. R. Tanhum/Tanhuma taught us about the blessing Yosef made in order to teach us about the deeper relationship between Yosef and Hanukah.

The Wildness of Purim

> Rava said: "A person must drink on Purim until he cannot distinguish between cursed Haman and blessed Mordekhai." Rabba and R. Zeira held a Purim feast together. They became intoxicated. Rabba arose and slaughtered R. Zeira. The next day, he asked for mercy and R. Zeira was revived. The following year, Rabba said to him: "Let the master come and we will make a Purim feast together." R. Zeira answered: "A miracle does not happen every time."
>
> (*Megilla* 7b)

Before beginning to comment on the humorous story at the end of this gemara, I must mention the possibility that it is a halakhic text, not solely an aggadic addition. A major debate exists as to the extent of the obligation to drink on Purim. Some authorities understand that a person should truly become drunk. Of course, even those authorities would condemn a drunkenness that leads to immoral and improper behavior. Rema (*Orah Hayyim* 695:2) recommended that one drink enough to become tired, thus creating a situation in which one cannot distinguish between blessed Mordekhai and cursed Haman. *Ba'al haMaor* (on *Rif* 3b) understands that the whole point of the Rabba/R. Zeira episode is to reject the rule that one should drink on Purim. The gemara places the story after a discussion of this obligation to argue that the Halakha could not obligate something with such destructive potential.

On an aggadic level, what does the story illustrate? Maharsha refuses to take the tale at face value. It simply cannot be true that Rabba killed his colleague. Instead, Maharsha suggests that Purim's wild merriment led R. Zeira to drink too much and become seriously ill. When Rabba prayed for him, he was restored to health. Even if we accept this reading, the story still illustrates the perils of alcohol, as it endangered R. Zeira.

R. Yizhak Hutner raises a different possibility in his *Pahad Yizhak* (*Purim* 32). He begins with the midrashic idea that at Sinai, every word of God caused the souls of the people to depart, but eventually their souls came back and revived them. For R. Hutner, this conveys something about the experience of receiving Torah. In its ideal form, *kabbalat haTorah* serves as a transformative experience that renders the recipient other than he or she was before. The midrash about souls departing and returning conveys the sense of renewal brought about by the Torah. The gemara (*Shabbat* 88a) famously views Purim as a second accepting of the Torah, done freely without the element of coercion present at Sinai. If so, Purim should also include the element of vitality and renewal. The death and return to life of R. Zeira indicates this novel identity achieved through the fresh acceptance of Torah in a successful Purim.

I admit that Rav Hutner may intend this interpretation as a good homily more than a simple reading of this story. He explicitly states that he interprets the story differently on the actual day of Purim than all the rest of the year. Still, let us work with this interpretation and raise a question that he does not mention. According to Rav Hutner's reading, why is R. Zeira reluctant to come back the following year? Perhaps this kind of identity-altering experience includes an intimidating element. Change frightens us, so it might seem safer to maintain one's current Torah personality, especially if it already incorporates much of worth. If so, this story challenges us not to fear the attempt to make this holiday an acceptance of Torah with far-reaching implications for religious growth. The attempt also mandates realizing that it depends much more on authenticity and inwardness than on the quantity a person drinks.

Accusing Achasverosh and the Nature of the Purim Salvation

> And Esther said: *The adversary and the enemy is this wicked Haman* (*Esther* 7:6). R. Elazar said: "This teaches us that she was pointing toward Achasverosh and an angel came and moved her hand toward Haman."
>
> (*Megilla* 16a)

Two questions arise from R. Elazar's statement. On what textual grounds does he argue that Esther first pointed to Achasverosh? Furthermore, why would Esther do such a thing when her target is clearly the wicked Haman? R. Baruch Epstein offers two answers to the first question in his *Torah Temima* on *Esther*. The original Hebrew reads *ish zar ve'oyev Haman ha'ra ha'zeh*. According to Rav Epstein, the pronoun *ha'zeh* renders the mention of Haman's name superfluous because Esther is pointing to the culprit. He also argues that the proper noun "Haman" should not appear in the middle of a series of negative adjectives describing Haman. Apparently, Esther began talking about someone else and only switched to Haman in the middle.

Assuming we have textual grounds for this homily, what does it imply? R. Epstein argues that Esther was furious with Achashverosh for the capriciousness and hatred he exhibited when consenting to the decrees proposed by Haman. She wanted to verbalize her disgust with her beast of a husband. However, the angel reminded her that even though Achashverosh deserved censure, it was far more important at the moment to oppose Haman and overcome the decree against the Jews.

The Vilna Gaon takes Esther's accusation in a different direction in his commentary on *Megillat Esther*. He points out that the images running through our mind often influence the words that escape from our mouths. At times we want to say Shimon but instead say Reuven because we were thinking about Reuven. As this shows, people were familiar with the Freudian slip even before the time of Freud. Esther was beseeching God to deal with Achashverosh. This thought, lurking in the back of her mind, led her finger to point initially at the king until the angel straightened things out.

Torah Temima understands that Esther consciously wanted to accuse the king, whereas the Gaon thinks that her subconscious pushed her in that direction. Both agree that she harbored justified resentment toward the Persian monarch. This highlights the heroism of Esther and helps us appreciate another gemara about the holiday of Purim. Esther bravely enters a contest that leads her into marriage with a man capable of terrible things. Even after the Jews emerge victorious, she must go on living with him. The story ends on a high note for the Jewish people, but the heroism of Esther does not come to an end.

The gemara (*Megilla* 14a) questions the absence of *Hallel* on Purim and provides three explanations. Perhaps we do not say

Hallel for a miracle that occurred in the diaspora. Perhaps the recital of the *Megilla* functions as the *Hallel*. Finally, perhaps it is because the joy of the story remains incomplete, since the Jews are still "servants of Achashverosh." The Pesach story reflects total salvation, but the Purim story recounts a reprieve that has great significance but does not permit a sense of complete redemption. Esther's desire to point her finger at the Persian monarch gives us a sense of the ongoing dilemma at the story's end.

As a final point, let us note that the absence of *Hallel* does not mean an absence of celebration. We do make Purim a holiday, quite a joyous one at that. R. Zadok haKohen of Lublin (*Divrei Soferim* 32) sees Pesah and Purim as two alternative paradigms. As mentioned, Pesah represents leaving the darkness. Purim, on the other hand, is a model for finding the ability to cope with remaining in the darkness. Even a holiday that does not merit *Hallel* remains worthy of celebration. It behooves us to remember this, because instances of complete salvation are few and far between. We must take joy in and show gratitude for the ability to make it through difficult times, even when our problems do not depart entirely.

The Roots of Disrespect

> It is told that R. Akiva had twelve thousand pairs of students from Gabbath to Antipatris, and they all perished during the same brief period because they did not act respectfully toward one another. The world was then desolate until R. Akiva came to our Rabbis in the South and taught them – R. Meir, R. Yehuda, R. Yossi, R. Shimon, and R. Elazar ben Shamua – and they sustained Torah at that time. It was taught: "They all died between Pesah and Azeret [Shavuot]." R. Hama bar Abba, and some say R. Hiyya bar Avin, said: "They all died a harsh death." What was it? R. Nahman said: "Croup."
>
> (*Yevamot* 62b)

41

The basis for our mourning rituals during the *omer* period lies in this gemara. The massacres of the Ashkenazic Jewish communities during the First Crusade, which occurred during this time period, added further impetus to the adoption of certain mourning practices (see *Arukh haShulhan, Orah Hayyim* 493:1). As a result, we have a situation in which two practices overlap despite the lack of an apparent connection between them. We fulfill the biblical *mizva* of counting the *omer* as we also mourn the tragedies that occurred in this period. The former aspect links the exodus from Egypt with our receiving the Torah at Sinai, and therefore would seem to be source of joy. The latter, a post-talmudic custom, clearly assumes a sense of sadness. I have often taught my students that these two rituals happen to coincide but bear no intrinsic relationship.

But perhaps this misrepresents the situation. R. Akiva's students presumably did not suddenly begin to act poorly toward one another. The difficulties between them must have unfolded gradually during the course of the year. If so, we can ask why they all passed away specifically during the *omer* period? Obviously, we could argue that God had to pick some time for the punishment, and perhaps there is no particular reason. At the same time, some implicit message may indeed lie behind the choice of timing.

Let us also raise a second question. We may assume that R. Akiva emphasized interpersonal decency as a crucial ideal in his yeshiva. How did his students come to stumble in this respect? We could explain that even the best efforts of excellent teachers do not always bear fruit, and perhaps the ubiquitous challenges of sheer selfishness and the clash of egos were not met successfully. Alternatively, some deeper flaw in understanding could have generated their behavior.

R. Shemuel Borenstein of Sochatchov was the son of the *Avnei Nezer* and a grandson of the Kozker Rebbe. He offers an approach (*Shem miShemuel, Emor*) that addresses both of our questions and attempts to tie quite a few apparently disparate details together into a unified whole. He postulates that it was not selfishness that led R. Akiva's students astray. Quite the contrary, their teachers in the *beit medrash* had constantly emphasized the goal of unity, and the students had so thoroughly internalized it that they began to view the yeshiva as a large, collective entity in which they were all merely cogs. This being so, there was no point in one student giving honor to another. After all, does your leg give credit to your arm for a job well done?

This is an example of a good idea pushed so far that it turns destructive. Without denying the importance of unity, joint co-operation, and a sense of a shared destiny, it is important to emphasize that the individual remains an important category worthy of respect. Ideological movements that focus only on the collective tend to do terrible things to individuals in their pursuit of communal goals. Communism is a prime example. As the Communists only took cognizance of the collective entity, it did not matter how many innocent people were sent to Siberia, as long as the nation as a whole moved closer to the realization of its communal utopia. R. Akiva's students did not deteriorate to that extent, but a similar error brought about their downfall.

Why were they punished in between Pesah and Shavuot? The *Shem miShemuel* argues that this period instructs us about the necessary balance between individualism and collectivism. The astrological sign for Nisan is a sheep. As in the idiom, "like sheep," this animal symbolizes the collective. Indeed, the historical event of Nissan, the exodus from Egypt, was a grand collective endeavor that formed Am Yisrael. The astrological sign for Iyyar, by contrast, is Taurus (an ox), which the *Shem miShemuel* believes emphasizes the individual. Note that no grand collective events in biblical history ever happened in Iyyar. Finally, the sign for Sivan is Gemini (twins), representing the twin themes of individualism and collectivism. The major historical event of this month also conveys this dialectic. *Matan Torah* could not have occurred without the presence of the entire Jewish collective. At the same time, each individual received a personal share in the Torah, and there were boundaries dividing the place designated for Moshe from that of Aharon, and so on.

The counting of the *omer* also reveals this theme. Every individual must conduct a personal count and may not rely on a communal counting by the court. Nonetheless, everyone counts the same number each day. The counting of both days and weeks points to the dual focus on individual units and collective units. It now becomes clear why R. Akiva's students perished at this time of the year. They had failed to internalize a central message of this period – the need to balance collectivism with individualism.

Another *aharon* provides a different answer to the question of where the students erred, but without reference to the time of year. R. Hazkel Levenstein was the *mashgiah* in the Mir and Ponivezh yeshivot. In his *Or Yehezkel* (*Middot*, pp. 21–23), he provides an insightful explanation for the error of R. Akiva's students. Basing himself on the teachings of R. Isaac Blazer, the foremost disciple of R. Yisrael Salanter, R. Hazkel notes an interesting moral asymmetry often reflected in people's attitudes. We evaluate certain traits differently in reference to ourselves, and to others. For example, *bitahon* is a significant ideal. At times, we must tell ourselves not to lose heart and to have faith that *Hashem* will give succor. However, we should be quicker to employ this concept with regard to our own problems than when approaching the trials confronted by others. We should make a great effort to help those in distress without preaching about the virtues of *bitahon*. The same principle applies to *perishut*. Without entering into the question of the place of asceticism in our tradition, there are times when we need to desist from our pursuit of physical indulgence. Again, we should apply this principle to ourselves sooner than to others. I should not justify my withholding dessert from you on the grounds that I am working to enhance your quality of *perishut*.

Finally, this ideal also applies to honor. On a personal level, I should not pursue honor and public recognition. However, I should not withhold honor from another person on the grounds that honor is religiously problematic. Herein, Rav Hazkel claimed, lies the mistake of R. Akiva's students. They had heard many lectures denigrating the pursuit of honor, and they decided that this ideal mandates withholding honor from others. The flawed conclusion they drew from the ideal of not seeking recognition resulted in their improper treatment of one another.

What causes this asymmetry? Perhaps we are suspicious of people's motives. Those who withhold honor or pleasure from others may be cloaking their own selfishness in a veneer of religious idealism. It may be that things we usually enjoy, such as honor and gratification, tend to become excessive when applied to ourselves. When applied to others, we find the ability to portion rewards out in the right measure.

I find it striking that both the *Shem miShemuel* and R. Levenstein focus on positive religious concepts that the students extended too far. This reveals that almost any positive value can be applied disproportionately, to the point where it becomes problematic. It also reveals that good intentions are not enough to produce interpersonal excellence. Authentic understanding must guide good intentions if we are to find the proper way of treating ourselves and others.

Freedom, Coercion, and the Nature of the Covenant

They gathered at the foot of the mountain (*Shemot* 19:17). R. Avdimi bar Hama bar Hasa said: "This teaches us that God suspended the mountain above them like a barrel and said, 'If you accept the Torah, good. If not, there will be your burial place.'"

R. Aha bar Yaakov said: "From here emerges a great protest about the Torah" [i.e., since the people were coerced into the covenant, they are not responsible for the agreement]. Rava said: "Nonetheless, they reaffirmed their acceptance in the days of Achasverosh, as it says: *The Jews established and accepted* (*Esther* 9:27). They established what they had already accepted."

(*Shabbat* 88a)

The wordplay that generates Rav Avdimi's idea is quite clear. Instead of understanding *be'tahtit ha'har* as "at the foot of the mountain," he translates the phrase as "underneath the mountain." However, Rav Avdimi's theological motivation is much cloudier. Rav Avdimi seems to introduce a shocking thought into our understanding of the biblical account of this event. As traditionally understood, the text in *Sefer Shemot* portrays the Jews as freely choosing to enter into the covenant at Sinai. In fact, *Hazal* praise the Jews of that time for affirming their acceptance even before hearing all the details of the *mizvot*. Why detract from that praise by introducing an element of coercion into the story? Furthermore, does Rav Avdimi truly think that the Jews were not accountable for their religious observance until the Purim events in the time of Mordekhai and Esther? After all, Jews were punished throughout the period of the First Temple for their religious shortcomings.

One approach to this question is to try to minimize the impact of the gemara. Ritva argues that Rav Avdimi does not truly contend that Jews were exempt from upholding the covenant. Rather, he maintains, R. Avdimi is making a rhetorical point in order to counter critics. In other words, even those who think that the Sinai covenant was accepted under duress should realize that the Jews subsequently accepted it of their own free will. Rav Soloveitchik (*The Lonely Man of Faith*, p. 45) also affirms that the Jews freely accepted the Torah at Sinai. He suggests that the coercive component related only to the implementation of the agreement, but not to the initial foundation of the covenant.

Along similar lines, R. Yaakov Kamenetsky (in his *Emet le-Yaakov*) sees God's threat with the mountain as a necessary supplement to the free acceptance that preceded it. In his view, the talmudic account combines the twin components crucial for religious life: fear and love. Without the mountain hanging over-head, the formative covenantal experience would have consisted only of a loving agreement. As religious success sometimes de-pends on fear of God, R. Avdimi introduced a more intimidating element into the story to provide the proper balance.

Midrash Tanhuma states that the Written Law was freely ac-cepted, but that the Oral Law required coercion. Apparently, there is something frightening about *Torah she'be'al Peh*. This could be because the Oral Law expands the parameters of what Halakha demands. Alternatively, the need for human interpretation and initiative generated a certain amount of reluctance and resistance. One can imagine the people saying, "Give us a definitive written Torah, but do not make us responsible for utilizing our intellect in order to understand it."

Another approach accepts that the covenant had a coercive element, but understands the gemara in a nonliteral fashion. R. Meir Simha haKohen of Dvinsk explains (*Meshekh Hokhma* on *Shemot* 19:17) that the awesome experience of revealed divinity at Sinai made it impossible not to accept the covenant. According to R. Meir Simha, the mountain may have been figurative, but the coercion was very real. This returns us to our second ques-tion: Weren't Jews punished for their sins long before the events of Purim occurred? R. Meir Simha answers that the Jews were responsible for the seven Noahide laws even without a special Sinaitic covenant. He notes that the First Temple was destroyed for sins included in the Noahide laws, such as idolatry and murder.

The idea that Jews were not responsible for violating Shabbat or *Shemitta* before the Persian exile is quite radical. Indeed, the Spanish school of *rishonim* found the idea unacceptable. Begin-ning with Ramban (commentary on *Shabbat* 88a), they discovered a way to concede that Sinai had a coercive element but still see the *mizvot* as binding. Ramban explains that receiving the Land of Israel comes with certain conditions. In other words, the rental agreement for living in Israel includes a commitment to a life of religious observance. Since the Jewish people lived in Israel during the time of the First Temple, they needed to observe the *mizvot* if they did not want to be evicted from the land.

The end of the gemara works beautifully with Ramban's interpretation. Until the Babylonian exile, the Jewish people remained committed, at least in theory, to Torah and *mizvot* as part of the deal enabling residence in Israel. When they were driven into exile, the ongoing relevance of religious observance was called into question. The Purim episode, taking place during that first exile, included a communal decision that the covenant should continue despite the exile. This idea gives an added dimension to the significance of Purim.

Hiddushei haRan echoes this interpretation, but adds a novel reading of a phrase from our gemara. God says: "If not, there will be your burial place." Ran emphasizes the word *sham*, "there." If you choose not to accept the Torah, you forfeit entry into Israel and will be buried in the desert. God is not so much threatening them as explaining the nature of the lease on the land.

Although we have seen a number of fine interpretations, I believe that Maharal (*Gur Aryeh* on *Shemot* 19:17) provides the most profound of them all. He explains that the gemara does not refer to threats, intimidation, or coercion. Rather, it instructs us about the nature of Torah and the gravity of our choices. Maharal understands that the Jewish people did indeed freely choose to accept the Torah. At the same time, it was crucial for the world that the Torah be accepted, and rejection of the Torah was sure to have catastrophic consequences. "Here will be your burial place" is not a threat of immediate punishment, but a statement about the seriousness of the choice and the potential consequences for humanity if the Jews make the wrong choice.

This idea has special resonance for modern man. People today value free choice and sometimes even maintain that the choices we make, whatever they may be, are always the best choices for us as individuals. According to Maharal, we should take the first step, but reject the second. Judaism greatly values free choice, and methods of coercion should be employed only sparingly. This does not mean that our choices are comparable to selecting a particular flavor of ice cream. We can recognize our freedom of choice even as we also affirm the ultimate significance and weighty ramifications of our choices. Rather than being dismayed by the gravity of our choices, we can find joy in the ability of our decisions to change the world.

Note that this discussion does not address the question of why a divine command should need human agreement to begin with. One religious position argues that God can command whatever He wants, irrespective of human consent. Since this gemara apparently views human consent as crucial, we have followed that path and avoided the broader theological question. *Ve'od hazon la'moed.*

The Placement of a Blemish and the Placement of an Aggada

> Jerusalem was destroyed because of [the incident involving] Kamza and Bar Kamza. There was a man who was a close friend of Kamza and an enemy of Bar Kamza. He made a party and told his servant to invite Kamza. He brought him Bar Kamza. He [the host] found him [Bar Kamza] sitting. He said to him: "Since you are my enemy, what are you doing here? Get up and leave!"
>
> He said to him: "Once I have come, leave me be and I will pay for everything I eat and drink."
>
> "No!"
>
> "I will pay for half the party."
>
> "No!"
>
> "I will pay for the entire party."
>
> "No!" He [the host] took him by the hands, picked him up, and threw him out.
>
> He [Bar Kamza] said: "Since the rabbis were sitting there and did not protest, it seems that they were pleased with what happened. I will go slander them before the emperor."
>
> He said to the Caesar: "The Jews are rebelling against you."

"How do you know this?"

"Send them a sacrifice and see if they offer it."

He [the Caesar] went ahead and sent with him [Bar Kamza] a healthy calf. While on the way, he [Bar Kamza] made a blemish on the animal's upper lip; some say he caused a cataract on the eye. These things are blemishes for us [and disqualify an animal for sacrifice] but not for them [the Romans].

The Rabbis wanted to offer it [despite its disqualifying blemish] to preserve good relations with the authorities.

R. Zekharya ben Avkolus said to them: "People will then think that blemished animals may be offered upon the altar."

They wanted to kill the person who had brought the animal, so that he could not go and inform on them. R. Zekharya ben Avkolus said [in opposition to this]: "People will say that anyone who places a blemish on a sacrifice should be killed."

R. Yohanan said: "The humility of R. Zekharya ben Avkolus destroyed our Temple, burned our sanctuary, and exiled us from our land."

(*Gittin* 55b–56a)

Lurking in the background of this well-known story may be another famous gemara (*Yoma* 9b) that attributes the destruction of the First Temple to the sins of murder, idolatry, and sexual immorality, and the destruction of the Second Temple to groundless hatred (*sinat hinam*). Our story in *Gittin* certainly involves a good deal of hatred. R. Yosef Hayyim of Baghdad (the *Ben Ish Hai*, in his work *Ben Yehoyada*) points out that the gemara purposely identifies what at first looks like an episode of minor importance as the cause for the destruction. Unlike the sins that led to the first *hurban*, groundless hatred often involves low-key offenses that the average person would not deem a major transgression. This gemara is teaching us to take minor slights and squabbles seriously.

Maharal suggests an interesting reading of the introductory sentence of this passage. Taken literally, it says that Kamza and Bar

Kamza caused the destruction. Maharal asks how Kamza could be faulted for what happened when he was not even present at the party. Maharal explains that in an atmosphere of great enmity, people look for friends as allies in their disputes with their many enemies. Such friendships do not reflect true human warmth, but are calculating partnerships exploited by those seeking supporters for their belligerence. If so, even the host's friendship with Kamza was part of the corruption that characterized the Jewish society of the time.

As with any talmudic tale, we should ask whether the story's details are simply items of information or have symbolic import. As Maharsha explains, the locations of the blemish clearly belong to the latter category. Blemished lips represent the terrible speech of the Jewish people before the *hurban*. Slander, insults, and mean-spiritedness dominated the society's discourse; the animal's blemish reflects the blemished lips of the people as a whole. The blemished eye suggests the pettiness with which they looked at each other. Pettiness of this sort features prominently in the decision to throw someone out of a party even after he offers to help foot the bill.

The story includes a condemnation of the "humility" of R. Zekharya ben Avkolus. Although R. Zekharya's statement is not obviously a product of humility, R. Yohanan understood that this character trait was R. Zekharya's Achilles' heel. The Rabbis wanted to take drastic measures to avert catastrophe: either allowing a blemished sacrifice or killing an individual bent on endangering them. R. Zekharya was afraid to make so momentous a decision because he considered himself unworthy. Leaders must make fateful decisions in times of crisis, and a humble declaration of inadequacy cannot substitute for a decisive response.

Another version of the story (*Eikha Rabba* 4:3) places R. Zekharya ben Avkolus at the party as one of the rabbinic authorities who remained silent when Bar Kamza was tossed out. If so, his excessive humility hindered him earlier in the story's development.

He thought himself unworthy of making a scene, and therefore allowed the gratuitously cruel treatment of an unwanted guest to proceed without protesting.

At first glance, one might think that this story found its way into *Massekhet Gittin* due to a linguistic tangent related to the word *sikrikin*, a term that appears both in the preceding mishna and later in this story. It is likely, however, that the editors of the Talmud could have employed associations in many tractates as a springboard for introducing this story. If so, then perhaps they had a particular reason to include the Kamza/Bar Kamza narrative here in *Masekhet Gittin*.

R. Zadok haKohen of Lublin asserted that the placement of all aggadot in the Talmud reflects deep thematic significance. In his *Peri Zaddik* (*Bereishit, Kedushat haShabbat* 3), he creatively explains the placement of the story of Kamza/Bar Kamza. *Gittin* deals with divorce, and the Temple's destruction resembles a divorce between God and the Jewish people (note the imagery in *Yirmiyahu* 3:1). Yet the name of the chapter in which this account appears is *HaNizakin* ("Damages"), a name that makes no reference to the issue of divorce. R. Zadok explains that the destruction of the Temple and the resultant exile are more similar to an instance of damages than to a divorce. While a divorce tends to be final, damages can be undone fairly quickly through restitution. *Sefer Yeshayahu* (50:1) explicitly denies that God has divorced us. On the day we prove worthy, God intends to compensate us for the damages, and the apparent divorce will turn out to have been but a temporary rift in the fabric of an enduring union.

The Fears of Resistance Fighters

The background of this aggada has the Romans laying siege to Jerusalem prior to the destruction of the *Beit haMikdash* in the year 70 C.E. The Jewish faction known as the *biryonim* wants to fight the Romans, and they destroy the storehouses stocked with provisions to force the people to support them. Rabban Yohanan ben Zakkai thinks that military action is futile and wants to salvage what he can.

> Abba Sikra, the head of the *biryonim* in Jerusalem, was the nephew of Rabban Yohanan ben Zakkai. [R. Yohanan] said to him: "Come to me in secret."
>
> He came. [R. Yohanan] said: "How long will you do this – until you kill everyone through famine?"
>
> [Abba Sikra] said: "What can I do? If I say anything, they [the other *biryonim*] will kill me."
>
> He said: "Think of a method to get me out, and we may have a partial salvation."
>
> He said to him: "Pretend that you are sick; let everyone come and ask about your welfare. Then bring something that stinks, lie next to it, and let them say that you have passed away. Let your students carry you out [of the city], not anyone else, so that the others will not notice that you are light; people know that a live person is lighter than a dead person."
>
> He did so. R. Eliezer carried him on one side and R. Yehoshua on the other. When they arrived at the gate, [the *biryonim*] wanted to stab him [to confirm that he was dead]. [Abba Sikra] said to them: "*They* will say that they stabbed their rabbi!" They wanted to shove him. He said to them: "They will say that they shoved their rabbi!" So they opened the gate and he went out.
>
> (*Gittin* 56a)

The key word in this story is the ambiguous pronoun "they," printed in italics in the preceding text. Whose murmurings are the *biryonim* afraid of? Rashi explains that "they" refers to the Romans. If so, it is striking that ardent Jewish nationalists ready to fight for independence still care what the Romans say about them. Their decision to employ drastic means (such as burning the Jewish food supply) in order to fight a losing battle for independence may actually reflect the adoption of certain Roman ideals. If so, it makes sense that they care what the Romans would say.

FRESH FRUIT AND VINTAGE WINE

R. Yosef Hayyim disagrees with Rashi in his *Ben Yehoyada*. He says that the Romans would have no way of knowing how the Jewish guards at the gate treated the casket, so the *biryonim* could not possibly be concerned about what the Romans would say. Instead, he suggests, "they" refers to other *biryonim*. This interpretation perceptively highlights one of the dangers of militant revolutionary activity. Once violent forces are unleashed, it is difficult to control them, and rival factions may seize any opportunity to attack each other.

Note that earlier in the story Abba Sikra agrees with Rabban Yohanan's evaluation of the situation but could not do anything because the others would kill him. Having unleashed the passions of the masses, Abba Sikra turns from a leader into the pawn of stronger forces. Similarly, any act that might dishonor the *biryonim* could cause another faction to put the guards to death.

The tyrannies that emerged from the Russian and French revolutions are ample evidence of these concerns. Resistance, rebellion, and force have a place in the Jewish worldview, but the dangers of their getting out of hand must always be kept in mind.

CHAPTER 4

Learning

R. Nehunya's Prayer and the Dangers of the Study Hall

R. Nehunya ben haKaneh would pray a short prayer upon entering and leaving the *beit midrash*. They said to him: "What is the nature of this prayer?" He said to them: "When I enter, I pray that no mishap should occur because of me, and when I depart, I give thanks for my lot."

The Rabbis taught: What does he say when he enters? "May it be your will, Lord my God, that no mishap occurs because of me, and that I not err in a halakhic matter and my colleagues rejoice over me, and that I not declare the impure pure or the pure impure, and that my colleagues not err in a halakhic matter and I rejoice over them."

What does he say when he leaves? "I am thankful to You, Lord my God, that You have placed my lot among those who dwell in the *beit midrash* and not with those who hang around street corners. They arise early, and I arise early. I arise early for words of Torah, and they arise early for idle matters. I toil, and they toil. I toil and receive reward, and they toil and do

not receive reward. I run, and they run. I run to the life of the
world-to-come, and they run to the pit of destruction."

(*Berakhot* 28b)

As with many *gemarot*, this passage lies somewhere along the
boundary line between Halakha and Aggada. Rambam, in his
commentary on the Mishna, understands this prayer as a concrete
obligation incumbent upon everyone who enters the *beit midrash*.
He draws proof from the formulation of the *beraita*'s opening
question: *Ma hu omer* ("What does he say?") as opposed to *Meh
haya omer* ("What would he say?"). This indicates that the *beraita*
is not merely describing the personal practice of R. Nehunya, but
is establishing an obligatory practice for everyone. Ritva, on the
other hand, sees this as a voluntary prayer. Those of us who do
not recite the prayer rely either upon Ritva's position or upon the
theory advanced by the *Arukh haShulhan* (*Orah Hayyim* 110:16)
that the prayer is obligatory only for *poskim* attempting to render
halakhic decisions.

Turning to the meaning of the prayer brings us closer to
the aggadic realm. Why do the sages ask, *Ma makom le'tifila zo*
(translated above as "What is the nature of this prayer")? We could
explain that they simply wanted to hear the text and themes of the
prayer. R. Kook (*Ein Aya*), however, suggests a deeper interpretation. We often associate prayer with an appeal to God in situations
of physical or spiritual danger. The sages saw R. Nehunya praying
before entering the study hall, and they wondered what could possibly be so threatening about time spent learning. After all, he is
entering a holy place to perform an important *mizva*. However, R.
Nehunya understood that the *beit midrash* poses its own religious
and ethical challenges. Indeed, *yesh makom le'tefilla zo*.

R. Nehunya is concerned that he might make an erroneous
halakhic judgment. He adds a request that his colleagues will
"rejoice over him," which Rashi explains as a further expression
of fear. R. Nehunya is afraid that his peers might laugh at and
ridicule him if he makes a halakhic error. Then he will have not

only distorted the given halakha, but will also have caused his friends to engage in improper behavior. In a slightly different vein, Maharsha suggests that the "rejoicing" refers to part of what R. Nehunya prays for, not what he fears. Namely, R. Nehunya prays that his friends will react with joy to his success at expounding the *halakha*.

Perhaps we can best appreciate this point by envisioning an academic conference at which some of the professors devote all their energy to attacking the theories of rival scholars. At some point, we must conclude that personal pettiness has supplanted the intellectual search for truth. Let us admit that such instances are not unknown in the world of the *beit midrash*. Rashi emphasizes an environment in which people do not take pleasure in others' mistakes. Maharsha goes further and aspires to an atmosphere in which people take active joy in the achievements of others. It behooves us to think about how to generate such an atmosphere in our own places of learning.

Ahavat Eitan adds another suggestion in his commentary, found in the *Ein Yaakov*. He notes that mistakes are usually an indispensable part of the learning process. Indeed, the gemara (*Gittin* 43a) explicitly states that "a person cannot understand matters of Torah unless he first stumbles in them." Yet the one who recites R. Nehunya's prayer would like to avoid even the initial error. The method for doing so, the *Ahavat Eitan* contends, depends upon *yismehu bi haverai*. Only a positive collective learning environment, in which the participating scholars complement one another's strengths, can avoid the errors inherent in a solitary individual's approach to a topic.

Finally, let us analyze the prayer of thanksgiving offered upon leaving the study hall. We can certainly appreciate the feeling of contentment after having engaged in meaningful activity rather than frivolously killing time. At the same time, we might question the phrase "they toil and do not receive reward." Many people involved in foolish activities receive some reward, financial or otherwise, for their efforts. The simplest answer might be that the reward mentioned in the prayer refers to otherworldly compensation. If so, we can understand why only those engaged in more meaningful work receive it.

R. Yisrael Meir Kagan offers a different answer (see *Hafez Hayyim al haTorah*, beginning of *Behukotai*). He admits that toilers of both kinds receive some type of reward. However, the reward of one rests solely in the results, while the others receive a reward for the effort involved in the process. The card shark on the street corner measures success solely in terms of the amount of money pulled in on a given day. The toil, per se, is not grounds for the reward. By contrast, a student struggling to attain understanding in the *beit midrash* views the endeavor as inherently valuable even if on a given day comprehension remains elusive. In this sense, a person leaving the study hall can truly declare: "I toil and receive reward."

Many of us do not recite this *tefilla*, but its inherent themes should animate everyone who spends time learning. Following a learning session, we should appreciate our good fortune at having engaged in significant activity rather than wasting the day in mindless entertainment. Before a learning session, we should think about the seriousness of purpose that is necessary in trying to understand the *peshat*, and also about setting the correct interpersonal tone for the give-and-take of academic discourse. Without denying that pride in Torah achievements has its place in the study hall, we can and must avoid an atmosphere in which the clash of egos supplants the sincere *milhamta shel Torah*.

The Proper Amount of Torah Study

> These are the things that have no fixed amount: The corner of the field, the first fruits...and the study of Torah (*talmud Torah*).
>
> (*Peah* 1:1)

> R. Yohanan said in the name of R. Shimon bar Yohai: "Even if one recites only *Keriat Shema* in the morning and the evening,

he has fulfilled *This book of the Torah must never depart from your mouth* (*Yehoshua* 1:8), but it is forbidden to teach this to the ignorant." Rava said: "It is a *mizva* to teach this to the ignorant."

(*Menahot* 99b)

The closing debate in *Menahot* raises an interesting pedagogical question: Is it preferable not to inform the masses about the ease with which one can technically fulfill the *mizva* of Torah study, thereby encouraging them to learn more than is required? Or is it better to teach them the minimum requirement, in the hope that this will encourage them to begin the endeavor with small steps and grow from there?

In the continuation of this gemara, R. Yishmael seems to take the position that we should spend the entire day learning Torah. The ambiguity about how demanding the obligation of *talmud Torah* is emerges from the mishna in *Peah* as well: What does it mean that this *mizva* has no fixed amount? *Tiferet Yisrael* and others explain that there is neither a minimum nor a maximum. If one recites only the *Shema*, already obligatory in its own right, one has fulfilled the *mizva*; but the more one learns, the better.

R. Meir Simha of Dvinsk offers an insightful explanation for this flexibility in his *Or Sameah* (*Hilkhot Talmud Torah* 1:2). He explains that the *mizvot* are meant, for the most part, to be equally binding on all Jews. This universalizing quality of *mizvot* conveys the idea that Judaism is not reserved for a small elite and applies equally to all. Every Jew has the same obligation to eat *matza* on Pesah or to make *Kiddush* on Shabbat. However, the extent to which some Jewish ideals should be applied depends a great deal upon the person being commanded. For example, the Torah does not give precise guidelines with regard to character traits, such as pride or anger, because the proper amount of these traits depends a great deal on the person and the context. When it comes to such subjective *mizvot*, the Torah does not explicate all the variables; instead, it offers a baseline obligation that applies to each and every Jew.

According to R. Meir Simha, the study of the Torah is just such a *mizva*. It depends a great deal on such factors as whether one has to support a family, one's intellectual abilities, and one's ability to concentrate diligently. Therefore, the Torah demands just a modicum of learning each morning and evening as a minimum obligation for everyone. Of course, we should all challenge ourselves to learn more, to the best of our capability.

I would add that the desired amount of Torah study not only varies from person to person but also from stage to stage in a person's life. When you have to work long hours and then take care of children when you return home, a relatively short dose of daily learning is heroic and impressive. When you study in yeshiva, the goal is nothing less than a full day. May we all succeed in reaching our learning potential and understanding how much energy to invest in *talmud Torah* at the different stages in our life.

Halakha and Gemara

> It was taught: "The *tannaim* [scholars of the Mishna] destroy the world." Could one truly think they destroy the world? Ravina explains that the above source refers to those who make halakhic decisions based on *mishnayot*. We also learn this idea in a *beraita*: R. Yehoshua said, "Are they destroyers of the world? Do they not build the world …? Rather, we are talking about those who decide halakha straight out of *mishnayot*."
>
> (*Sota* 22a)

What is the problem with making halakhic decisions based solely on *mishnayot*? Rashi explains that such a methodology invariably leads to mistakes. A scholar who does not know the gemara's rationale for a mishnaic ruling could not possibly apply that ruling correctly. The ability to extend or limit the scope of a particular halakha depends on knowledge of the talmudic argumentation that led to that halakha. For example, someone who knows that we light Shabbat candles before reciting the *berakha* but does not know the rationale for this practice might easily assume that the same sequence applies for lighting Yom Tov candles. Only if you understand the reason for our Shabbat practice (namely, that making the blessing might constitute accepting of Shabbat, and thereby prohibit the subsequent candle lighting) will you realize that this rationale does not apply to the festivals. On the festivals, it is permissible to light from a prelit fire.

Furthermore, we do not always decide in accordance with the Mishna, because there may be other tannaitic evidence that overrides a particular mishna. There are situations in which our tradition follows a *beraita* rather than the opinion recorded in the Mishna. Finally, those who attempt to bypass the gemara will frequently rule incorrectly in the cases where a mishna incorporates multiple positions. Thus, Rashi explains how several pitfalls will cause those who derive *pesak* (halakhic ruling) from *mishnayot* to lead their adherents astray.

Maharal offers quite a striking alternative explanation in his *Netivot Olam* (*Netiv haTorah* 15). He rejects Rashi's explanation on linguistic grounds. The gemara refers to those who derive "halakha" from *mishnayot*. Maharal argues that the term "halakha" implies a correct ruling, and not a mistaken ruling. If so, the gemara speaks negatively about those who rule out of the mishna, even if they get all their rulings right. The problem is not about the correctness of the *pesak*, but rather about the entire endeavor of Torah learning. Authentic Torah is not just a fixed set of rulings, but a whole system of learning. Apparently, we are not meant to experience Halakha as a set of arbitrary commandments and prohibitions. Instead, we are to follow the halakhic argument through its talmudic pathways until we understand the thought process that leads to a given conclusion. Learning the full depth of a talmudic topic enables us to see that halakha emerges from a rigorous, serious, and profound system of analysis. It is not at all arbitrary.

Many students wonder why we emphasize gemara study when it would be more effective to concentrate our intellectual energies on practical halakhic conclusions. The sources we have seen suggest a dual counter-argument. If we learn only the conclusions, we will invariably generate mistaken conclusions, and we will also have a misleading impression of God's Torah. The constant quest for growth in learning should combine the ideas of Rashi and the Maharal. We learn both in order to know what to do in a particular case and to understand the profound nature of Torah.

Intensity, Integration, and *Talmud Torah*

> Rav asked a question of Rabbi [Yehuda haNassi]…R. Hiyya said to Rav: "Child of great ones, did I not tell you that when Rabbi is involved in one tractate, you should not ask him about another, lest it be difficult for him to focus on it? If not for the fact that Rabbi is a great man, he would have been embarrassed for answering incorrectly."
>
> (*Shabbat* 3a–b)

Rav Yizhak Hutner points out (*Pahad Yizhak, Shavuot* 9) that the simple reading of this gemara is that R. Hiyya is referring to a difficulty stemming from a certain shortcoming of the scholar in question. He cannot easily make the transition to different material because he lacks complete mastery of all the tractates; had he been a truly great scholar, the issue would be of no concern. Indeed, R. Yehuda haNassi's excellence enables him to avoid this problem and answer a question from afar. R. Hutner suggests that, on the contrary, R. Hiyya's caution actually reflects the scholar's greatness. A great scholar so immersed himself in the topic at hand that it is difficult for him to tear his focus away and think clearly about something else. Someone who can easily and swiftly shift gears to another topic may not have been thinking that deeply about the first topic.

Rav Hutner contends that this idea reflects the fact that our personal Torah study is modeled after the original Torah study, the giving of the Torah at Sinai. A gemara (*Shabbat* 88b) says that each *dibbur* from the *Aseret haDibberot* filled the entire world; if so, asks the gemara, how did the second *dibbur* find room to enter? It is clear that this gemara does not refer to physically taking up space. For R. Hutner, the gemara utilizes the image of a *dibbur* filling the world as a metaphor for a total focus on the aspect of Torah being studied at any given moment. We emulate this intensity in our own narrowing in on the text in front of us.

In our gemara, Rabbi's greatness allows him to answer the question regardless. According to the conventional approach, this works well, because Rabbi did not have the shortcomings of the ordinary scholar. However, according to Rav Hutner's idea that the inability to quickly change topics itself reflects a positive intensity and focus, it seems that Rabbi lacks this intensity. Why then does the gemara state that Rabbi's greatness would enable him to answer the question correctly?

R. Kook makes an insightful suggestion in *Ein Aya* (*Shabbat* 3a) that resolves our difficulty. Some unusual scholars are able to so integrate the many texts of Torah that the other topic does not represent an invasion from an external source; instead, it represents a natural continuation from the original source. For a scholar at this level, there is no such thing as being asked a question from an unrelated tractate, for all of talmudic thought forms part of a coherent whole.

This interpretation points to a broader concept in Rav Kook's thought. In other contexts (See *Orot haKodesh* 1, p. 49), Rav Kook distinguishes between academic specialists, who know one thing very well but lack breadth, and polymath scholars, who can integrate various disciplines into a coherent whole. There is no doubt that specialization has enabled impressive achievements in many fields, and especially in the sciences. On the other hand, the specialist often lacks the sweeping vision to realize how a particular piece of information relates to a broader worldview.

R. Kook says that specialists "offer us dry kernels of matters, which are, fundamentally, full of freshness and ultimate vision" (trans. by R. Shalom Carmy in *Torah u'Madda Journal*, vol. 2, p. 20). He counsels that we should learn the individual bits of wisdom these scholars offer but revitalize them by seeing them as part of a greater whole. Indeed, for R. Kook, the truly great thinkers are the ones who are able to weave the many branches of wisdom into a grand tapestry.

The challenge to achieve the depth and intensity spoken of by R. Hutner while still maintaining a larger vision awaits all aspiring *talmidei hakhamim*.

The Ideal *Chavruta*

One day R. Yohanan was swimming in the Jordan. Reish Lakish saw him and jumped into the Jordan after him.

He [R. Yohanan] said: "You should use your strength for Torah." He [Reish Lakish] said: "You should use your good looks for women." He said: "If you return to Torah, I will give you my sister [for a wife], who is better looking than I am."

[Reish Lakish] accepted this offer. He tried to do a return jump to get his clothing and was unable. He then learned Tanakh and studied the Talmud and became a great man.

One day, they were arguing in the *beit medrash*. "A sword, a knife, a dagger, a spear, a sickle, and a scythe: from what point are they susceptible to ritual impurity? From the time that they are completed." When is the point of completion?

R. Yohanan said: "When they are forged in the fire."

Reish Lakish said: "When they are rinsed with water."

[R. Yohanan] said to him: "The bandit knows his trade."

[Reish Lakish] said to him: "And how did you benefit me? There[, when I was a bandit,] I was called the master, and here I am called the master."

He said to him: "I helped you because I brought you closer under the wings of the divine presence."

R. Yohanan became depressed. Reish Lakish became sick. His sister came crying to R. Yohanan.

She said: "Do it [i.e., forgive Reish Lakish or pray for him] for my son."

He said: *Leave your orphans; I will revive them* (*Yirmiyahu* 49:11).

She said: "Do it because of my widowhood."

He said: *The widows should trust in Me* (ibid.).

R. Shimon ben Lakish passed away. R. Yohanan was very pained by his passing. The Rabbis said: "Who will go and help calm R. Yohanan? Let R. Elazar ben Pedat go, for he is sharp in learning."

He went and sat before R. Yohanan. Every time R. Yohanan said something, R. Elazar cited a supporting tannaitic source.

R. Yohanan said: "Are you like the son of Lakish? When I said something, the son of Lakish would ask me twenty-four questions, and I would respond with twenty-four answers. As a result, learning increased. And you tell me a tannaitic support. Do I not know that I say good ideas?"

He walked, and tore his garment, and wept.

He said: "Where are you, son of Lakish? Where are you, son of Lakish?" He kept crying out until he lost his mind. The Rabbis asked for mercy on him and he passed away.

(*Bava Mezia* 84a)

Many elements of this tragic story require analysis. First, let us assume that, before their meeting in the Jordan, R. Yohanan already knew something about Reish Lakish's character and potential. We may take it for granted, after all, that R. Yohanan did not offer his sister to every straying Jew as his standard method of *kiruv* (bringing unaffiliated Jews closer to Torah). In this case he must have foreseen the greatness that Reish Lakish would achieve. This idea finds support in Tosafot's contention that Reish Lakish was already learned before he abandoned the *mizvot*. (They infer this from the words "if you return.") R. Yohanan may have known Reish Lakish from his earlier history.

As the story jumps from their early meeting to their sad final conversation, the reader may get the mistaken impression that the two of them never had a fruitful relationship with one another. Missing from the story are all the intervening years in which the brothers-in-law studied together and debated the fine points of talmudic law. The record of these years is found in the many halakhic debates between R. Yohanan and Reish Lakish throughout the Talmud.

The most difficult part of the story is the harsh exchange between the two study partners. Did R. Yohanan really insult Reish Lakish by referring to his sordid past as a bandit? Did Reish Lakish really question whether his decision to return to Torah had been worthwhile? Some commentators refuse to take these lines at face value. Maharsha states that R. Yohanan was not trying to insult his *chavruta* (study partner). Instead, he was acknowledging that Reish Lakish knew more about knives, and was therefore correct in this debate. Tosafot argue that when Reish Lakish spoke about being called a master there, he was not referring to his time as leader of the thieves, but to his earlier time as a talmudic scholar. As he was given an honorific title both before he left the *beit medrash* and after he returned, Reish Lakish wondered whether he had benefited from his dramatic foray into banditry. While we can appreciate what motivated these commentators, it must be conceded that the simplest reading of the story indicates that a harsh exchange indeed took place.

R. Yohanan's displeasure at what Reish Lakish said may have caused the latter's illness. That is why R. Yohanan's sister pleads with him to intercede on her husband's behalf. Why does he refuse her request? One possible answer is that he was still angry with Reish Lakish for expressing doubt about rejoining the world of Torah. Alternatively, R. Yohanan may have felt that he had no special power to bring about his brother-in-law's recovery. The verses he cites from *Yirmiyahu* indicate that only God can help the destitute.

I believe that the key to the story lies in the exchange between

R. Yohanan and R. Elazar. The latter tries to console R. Yohanan by citing proofs for everything R. Yohanan says. R. Yohanan is incredulous that R. Elazar thinks this will replace Reish Lakish. It was precisely the ongoing argumentation between R. Yohanan and Reish Lakish that led to a flowering of Torah. This is what R. Yohanan feels cannot be replaced. R. Yohanan is teaching us that the ideal *chavruta* is not the person who quickly endorses everything his study partner says. On the contrary! The ideal *chavruta* challenges one's ideas. This process generates growth in learning. We should add that the same principle also applies to other forms of friendship. Instead of looking for friends who will always agree with us, we should seek out those who are willing to tell us when they think we have erred, whether intellectually, ethically, or religiously.

Assuming that the preceding idea reflects the essential theme of the story, we can now understand the harsh exchange. If the ideal study partnership involves argument, then there is a lurking danger that the arguing will get out of hand. In the heat of a verbal dispute, people will say things that they later regret but can no longer take back. Thus, the very strength of the partnership of R. Yohanan and Reish Lakish was the source of its downfall, as they temporarily lost themselves in the passion of talmudic debate.

My student Daniel Vinik added a profound postscript to my reading of this story. Even after the tragedy of Reish Lakish, R. Yohanan rejects R. Elazar's attempt to make learning an experience of constant agreement. This means that even when aware of the dangers, one cannot forsake the back-and-forth argumentation that constitutes the lifeblood of learning. We cannot forsake debate, but we must try to ensure that the debate remains respectful and dignified.

Maharsha adds two more insights. R. Yohanan tore his garment after the encounter with R. Elazar. The failure of Reish Lakish's substitute must have brought home the magnitude of the loss, and that is why R. Yohanan rent his garments. Maharsha also notes that other talmudic sources mention the forty-nine aspects of every Torah idea. When R. Yohanan presented an idea, Reish Lakish raised twenty-four questions and R. Yohanan responded with twenty-four answers, meaning that all forty-nine aspects of the idea (the original idea plus the two sets of twenty-four) had been addressed. Thus, the back-and-forth between these two giants had truly led to the deepest and most comprehensive understanding of Torah. The possibility of having such productive interactions without resorting to harsh or insulting words is a challenge beckoning to all of us.

Monetary Law and the Quest for Wisdom

> R. Yishmael said: "He who wants to become wise will study *dinei mammonot* [monetary law], for no subject of Torah is greater, and it is like an overflowing spring."
>
> (*Bava Batra* 175b)

R. Yishmael's statement anticipates the view frequently found in the yeshiva world that the tractates in *Seder Nezikin* lend themselves to the deepest form of talmudic analysis. One need only think of the justified admiration and love in learned circles for the works of the *Kezot haHoshen* and the *Netivot haMishpat*, classics of monetary law, to see this view. Yet we can still question why things developed in this way. What aspect of study does the mishna refer to when it ranks *Nezikin* as the greatest Torah subject?

R. Yisrael Lipshutz (*Tiferet Yisrael*, commentary on the Mishna) identifies two aspects unique to this field of study. He points out that the Torah gives the human intellect greater leeway to make decisions in monetary law than in any other area of Halakha. Unlike the laws of *kashrut*, where the Torah specifies many minute details, the laws of plaintiffs and defendants are summed up in Torah in the verse "Judge your neighbor with righteousness" (*Vayikra* 19:15). This broad imperative generated a situation in which human reasoning became paramount in this area of learning.

Additionally, R. Lipshutz points, monetary law prevents a kind of intellectual evasion. When it comes to *kashrut*, we can always respond to a doubtful situation by deciding to be stringent. In monetary law, the impulse to deal with doubt through *humra* is meaningless. What would be a stringency for the plaintiff will be a leniency for the defendant, and vice versa. Therefore, there is no choice but to reason things out to some conclusion. This pressure to decide also contributed to the intricate analysis of monetary law.

I would broaden the insight offered by R. Lipshutz to other areas of Jewish life. On the one hand, there is no denying the fact that halakhic decisors often choose to be stringent so as to avoid possible transgressions. At the same time, not every situation lends itself to this solution. Many communal and personal religious questions involve the clash of opposing Jewish ideals, so that there is no safe way out of the dilemma. In the clash for time between Torah and *hessed*, the *humra* escape route does not exist. We must utilize the best analytic abilities to the fullest to make such decisions and not attempt to avoid them. The search for safe answers reflects a profound misunderstanding of the questions.

R. Yosef Hayyim offers a more homiletical reading of this mishna in his *Ben Yehoyada*. He plays with the letters of the word *mikzoa* ("subject") and connects it to the word *zoek* ("to cry out"). Monetary law involves a certain amount of crying out. He illustrates this by telling the story of a man who loses money in a court case and proceeds to cry out in anger. The judge asks the man what his reaction would be to a *pesak* regarding *hamez* on Pesah that would cause him a comparable loss. When the man responds that he would accept the decision in silence, the judge asks him what the difference is between the hypothetical *hamez* case and the court case at hand. The man answers that he can accept financial loss but cannot tolerate someone else winning the money from him.

According to the *Ben Yehoyada*, this mishna hints at the heightened tension that comes into play when two people fight over money. It behooves us to keep this in mind the next time we face such a disagreement. I would add that this homily gives new meaning to the connection between monetary law and wisdom. It takes great wisdom to maintain one's equanimity when embroiled in a monetary dispute.

Ignorance, Arrogance, and the Wisdom That Edifies

> Rava says: "*It* [the Torah] *is not in heaven* [*nor is it over the sea*] (*Devarim* 30:12): You will not find Torah in a person who raises himself above it like the heavens, and you will not find Torah in a person who expands himself upon it like the ocean."
> Rav Yohanan says: "*It is not in heaven* (*Devarim* 30:12): You will not find Torah among the arrogant."
>
> (*Eruvin* 55a)

Rav Shemuel Edels (Maharsha) suggests that Rava's warning pertains to two different types of arrogance. The first person denies the need for a teacher, mistakenly raising himself above the need for guidance in learning. The second assumes that having a teacher suffices in and of itself. A student blessed with an outstanding teacher may haughtily assume that he is superior to others merely by virtue of his teacher's ability. The student who does this arrogates an expanse of knowledge to himself, not realizing that true expansiveness in learning depends upon one's own hard-fought efforts irrespective of the teacher's excellence. Rava tells us that both dispensing with the need for a teacher and relying solely upon the teacher get in the way of a good education.

R. Yoshiyahu Pinto offers an instructive reading in the *Rif* commentary that appears in *Ein Yaakov*. He argues that Rava and R. Yohanan are not making the same point. Rava refers to one's relationship to the material studied, R. Yohanan to one's relationship to others. For Rava, haughtiness toward the material can get in the way of knowledge. The intense desire to criticize a text blocks appreciation and understanding of it. Further, as R. Pinto points out, the proud student may deem more basic material as beneath him, and focus solely on esoteric knowledge. Students of this may never address the fundamental gaps in their knowledge. For example, the aspiring kabbalist may never set aside the time to develop a solid understanding of the basic storyline of *Humash*. I have encountered students more interested in delving into mystical, esoteric knowledge than in setting aside time to find out more about the life of Moshe Rabbenu.

For Rav Yohanan, it is the social blowhard who remains ensconced in ignorance. People of this kind refuse to learn from others or to dedicate the time needed for study and review. An arrogant interest in presenting a learned veneer rather than engage in actual learning renders them unable to ever admit publicly to not knowing something. For this latter type, the desire to show that wisdom comes easily prevents it from coming altogether.

Rav Zadok haKohen (*Divrei Soferim* 15) offers another perspective on the incommensurability of wisdom and arrogance. The Zohar says that a sign of Bilaam's ignorance is that he praised himself. Rav Zadok points out that as Bilaam actually seems to be quite learned, the Zohar must be referring to Bilaam's lack of internalized knowledge. When knowledge fails to penetrate into the deeper recesses of the human personality, arrogance results.

I believe that Rav Zadok offers us a profound psychological insight. If our knowledge has a positive effect upon the world, or enables us to become more ethically sensitive or spiritually alive, then that knowledge has found a worthy home, and we will find satisfaction in our learning. On the other hand, if our knowledge has no effect upon the world or upon our personality, then the knowledge finds no expression and we end up wondering what our years of study have produced. At that point, the only thing left to do with our knowledge is to brag about it. Envision two brilliant academics, one who goes about the day's scholarly work with quiet dignity, and the other constantly attempting to show off his or her knowledge. Rav Zadok's insight lies at the root of the difference between them.

Thus we see that arrogance can be both the cause and the effect of ignorance. Arrogance toward the material, or toward teachers and peers, prevents the accumulation of knowledge. At the same time, arrogance also reveals that the knowledge accumulated has failed to affect the knower. The Talmud refers to such knowledge as "from the mouth and outward" (*Sanhedrin* 106b). For Rav Zadok, this image conveys both the failure to internalize the knowledge and the need to brag about one's learning.

CHAPTER 5

Education

Breadth, Depth, and Choosing a *Rosh Yeshiva*

Rav Yosef was referred to as Sinai [meaning that he had very broad knowledge], while Rabba was said to be an *oker harim* [uprooter of mountains, i.e., excellent in analytical reasoning]. The time came that one of them was needed [to become the *rosh yeshiva*]. They sent a message to the Rabbis there: "A Sinai and an uprooter of mountains – which one of them takes precedence?"

They [the Rabbis] sent back: "Sinai takes precedence, for all need the master of the wheat [i.e., the one who has gathered all the talmudic teachings]." Nevertheless, Rav Yosef did not accept the position. Rabba ruled [as *rosh yeshiva*] for twenty-two years, and then Rav Yosef ruled for two and a half years. All the years that Rabba ruled, Rav Yosef did not even call a bloodletter to his house.

(*Berakhot* 64a, *Horayot* 14a)

This story begins with an important educational question and ends with a note of ethical excellence on the part of R. Yosef. The commentaries offer three explanations of the latter. According to Rashi, the bloodletter made house calls as a sign of respect for distinguished people. R. Yosef refused to accept that honor so as not to set himself up as a challenger to Rabba. We can easily understand that situations calling for a change in leadership often divide people into rival camps, and that negative feelings between the partisans of each candidate frequently linger on even after a decision has been finalized. R. Yosef understood this and took steps to publicly demonstrate that he was not a challenger to Rabba's reign.

Rashi cites another explanation, this one holding that R. Yosef did not have time for bloodletting because he was too busy learning from Rabba. R. Yosef's insistence on not missing any time in yeshiva may also have been a way of conveying his contentment with Rabba at the helm. One who refuses to miss a single lecture clearly assumes the self-definition of a student and not a rival. Additionally, R. Yosef may have recognized that Rabba had reasoning skills he lacked and therefore wanted to hear Rabba's *shiurim* and learn a new set of analytical skills.

Tosafot haRosh cites a different explanation in which the closing line about the bloodletter actually reflects the reward for R. Yosef's decision to allow Rabba to accept the position. No bloodletter came to R. Yosef's house because no one in this house fell ill during this time period. If so, the sterling character of R. Yosef manifested itself in his humble ability to step aside, and divine providence arranged an appropriate reward.

Let us return to the educational question raised at the beginning of the gemara. Is breadth of knowledge or depth of reasoning the crucial qualification for heading the yeshiva academy? Note that we are not talking about two extremes. If the "uprooter of mountains" knows nothing about Halakha, then he has nothing to analyze. Conversely, if the fellow who has learned it all shows little understanding of the material, he too cannot function

productively in the *beit midrash*. For this reason, Meiri explains
the Sinai as someone who can make analogies and extrapolations,
but lacks the creative reasoning of the *oker harim*. Presumably, the
uprooter of mountains has learned a good deal of material. The
gemara's question refers to rabbis with different emphases and
diverse strengths, but not to those totally inadequate with regard
to either knowledge or reasoning.

The Rabbis prefer that the scholar with vast knowledge assume
the mantle of leadership. Rav Shlomo Kluger argues (in his notes
on *Peri Megadim, Orah Hayyim* 136) that this was only true in the
time of the Talmud, before the entire Oral Law was committed to
writing. At that time the most crucial issue was finding someone
who had memorized and could recall all the traditional material
needed for discussion. Once the Oral Law was easily available
in writing, the uprooter of mountains would take precedence.
Rav Ovadia Yosef, in his introduction to *Yabia Omer*, cites many
authorities who still maintain, contra Rav Kluger, that a Sinai
takes precedence. This debate has a certain poetic appropriateness in that R. Kluger offers innovative, reasoned support for the
oker harim, while R. Ovadia Yosef utilizes his great knowledge to
support the Sinai.

One might conclude that every educational institution needs
both types of scholars. Indeed, Neziv (*Meromei Sadeh* on *Horayot*)
argues that R. Yosef was able to step aside only because he remained in the yeshiva and provided his knowledge. The yeshiva
was able to draw on the knowledge of R. Yosef even as it was directed by the sharp reasoning of Rabba. Thus, R. Yosef's continuing presence in the *beit medrash* not only indicated his acceptance
of Rabba's authority; it also enabled the combined abilities of these
two scholars to generate a stronger learning environment.

When I think back to my days as a youthful yeshiva student
and recall the many intense debates about the relative merits of
bekiut ("breadth") and *beiyyun* ("depth"), I conclude that youthful
exuberance sometimes got in the way of more nuanced positions.
While students can certainly take pride in their teacher's or their

yeshiva's approach to these issues, they should also have a healthy awareness of the need to integrate these two strengths on both an individual and an institutional level. No one who is sorely lacking in knowledge or analytical ability can succeed in learning. No *beit midrash* can truly flourish without a healthy mix of scholars with different strengths.

Rav Kook (*Ein Aya* on *Berakhot*) frames the question differently. He suggests that the Sinai is able to teach the masses, but the *oker harim* cannot because ordinary Jews find his abstract reasoning incomprehensible. Nevertheless, both together can educate the entire population. The Sinai has a direct effect on the masses because they understand his more straightforward approach to the material. The *oker harim* teaches the learned and scholarly, who then in turn pass on some of his teaching to the broader populace. When the Rabbis decided that "All need the master of the wheat," they indicated a preference for the teacher with the ability to speak to the common Jew without the help of an intermediary.

Of course, the opposite can be true as well. Breadth of knowledge sometimes makes things difficult for the average reader. One of the difficulties in reading an essay by Isaiah Berlin or George Steiner is simply keeping up with the massive number of references. In the Torah world, the sweeping erudition of some *aharonim* presents a similar challenge. Perhaps Rav Kook is offering a charge to the leading scholar, be he a Sinai or an *oker harim*. While there is tremendous value to influencing the community through an intellectual trickle-down effect, a leader ultimately has to find a more direct way to teach the broader community. Knowing how to simplify things when necessary, without sacrificing the profundity of Torah, makes a person ready for rabbinic leadership.

From Mother's Milk to Butter: The Toil of Torah

> They said in the study hall of R. Yannai: "What does it mean when it says, *The churning of milk brings forth butter, the wringing of the nose brings forth blood, and the forcing of anger brings forth strife* (*Mishlei* 30:33)? In which individual will you find the butter of Torah? In the one who spits out the milk he sucked at his mother's breast for it [the Torah]."
>
> (*Berakhot* 63b)

This forceful statement certainly calls for an explanation. What does the imagery of spitting out mother's milk mean, and how does doing this enable a person to achieve success in Torah learning? We are fortunate to have R. Avraham Yizhak haKohen Kook's commentary on the aggadot in *Berakhot*, a tractate packed with Aggada. Rav Kook interprets this gemara as a message to all educators and pedagogues. Many teachers conceive of their job as requiring them to constantly make learning easier for their students. They think that the goal of education is to create a learning environment that enables student achievement with a minimum of toil and effort. The perfect symbol for such a vision is the nursing baby, who need not work to obtain a good meal.

For R. Kook, this educational approach has two shortcomings: it mistakenly prizes quantity over quality, and it misjudges the impact of this type of learning on the student's personality. It is true that a teacher can invent ingenious methods for imparting masses of information fairly quickly, but there are no clever tricks for teaching depth of understanding. A focus on easing the student's burden invariably sacrifices depth in the quest to cover more material.

A student accustomed to this easy style of learning will not undergo the personal growth necessary for true academic excellence. Ultimately, there is no personal or educational greatness without the ability to persevere in the face of massive difficulties. It is the hard-won insight that usually bears retelling. Only intense effort expended in trying to understand a text enables the student to truly internalize its message and meaning.

Any educational environment that fails to make real demands of its students does them a great disservice. In Rav Kook's understanding of the talmudic imagery, the growing child eventually refuses his mother's milk despite the ease with which it provides dinner. Real growth depends upon a decision to procure food that involves more effort.

R. Kook's message should have great resonance for our generation. The broader society, influenced by the achievements of modern technology, often seems dedicated to making life easier. From this standpoint, it seems as if the final goal of human existence would entail sitting on a couch with a remote that controls everything else in the house and brings you whatever you need without your ever having to get up. This atmosphere has influenced all religions, and Judaism is no exception. The current publishing flood of English translations of traditional works and of collections summarizing vast amounts of material is intended to make learning easier. Without denying that these works can often be helpful, we should still realize that an over-reliance upon them does not produce real *talmidei hakhamim*. A student can finish *Shas* with the help of ArtScroll or a short *daf yomi shiur*, but still not learn how to read gemara independently in the original Aramaic. I have encountered several students in recent years who fit this description.

Rav Kook's contention does not mean that a teachers should impose arbitrary difficulties in order to enhance student growth. We should avoid difficulties that crush the student's spirit, as well as those that are really pointless. At the same time, we should be wary of frequent searches for ways to ease the burden of learning. The constant attempt to remove difficulties ultimately diminishes the depth of the material, lessens its impact, and stunts the student's personal development.

Søren Kierkegaard tells how he was once sitting in the Frederiksborg Garden in Copenhagen one Sunday afternoon, thinking about how the great benefactors of modern-day life are dedicated to making life easier.

> ...the many benefactors of the age who know how to benefit mankind by making life easier and easier, some by railways, others by omnibusses, and steamboats, others by the telegraph, others by easily apprehended compendiums and short recitals of everything worth knowing, and finally the true benefactors of the age who make spiritual existence in virtue of thought easier and easier, yet more and more significant.... seeing that I had accomplished nothing and was unable to make anything easier than it had already been made, and moved by genuine interest in those who make everything easy, I conceived it as my task to make difficulties everywhere.
>
> (*Concluding Unscientific Postscript* pp. 165–166)

Kierkegaard expresses the point beautifully in his *Attack Upon Christendom* (p. 100). In the following passage, he distinguishes between procuring water and achieving eternal blessedness.

> Far be it from me to speak disparagingly of the comfortable! Let it be applied whenever it can be applied, in relation to everything which is in such a sense a thing that this thing can be possessed irrespective of the way in which it is possessed, so that one can have it either in this way or in the other, for when such is the case, the convenient and comfortable way is undeniably to be preferred. Take water for example: water is a thing which can be procured in the difficult way of fetching it up from the pump, but it can also be procured in the convenient way of high pressure; naturally, I prefer the more convenient way.
>
> But the eternal is not a thing which can be had regardless of the way in which it is acquired; no, the eternal is not really a thing, but is the way in which it is acquired.

Even if we reject Kierkegaard's overly strong formulation that the eternal is identical with the way in which it is acquired, we can accept his point that we cannot achieve the most important things in life by circumventing the arduous path that leads to them. This rings true for all religious, moral, and personal growth, and certainly for the world of Torah learning. As this Danish philosopher did a century and a half ago, we must understand the tide of our time, which is always in search of greater ease, and swim against it. In the long run, only a life of toil and striving produces the sweet butter of Torah.

Eulogizing, Teaching, and Authenticity

> When Rav Huna passed away, they wanted to place a Torah scroll on his bier.
>
> Rav Hisda said to them: "You are now going to do for him something which he thought was incorrect during his lifetime?" For R. Tahlifa said: "I saw that R. Huna wanted to sit on a bier, and a Torah scroll was on it. He placed a vessel on the floor, and moved the Torah to it." Apparently [R. Huna] held that it is forbidden to sit on a bed that a Torah scroll is resting upon.
>
> His bier would not fit out the door, so they wanted to lower it from the roof. R. Hisda said to them: "We learned from him that the honor for a sage is to go out the regular entrance."
>
> They wanted to move him to a different bier. R. Hisda said to them: "We learned from him that the honor for a sage is to go out in his original bier."…They enlarged the entrance and took him out.
>
> (*Moed Katan* 25a)

The first part of this story reflects the tension between wanting to honor a great talmudic sage by asserting his intimate relationship with the Torah and yet trying to maintain a sense of the unique honor reserved for a Torah scroll. The second part of the story requires further elucidation. Although the halakhic details prohibiting changing biers or exiting the building in an awkward fashion are certainly valuable, they may contain an aggadic message.

Rav Yosef Dov Soloveitchik offers a brilliant metaphorical reading in his eulogy for R. Hayyim Ozer Grodzinski ("*Nossei haZitz ve'haHoshen*" in *Divrei Hagut ve'haArakha*). According to R. Soloveitchik, the physical inability to move R. Huna's bier outside reflects a metaphorical inability to convey the greatness of Rav Huna to the masses waiting outside the door. The simple artisans and farmers could not understand the complexity and depth of this great personality. It is in this sense that the bier could not fit through the door.

The eulogizers thought that they could solve the problem by making the masses feel the loss through easy emotion and cheap sentiment. They would wail and cry as they spoke about the tribulations, sufferings, and death that await all mankind. The audience would be overcome by a sense of their own mortality and weep with great emotion. The eulogizers wanted to bring R. Huna out to the masses through the roof of shallow emotions and false tears. R. Hisda insisted that the sage must be brought out through the main door. A roundabout way of achieving emotional impact was no substitute for authentic recognition of a special person.

The eulogizers then suggested a different strategy. If they could not rely upon emotions, they could still portray R. Huna in a way the masses would find appealing. They could depict R. Huna as a public figure, a great diplomat and politician, a compelling orator. They could move him to a new bier that would easily find its way outside. R. Hisda taught them that we refuse to distort a rabbinic portrait in order to achieve popular recognition. Either the populace will learn to appreciate R. Huna as he truly was or he cannot be taken out to them at all. The only remaining option is to break down the door and enlarge the opening. Extend the emotional range and intellectual depths of the listeners! Fight against the darkness of ignorance and falsehood! Show them the personality of a truly great man!

The last few sentences, paraphrased from Rav Soloveitchik,

pertain both to the narrow issue of portraying great individuals and to the broader issue of education in general. Regarding the narrow issue, contemporary eulogies and biographies tend to reduce all *gedolim* to one fixed form, with no sense of the color and vibrancy of each individual personality. No one is willing to share an authentic portrait of greatness with the masses. Regarding the broader issue, all educators face the temptation of appealing to their students through cheap appeals to emotion (such as gratuitous mentioning of the Holocaust) or by presenting something differently from the way it really is. R. Hisda reminds us that teachers must aim to expand the capabilities of their students, rather than compress the subject matter they are attempting to convey.

The Business of Yeshiva

> Hillel used to earn a *trepik* a day, half of which he gave to the guard at the house of study and half he used to support himself and his family. One day he earned nothing and the guard would not let him in. He climbed up and sat on the skylight so that he could hear the words of the living God from Shemaya and Avtalyon. It happened that it was a Friday in the winter and the snow from the sky fell upon him. At the break of dawn, Shemaya said to Avtalyon: "My brother, usually it is light, but today it is dark. Perhaps the day is cloudy." They looked up and saw the shape of a man against the window, and they found three cubits of snow upon him. They took off the snow, washed him, anointed him, and put him by the fire. They said: "He is worthy for Shabbat to be profaned for his sake."
>
> (*Yoma* 35b)

Why did they charge an admission fee to those who wanted to attend the *beit medrash*? Maharsha raises two possibilities. The study halls in talmudic times were often out in the country and not in the heart of civilization. Out in the wild, people need a guard, and someone has to fund the guard's salary. Alternatively, some study halls only let high-quality students in (see *Berakhot* 28a), and someone needed to pay for whoever was responsible for administering this policy. We might also suggest that the money went to pay for teacher salaries, buying *seforim*, cleaning, and general maintenance.

Beyond the specifics of the yeshiva's budget, Maharsha's explanations raise a significant point. *Yeshivot*, shuls, and other Jewish institutions have financial needs, and to some degree they need to function like businesses. At the same time, if they function only like a business, something has gone very wrong. When a student with the dedication of Hillel is locked out because this one time he could not pay, the business side of the yeshiva has become too dominant. An overemphasis on the business angle may be reflected in the admission fee. As Professor Yonah Frankel points out (in his *Iyyunim beOlamo haRuhani shel Sippur haAggada*, pp. 66–69), the fact that the fee equaled the amount needed to support Hillel's family indicates that it was too high. Professor Frankel also argues that Shemaya's comment about Hillel blocking the skylight has symbolic import. The study hall is normally a great source of spiritual illumination. When small-mindedness forces a Hillel to endanger himself in order to hear a *shiur*, it is a dark day in the *beit medrash*.

Isolation and Education

> The Rabbis taught: A person may not clear stones from his own domain into the public domain. An incident occurred with a certain person, who was clearing stones from his own domain into the public domain. A pious person found this fellow and said to him: "Empty one! Why are you clearing stones from a domain that is not yours, into a domain that is yours?" The fellow scoffed at the pious person. After some time, he needed to sell his field, and he was walking in that public domain, and tripped over those stones.

He said: "Fittingly did that pious person tell me, 'Why are you clearing stones from a domain that is not yours into a domain that is yours?'"

(*Bava Kama* 50b)

The straightforward meaning of this story revolves around one's attitude to property. As a basic moral obligation, we need to respect public spaces and avoid littering or leaving items about that could hurt others. In addition, we must understand that our hold on our own property remains ever tenuous. From this perspective, the public domain belongs to us in a deeper and more enduring way than our own private property. When the pious fellow's apparently erroneous statement proved prophetic, the former owner of the field, who had lost his fortune, understood the wisdom of a different attitude to property.

One of the guiding principles of my Aggada interpretation is that finding a good commentary on aggadot often demands expanding the search beyond the standard commentaries on the Talmud. This story provides a good example of the benefits of widening the search for the accumulated wisdom of our sages regarding aggadot. Rav Reuven Katz, former chief rabbi of Petah Tikva, wrote a book on *Humash* called *Dudaei Reuven*. It contains many sharp insights, including some wonderful readings of aggadot. The following is based on his sermon for *Parashat Bo*.

Rav Katz locates an additional metaphorical layer of meaning in our story. According to Rav Katz, the story revolves around an educational decision. Some parents decide to withdraw completely from the community, and educate their children separately, in an effort to avoid the problematic ideals of the broader community. They focus all their resources on their own children and ignore communal educational needs. They think that these stones of poor ideals will be safely removed to the public domain. Such an approach is mistaken on two accounts.

First, it ignores the responsibility we all have to others, and, in particular, to those without the financial or religious resources to educate their own children.

Second, it is mistaken even with regard to one's own children, as they will invariably be affected by the ideals outside their own doors. Total isolation from one's communal culture is not possible. Therefore, if that culture has problematic aspects, one must fight to change them. If we do not try to clear the stones of culture on the street outside, they inevitably will trip us up.

R. Katz does not advocate exposure to every aspect of the surrounding culture, but he does note the pitfalls of extreme isolation. The isolationist approach lacks communal responsibility and shows a narrowness of vision regarding social influences on one's children.

CHAPTER 6

Interpersonal Obligations

Torah-Only and Having a God

When R. Elazar ben Parta and R. Hanina ben Teradyon were captured, R. Elazar said to R. Hanina: "You are fortunate, because you were captured for one offense. Woe is me, for I was captured for five offenses."

R. Hanina said to him: "You are fortunate, because you were captured for five offenses and you will be saved. Woe is me, who was captured for one offense, and I will not be saved. For you engaged in Torah and *gemilut hassadim* [acts of compassion], and I was only involved in Torah."

It is as Rav Huna taught. R. Huna said: "Whoever is only involved in Torah, it is as if he has no God, as it says: *And there were many days in Israel without a true God* (II *Divrei haYamim* 15:3). What does the verse mean when it says *without a true*

87

God? That anyone who involves himself only with Torah is
compared to someone without a God."

(*Avoda Zara* 17b)

R. Huna's sharp formulation demands explanation. While we can
easily understand that Torah learning without acts of compassion
leaves a person religiously incomplete, that hardly constitutes
lacking a God. Why does R. Huna employ such a harsh and sweeping formulation? Rashi explains that the person so described lacks
a God to protect him, because God will only step in to aid the
compassionate. If so, the "Torah-only personality" obviously has
a God, but not a God who will provide succor.

R. Shemuel Edels, the Maharsha, offers a beautiful alternative explanation. He points out that among the divine attributes
(see *Shemot* 34:6–7) compassion predominates. Furthermore, the
attempt to emulate God, to the best of our human ability, represents a significant religious ideal. Our Rabbis state on several
occasions that human acts of mercy fulfill the *mizva* of imitating
God (e.g., *Sota* 14a). Thus, one who downplays acts of kindness
has a fundamentally flawed conception of the divine. A person
who truly understands the nature of God will be drawn to emulate
His compassion. If so, the Torah-only personality is, in reality,
"without a true God."

This argument finds support from the magnificent closing
chapter of *Moreh Nevukhim* (3:54). There Rambam discusses the
true goal of human life. He rejects wealth as a goal, because wealth
is a means more than an end. He rejects physical prowess as the
goal, because members of the animal kingdom accomplish feats
of speed and strength more effectively. Rambam initially states
that human ethics could not be the goal, because they apply only
in an interpersonal context, whereas the true goal must have universal applicability. Therefore, he asserts, intellectual cognition of
divine truth represents the ultimate purpose of human striving.

Had Rambam stopped here, his vision of the good life would
have been purely intellectual. However, he goes on to say that

those who authentically comprehend the nature of the divine are drawn to emulate God's acts of compassion and justice. Thus, only ethics that do not stem from *imitatio Dei* are excluded from the true goal of mankind. For a religious people intending to emulate their Maker, compassionate behavior is an indispensable component of the *summum bonum*. We cannot truly understand God unless we have a desire to follow in His ethical footsteps.

Some verses in *Yirmiyahu* beautifully convey the Rambam's vision. The prophet (9:23–24) tells the wise, the strong, and the wealthy not to glory in their achievements. For the Rambam, this means that riches, physical might, and ethics (here identified with a kind of wisdom) are not mankind's central achievements. Yirmiyahu continues: *"But let a man glory in this, that he understand and know Me, that I am the God who does beneficence, justice, and righteousness in the earth."* This verse clearly links knowledge of God with knowledge of His ethical actions. If we fail to make this connection, and do not draw the implications for our own actions, we have a faulty conception of the Master of the Universe.

Meiri interprets the gemara somewhat differently, but a similar point emerges. He points out that while many people do not observe various *mizvot*, we do not accuse them of lacking a God. He explains that from a certain perspective, it is worse for one who is engaged in Torah not to be engaged in *hessed* than for a person to be religiously uninvolved altogether. Someone who learns Torah should understand the interpersonal obligations it mandates. This knowing rejection of the Torah's authority makes the person fall into the category of those "without a God." To rephrase Meiri's point in our own words, someone who has truly learned and internalized the message of Torah could not possibly be indifferent to the call of *hessed*.

The continuation of the gemara in *Avoda Zara* strengthens the point.

> And did not [R. Hanina] engage in acts of benevolence? Did we not learn: R. Eliezer ben Yaakov taught: "One should not

give money to the charity fund unless the person in charge is a sage like R. Hanina ben Teradyon"?

[The gemara answers:] He was very trustworthy but was not actively engaged.

But did we not learn: He [R. Hanina] said to him: "Money for Purim became mixed up with money for charity, and I divided it among the poor"?

[The gemara answers:] He was involved, but not as much as he should have been.

Rashi offers two interpretations of the money mix-up. R. Hanina may have confused the money for his own Purim feast with the money for the poor, and thus gave the entire amount to charity. Or perhaps he used the Purim funds for a different charitable cause and replenished the Purim fund from his own pocket. According to either interpretation, R. Hanina was a person of honesty, integrity, and benevolence. Nonetheless, he felt that he had performed inadequately in this regard. Apparently, the mere fact of engaging in charitable work does not discharge our duties in the realm of *gemilut hassadim*. This story calls for a more serious and ongoing attempt to strike the right balance between the competing claims of Torah and *hessed*.

The balance need not be attained on a daily, or even yearly, basis. It is reasonable to argue that the yeshiva years will be more dedicated to Torah, whereas our middle-aged years, when we have greater financial means and a home in which to host guests, may offer more opportunities for *hessed*. However, even one's time in yeshiva offers numerous opportunities for acts of compassion within the very walls of the *beit midrash*. Beyond this, the aspiring scholar should view the time in yeshiva as an investment, enabling greater contributions to the community at a later date.

One might add that this gemara clearly rejects the idea that *hessed* can be accomplished in a metaphysical manner. Some say that everyone who learns Torah engages in an act of compassion, because Torah learning improves the world in some grand cosmic way. If we push this idea too far, there would be no category of Torah without *hessed*. Compassion must be expressed in a naturalistic way, with our own efforts and resources directed toward helping other flesh-and-blood human beings. May we successfully integrate the great twin religious callings of Torah and *hessed*.

Circles of Ethical Responsibility

Kohelet 12:14 states, "For every action God shall bring to judgment, on every hidden thing, whether good or evil." The following gemara comments on this verse:

> What does *whether good or evil* mean?
>
> It was taught in the house of R. Yannai: "This refers to a person who gives charity to a poor person in public." In this vein, R. Yannai once saw a fellow giving a coin to a poor person in public; he said to [the donor]: "Better that you should not give him anything at all than that you should give to him and embarrass him."
>
> In the house of R. Shila, they taught: "This refers to a person who gives charity to a woman in private, because he brings her under suspicion."
>
> Rava said: "This refers to the person who sends his wife uncut meat [from which the non-kosher parts have not been removed] on Friday." But did not Rava send [such meat to his own wife, R. Hisda's daughter]? The daughter of R. Hisda is different, because her expertise is established.
>
> R. Yohanan would cry when he arrived at this verse: *And it shall come to pass, when ra'ot* (evils) *that are many and zarot shall find them* (Devarim 31:21). [He would say:] "A slave whose master causes *ra'ot* and *zarot* to be found for him, what hope does he have?" What are *ra'ot* and *zarot*? These are evils (*ra'ot*) that become rivals (*zarot*) to one another, such as the wasp and the scorpion.

> Shemuel said: "This refers to the person who causes money
> to be found for a poor person at the time of his distress."
>
> (*Hagiga* 5a)

The preceding gemara expresses one idea with great clarity, but it has an ambiguous element. It clearly teaches that acts of giving can be performed in a problematic fashion. An act of benevolence (*hessed*) can humiliate a pauper, bring undeserved suspicion on a poor woman, or encourage the recipient to eat non-kosher meat. For this reason, the verse in *Kohelet* tells us, God brings even our good behavior to judgment. Indeed, even our righteous deeds must be checked for such faults.

Shemuel's statement is more difficult. Why should providing for a pauper be problematic? Furthermore, if Shemuel offers another example of improper giving, why does the gemara place his statement after the quotation from R. Yohanan about *ra'ot* and *zarot*? Despite the intrusion of R. Yohanan's idea, Rashi explains, Shemuel's example belongs to the previous discussion. Shemuel criticizes those who do not give to the poor in a timely fashion, but instead wait until the pauper is in distress and unable to shop around for more reasonable prices when spending the money.

In contrast, Rabbeinu Tam understands that Shemuel is providing an example of rival evils. His example is that of a poor person who is capriciously imprisoned by the ruler and then is offered a loan against his property. Had the poor man not been offered a loan, the ruler would have reduced the ransom; now that the poor person has access to funds, the ruler demands the more exorbitant ransom. Captivity followed by a forced loan can be termed "rival evils." Although this interpretation docs not connect Shemuel with the earlier discussion, it certainly represents another kind of problematic giving.

Many commentaries point out that Shemuel's criticism apparently contradicts another gemara which praises the person who gives the pauper a gift at the time of his distress.

A person who loves his neighbors, who brings close his relatives, who marries the daughter of his sister and lends a *sela* to a pauper at the time of his distress – about [such a person], Scripture says: *Then shall you call, and God will answer; you shall beseech and He will say: "Here I am"* (*Yeshayahu* 58:9).

(*Yevamot* 62b)

Rabbeinu Tam's explanation of the gemara in *Hagiga* resolves the contradiction. The gemara only censures those who cause indirect economic damage by their charity; otherwise, helping the poor would certainly be laudable. Rav Yaakov Reisher (in his *Iyyun Yaakov*) suggests another resolution. Perhaps the gemara in *Yevamot* refers to the distress of the giver and not of the recipient; thus, it praises those who are willing to help others financially despite their own economic problems. The gemara in *Hagiga* criticizes the person who waits too long before aiding the destitute.

It may prove helpful to set aside the contradiction and analyze the source from *Yevamot* independently. There, helping the poor is listed together with love of neighbors, closeness to relatives, and marrying a niece. What common theme unifies these disparate elements? Maharal offers an insightful interpretation in his *Be'er haGola*. It bears noting that this work is a valuable tool for aggadic interpretation. In *Be'er haGola*, the Maharal defends *Hazal* from several different critiques. The second section focuses on *gemarot* that seem illogical or immoral; Maharal defends the coherence and ethics of our sages. At the end of this section, Maharal relates to this gemara, which it had come under censure for promoting marriages between uncles and nieces.

His answer to that specific problem need not concern us as much as the sterling insight emerging from his reading of the entire passage. Let us first note that Maharal assumes that the gemara refers to a Jewish pauper. He goes on to argue that this gemara advocates the importance of advancing an extra closeness to those to whom we already bear some kind of relationship:

neighbors, relatives, and fellow Jews. Marrying a niece reflects closeness to family, and the poor person of whom the gemara speaks is a another Jew with financial troubles.

I believe that Maharal here rectifies a potential error in our ethical thinking. We correctly regard impartiality as an important component of a moral philosophy. Any situation calling for just behavior will lean heavily upon objectivity; yet we err when we see impartiality as the dominant theme of all ethical decisions. From this perspective, we might view favoring friends, relatives, and the like with our time and money as immoral. In opposition to such a view, the gemara in *Yevamot* contends that the moral person will feel greater responsibility toward those with whom he already has some kind of relationship.

Lawrence Blum makes this point in the context of his critique of Immanuel Kant's moral theory:

> The Kantian view objects to our being beneficent towards friends on the grounds that in doing so we distribute our beneficence according to personal interest and attachment rather than need or desert. Against this objection I argue that impartiality as a moral stance is appropriate only in certain circumstances, which do not generally include those of friendship.
>
> (*Friendship, Altruism and Morality*, p. 5)

A moral person must behave decently to everyone, whether friend, relative, or total stranger. At the same time, the most ethically scrupulous feel a greater responsibility toward friends, relatives, neighbors, and those who share their heritage. Although time and resources are limited and we cannot always serve both particularistic and universalistic visions, some combination of the two helps forge the ideal ethical personality.

Rav Kook (*Orot haKodesh*, 3:337) contends that the two Jewish paragons of compassion, Avraham and Aharon, reflect this dual theme. Avraham represents benevolence to the entire world,

Aharon stands for kindness to the Jewish people. For R. Kook, the ideal ethical personality incorporates both goals.

We may sometimes choose to ignore of these principles because they seem invariably to conflict. R. Kook argues, however, that they complement, rather than contradict, one another. The scope of universal *hessed* and the intensity of particularistic *hessed* are mutually reinforcing. When we are truly ethical, we acknowledge that all groups are worthy of largesse, but we focus much of our charitable energy on smaller groups sharing a common identity.

Order, Compassion, and the Moral Society

> The people of Sodom had beds for guests: if the guests were too tall, they were cut down to [the] size [of the bed]; if the guests were too short, they were stretched.
>
> (*Sanhedrin* 109b)

Many of us recall hearing this aggada back in elementary school and being struck by the strong image of human evil. Without denying the validity of our childhood understanding, we should still try to comprehend the tale on a deeper level, as adults. Certainly, this gemara conveys the rampant cruelty of Sodom quite successfully. Yet we wonder about the rationale for its specific imagery. The gemara could have employed many different manifestations of cruelty, but it decided to go with the intriguing image of adjusting the size of the guest to match the bed.

Rav Moshe Avigdor Amiel, rabbi of Antwerp and then of Tel Aviv, was a master *darshan* as well as a fine *talmid hakham*. He won the election for the Tel Aviv chief rabbinate in 1935, when the other candidates were Rav Soloveitchik and Rav Herzog. Among his many published *seforim*, he has a wonderful work of *derush* called *Derashot el Ami* that once helped many congregational rabbis prepare for their Shabbat morning sermons. I mention his biography as a way of reiterating how good commentary on aggada can be located by expanding the search.

In his *Hegyonot el Ami*, Rav Amiel brilliantly elucidates the meaning of the imagery in the Sodom story. According to Rav Amiel, some societies perform acts of charity more as a solution to an aesthetic or bureaucratic problem than from genuine kindness. In such societies, the motivation for helping the poor and the destitute is primarily that these disadvantaged people blemish the landscape of the city or prevent maximum economic efficiency. An administrator who has this bureaucratic perspective on charity might well conclude that the needs of the poor must be adjusted to fit the help we give them, rather than our help be adjusted to match their need. People with this perspective refuse to acknowledge the real needs of the poor and figuratively adjust them to fit the beds we have prepared.

In a chilling passage, R. Amiel describes what happens to societies whose acts of benevolence are no more than a way to maintain order. He points out that it was the most orderly of twentieth-century cultures that produced the greatest atrocities. When a desire for efficiency and order supplant authentic compassion, the door leading to cruelty is opened. While Rav Amiel certainly is referring to both fascism and communism, the danger he warns of can be found in any political system. Let us first ascertain the reality of those in need and then proceed, with true sympathy and kindness, to find beds for them of the appropriate size.

Hidden Hatred

> Why was the First Temple (*bayit rishon*) destroyed? Because of three sins: idolatry, sexual immorality, and murder.... But why was the Second Temple (*bayit sheini*) destroyed, if the people were engaged in Torah, *mizvot*, and *gemilut hassadim*? Because of groundless hatred (*sinat hinam*). This teaches you

that groundless hatred corresponds in gravity to the three sins of idolatry, sexual immorality and murder....

R. Yohanan and R. Elazar both say: "The earlier ones [the generation of the First Temple], their sin was revealed and the end of their exile was also revealed; the latter ones [the generation of the Second Temple], their sin was not revealed and the end of their exile was also not revealed."

(*Yoma* 9b)

The gemara's distinction between the two destructions in respect to the end being is based on the fact that there was a prophetic prediction about the duration of the first exile (seventy years; see *Yirmiyahu* 25:11) but not about the second. In fact, the second exile is still in effect without a clear promise of when it will end. Yet what does this have to do with sins being revealed? Moreover, why were the earlier sins revealed but not the latter ones? Is there some aspect of groundless hatred that lends itself to being hidden?

Maharsha explains that the Jews at the time of *bayit sheini* pretended to love their friends and neighbors, but stabbed each other in the back at the first opportunity. The gemara refers to sins that were not revealed because they were covered up with a facade of false friendship. Maharsha bolsters his argument by citing the famous idea of *Hazal* (*Bava Kama* 79b) that the *gazlan* (mugger) pays a lesser penalty than the *ganav* (burglar) because the latter commits his crime secretly, thereby attempting to preserve a righteous veneer for society. According to this explanation, hypocrisy makes a sin much more grievous and difficult to repent of; the exile continues because we have not successfully combated this hypocrisy. In our age of advertising and public relations, this call for authenticity should certainly strike a chord.

The *Ben Yehoyada*, in contrast, suggests that people in the time of *bayit sheini* were up-front about their enmity, but did not treat it as a serious crime. What was hidden from them was an understanding that *sinat hinam* is a major transgression. When they evaluated the gravity of their crimes, the sin of hatred was not exposed for the horror it is. Even today, while people understand that murder and adultery are seriously wrong, they often make light of communal discords; the quarreling and enmities of shul or school politics seem to them a ubiquitous feature of Jewish life that need not overly concern anyone. However, Jewish history has shown us the terrible dangers of groundless hatred. Given all our contemporary internal squabbling, this second message should hit home.

R. Moshe Feinstein (*Darash Moshe Derush* 29) presents yet another view. R. Moshe explains that everyone was aware of the hatred but not of its baselessness. Unlike Maharsha, Rav Moshe contends that the people did not hide their feelings, but unlike the *Ben Yehoyada*, he argues that they fully appreciated the conceptual problem of groundless hatred: they simply did not think that their own hatreds and enmities qualified. When conflicts occur, each side usually considers its dislike of the other to be fully justified. No one repents of *sinat hinam*, because no one thinks that their *sina* is truly *hinam*. Rav Moshe reminds us to forthrightly face the question of whether our strong dislikes are justified by real reasons, or are due to such poor motives as feeling threatened, disliking competition, or something as silly as finding another's laugh irritating. Only when we recognize the groundlessness of much of our enmity will authentic repentance become a possibility.

These three interpretations emphasize three crucial themes. First, we need to show love rather than just make an external show of talking about it. Second, we need to see communal and personal strife as serious matters. And finally, we need to assess whether or not our carefully constructed grounds for disliking others are really justified.

Two Aspects of Gratitude

> The Rabbis taught: "*Who can ensure that this heart will remain
> theirs [to fear Me and observe My commandments for all time]?*
> (*Devarim* 5:26). Moshe called Israel 'Ingrates, descendants of
> ingrates!' For when the Holy One, blessed be He, said to Israel
> *Who can ensure that this heart will remain theirs*, they should
> have said 'You can ensure.' We see that they are ingrates from
> the verse *Our souls are disgusted with the unsubstantial bread*
> (*Bemidbar* 21:5); we see that they are the descendants of ingrates
> from the verse *The woman that you gave to be with me, she gave
> me of the tree and I ate* (*Bereishit* 3:12)."
>
> (*Avoda Zara* 5a)

This gemara has Moshe citing two previous instances of ingratitude: the Jewish people complaining about the manna God gave
to sustain them in the desert, and Adam blaming the partner
Hashem gave him for the sin in the Garden of Eden. It also mentions that Moshe calls the people ingrates when they do not request divine help in achieving sensitivity to religious ideals. What
connects this failure with ingratitude? Tosafot explain that people
who are not grateful often prefer to not have favors done for them,
because they resent feeling beholden to anyone else. Thus, the
same personality trait that prevents someone who receives a gift
from saying "Thank you" can also prevent that person from accepting gifts in the first place.

Rashi, on the other hand, explains that they did not recognize the things in question as a good. In other words, Adam
truly thought that Eve was no boon, the Jews in the desert truly
did not want manna, and the Jews that Moshe addresses did not
perceive a more religiously sensitive heart as something positive.
For Rashi, the central question is not whether one knows how to
express gratitude, but whether one can recognize the good in the
first place.

There seem to be two aspects to becoming a grateful person.
The first requires that we swallow our pride, admit that others have

done favors for us, and verbalize our feeling of thanks. The other demands an awareness of what things in life are truly valuable. A mistaken scale of priorities can lead us to reject or undervalue the beautiful gifts offered by others.

Rav Barukh Epstein (*Torah Temima, Bereishit* 3:12) discusses these two types of ingratitude and cites a linguistic proof in favor of Tosafot's understanding. He points out that the talmudic phrase for lack of gratitude is *kafui tova*. The word *kofeh* in the Talmud means "to cover," as in the phrase *kofeh alav et ha'keli*, "he covers it with a vessel" (Mishna *Pesahim* 6:1). This phrase sounds like a conscious attempt to pretend that no good was done, rather than a failure to recognize what the good is.

Yet perhaps we need not identify either of these two understandings as the correct one. After all, expressing appropriate gratitude depends upon avoiding both of the shortcomings mentioned above. To avoid the pitfall of ingratitude, we must take a two-pronged approach that includes both adopting a decent scale of values in recognizing that which is good and a capacity to acknowledge the good done for us by others.

(The preceding analysis does not deal with the question of why asking for divine help in acquiring a religious heart is not a violation of human free will. For one approach to this question, see Maharsha's commentary ad loc.)

Sensitivity and Visiting the Sick

> Rav Helbo fell ill, so Rav Kahana went out and announced: "R. Helbo is very sick." Even so, no one came [to visit him].
>
> [R. Kahana] said to them: "Did not the following story happen with a student of R. Akiva? He was sick and no one came to visit him, so R. Akiva went in to visit the student; because the floor of the sick fellow was swept and washed [in connection with the visit], that fellow recovered.
>
> "He said: 'Rabbi, you have revived me.'"

"R. Akiva then went out and taught: 'Whoever does not visit the sick is as if he sheds blood.'"

When Rav Dimi came [from Israel] he said: "Whoever visits a sick person causes him to live; whoever does not visit a sick person causes him to die." What is the nature of this causal relationship? If you say that the one who visits the sick person asks for mercy so that the sick person will live, whereas the one who does not visit the sick asks that the sick person should die, do you really think that anyone asks for the sick person to die? Rather, [R. Dimi meant that] the one who does not visit the sick fellow does not ask for mercy regarding whether he lives or dies.

Rava, on the first day that he was ill, said to [his students]: "Do not tell anyone about my illness lest I have bad fortune." After the first day, he said: "Go out and declare it to everyone in the marketplace."

...Rav Shisha the son of Rav Idi said: "Do not visit the sick during the first three hours of the day or during the last three hours of the day, so that you do not stop asking for mercy – for during the first three hours, the sick person looks healthy; during the last three hours, the sick person looks overcome with illness."

(*Nedarim* 40a)

Before we explain *Hazal*'s insights into the *mizva* of *bikkur holim*, visiting the sick, let us consider this *mizva* in some detail. Although *bikkur holim* does not appear on the Rambam's list of the six hundred and thirteen *mizvot*, it may still constitute the fulfillment of a biblical mandate. One gemara (*Sota* 14a) lists visiting the sick as an avenue for fulfilling the command to emulate the divine, *imitatio Dei*. Rambam (*Hilkhot Avel* 14:1) mentions visiting the ill as a way of fulfilling *ve'ahavta le're'iakha kamokha*, "You must love your neighbor as yourself" (*Vayikra* 19:18). Even though *bikkur holim* is only a rabbinic obligation, one who performs it fulfills a *mizva* from the Torah.

Our gemara certainly emphasizes the great worth of visiting the sick, suggesting that it can be a lifesaving endeavor. How precisely does this occur in the story of R. Akiva? *Ez Yosef* (in *Ein Yaakov*) and Rosh suggest that R. Akiva directs other people to clean the house, and its being clean helps the sick person to recover. In one of his two readings, Meiri explains that R. Akiva himself takes broom and mop in hand to clean the place. Clearly, R. Akiva does not consider menial labor for a good cause to be beneath the dignity of an important sage.

Two other explanations carry significant implications. In his second interpretation, Meiri says that the landlord of the house cleaned it up in order to honor R. Akiva. If so, this tale shows the problematic priorities of the landlord. The visit of a scholar of the caliber of R. Akiva was a reason to straighten up, but the serious illness of a tenant did not inspire much effort in this regard. R. Akiva simply intends to visit the sick, but his visit fortuitously generates a cleanup just when the patient needs it.

Rav Ahai (*Sheiltot* 93) cites another interpretation in which the landlord sees that R. Akiva values the patient and decides, as a result, that the patient is worth cleaning up for. Although this version has the landlord cleaning up for the sick person, the landlord exhibits greater insensitivity here than in the previous version. The landlord initially thinks that important patients deserve cleaning efforts but not the unimportant. Only a get-well visit from a major sage induces the landlord that to put in some effort on behalf of an unimportant tenant whose name does not appear on the list of a community board.

As this discussion demonstrates, visiting the sick has a ripple effect, with much broad implications. On the most basic level, one individual's visit may inspire others to follow suit. On a deeper level, a visit may put the sick person on the social map. Those who visit, even if not of the same stature as R. Akiva, show the community that the suffering individual matters and is worthy of attention.

According to Rav Dimi, visiting the sick does more than raise the awareness of other members of the community. It deepens the consciousness of the visitor that the ill person needs many forms of help. That is why in the gemara it is only the one who visits who prays for the sick with sufficient intent.

Rav Dimi says that someone who does not visit will not pray for the sick person to live or die. Rabbeinu Nissim infers from this gemara (and from *Ketuvot* 104a) that there are times when it is permissible to pray for the death of a sick person. He limits the possibility to a situation in which the sick person is suffering greatly and the doctors see no chance for recovery. According to Rabbeinu Nissim, Halakha rejects euthanasia but permits beseeching God to end a person's suffering. However, only someone who has visited the sick person knows when this unusual type of prayer would be appropriate.

Why does Rava not want the world to know about his illness on its first day? Some commentators explain that words have their own power and impact, and talking about an illness can strengthen it. I would add that sick people are sometimes embarrassed about their illness. They fear that others will see them as weak or unproductive. Perhaps this explains why Rava counsels against quickly turning every illness into a public story. On the other hand, once it becomes clear that the illness persists, it is important to inform everyone in the community who might lend a helping hand.

Rav Shisha's insight adds one final note of psychological sensitivity. Sometimes, when paying a sick call, we are surprised to find the bedridden patient looking fairly robust. It may be tempting to conclude that the patient is faking an illness to avoid responsibility or is a hypochondriac. Rav Shisha reminds us that illnesses have peaks and valleys, and an early morning visit when the patient looks better may give the wrong impression.

On the opposite extreme, a nighttime visit, when the patient looks exhausted and bedraggled, may mistakenly lead us to feel that the patient has little hope of recovery. This mistake may limit our efforts to help the patient. Moreover, if the sick person senses our dismay it may have a harmful effect. R. Shisha exhorts us to visit in a manner that avoids both of these errors.

Hazal do far more than emphasize the importance of visiting the sick. They provide detailed directions and nuanced guidance for fulfilling this *mizva* with sensitivity and kindness.

The Choice Between Intimidation and Pleasantness

> Rav Hisda said: "A person should never be excessively intimidating in his household, because in the story of the concubine of Giva, her husband did so, and it led to the deaths of tens of thousands from Israel."
>
> Rav Yehuda said in the name of Rav: "Whoever excessively intimidates his family will eventually come to three sins – sexual immorality, murder, and desecration of Shabbat."
>
> Rabba the son of Bar Hana said: "Regarding the rabbis' saying that 'A person should say three things to his family on Friday before dark: Did you tithe? Did you make the *eiruv*? Then light the candles' (*Mishna Shabbat* 2:7) – these must be said in a pleasant fashion, so that the family will accept it from him."
>
> Abbaye said: "I did not hear the teaching of Rabba the son of Bar Hana, but I fulfilled it in line with my own reasoning."
>
> (*Gittin* 6b–7a)

This aggada instructs us both about the negative implications of a home atmosphere based upon intimidation and about the positive benefits of a more tranquil family environment. The placement of Rav Yehuda's statement immediately after the earlier discussion of the "concubine of Giva" motivates Tosafot to assume that R. Yehuda refers specifically to that story. Locating murder in the concubine story is easy, for it includes a bloody war fought between the tribe of Binyamin and the rest of the Jewish people. Locating the Sabbath desecration is a bigger challenge. Tosafot, based on *Seder Olam*, argue that the incident recounted in the story took place on a Shabbat. Alternatively, they cite Rabbenu Hananel's assertion that the correct text of this gemara reads *hillul Hashem* ("profanation of the name of God") rather than *hillul Shabbat*. This makes the explanation simple. The poor behavior of almost everyone involved in this tale certainly constituted a significant profanation of the divine name.

Rashi differs from the above approach. He thinks that Rav Yehuda no longer has the "concubine of Giva" episode in mind when he mentions the pitfalls that come from fear and intimidation. In general, an atmosphere of trepidation felt by another human being paves the path toward sin. For example, a woman afraid of the shouts and insults of her husband might conceivably cook on Shabbat to quiet his capricious rage. In this way, the intimidation could lead to the three terrible sins mentioned by R. Yehuda.

Following the discussion of the problems of intimidation, the gemara moves on to the positive impact of speaking kindly. First, Rabba instructs us how to encourage our family members to finish all the requisite religious duties before Shabbat. Abbaye then points out that he came to the identical conclusion without hearing this teaching directly from Rabba. What is the import of Abbaye's remark? Why is it critical for us to know that he hit upon this idea without any help?

Rav Meir Schiff, the seventeenth-century rav of Fulda, whose novella are printed in the back of the Vilna *Shas*, offers an explanation. When Rabba derived this principle in a different way from Abbaye, it was based on a careful reading of the mishna in *Masekhet Shabbat*. The mishna utilizes the word *lomar* ("to say"). Rabbinic tradition teaches us that the verb *amar* reflects a softer utterance, while the verb *daber* reflects a harsher command. Moreover, the phrase *betokh beito* indicates that the speaker sees himself as part of the household unit, rather than as a captain barking orders from above. Thus, a close reading of the Tannaitic source led Rabba to his teaching. Abbaye, on the other hand, thought that logic dictated speaking kindly even without any textual inferences.

Maharam Schiff's comment illustrates the twin aspects of Jewish learning. On the one hand, we have traditional sources whose authority we accept. We engage in a painstaking reading of these sources, in order to catch all the subtle nuances and inferences. At the same time, we employ human reason – both analytic ability and intuitive insight – to help us understand the Torah. Rabba and Abbaye complement each other, together embodying the two aspects of Torah learning.

Another way to think about Abbaye's postscript sees it as a more pointed statement. Some people mistakenly think that all halakhic demands come to us as explicit details in the great codes of Jewish law. They fail to realize that the Torah gives us overarching directives to lead lives of holiness and moral goodness. These directives create demands even when the demands do not appear in the *Shulhan Arukh*. Perhaps Abbaye was saying that we should not need a traditional source to teach us to speak kindly to our family members. Abbaye spoke softly without hearing it from Rabba because no tradition is necessary for such basic ethical behavior.

Rav Avraham Yizhak haKohen Kook (*Ein Aya, Shabbat* 34a) offers another perspective on the difference between Rabba and Abbaye. Rabba explicitly adds that a person should speak this way "so that they will accept it from him." In other words, Rabba evaluates which approach is the more effective educational strategy in the long run. As many teachers have done since, Rabba wondered whether he would get better results by coming down hard on those he was instructing or by offering them words of gentle encouragement. He concluded that the softer path ultimately leads to better performance.

Abbaye, however, chose to speak kindly because of his own reasoning, which did not factor in the question of consequences and results. When Abbaye mentions his reasoning, he refers to a deontological ethic in which certain things must be done and other things must be avoided, without any connection to the possible results. Even if yelling would motivate the family to tithe the produce, it is not justified to yell at people who do not deserve to be yelled at. Abbaye is instructing us that even pedagogic issues of great importance cannot be settled by a utilitarian calculus that asks only what will produce finer results. Improper behavior remains improper irrespective of the good that might emerge from it.

Rav Kook's insight is a stern warning to educators who focus only on pragmatic results – teachers, say, who arbitrarily pick a student to yell at on the first day to set the right tone of intimidation in the classroom, or who choose to expel a student during the first month of school to make everyone else shape up. For Rav Kook, a teacher must evaluate the appropriateness of the act before asking about its possible ramifications.

We must recall, however, that Rabba came to the same conclusion as Abbaye from the perspective that focused on results. This suggests that both outlooks endorse speaking kindly. Most important, speaking gently is an independent value, and it will ultimately generate better results. Let us not be seduced into yelling as a form of righteous indignation, or as a quick fix for difficult students or children. From a multiplicity of viewpoints – textual and analytic, explicit norms and implicit values, deontological ethics and consequentialist morality – our sages taught us to speak with a gentle voice.

Argumentation and Peace

> R. Elazar said in the name of R. Hanina: *"Talmidei hakhamim* increase peace in the world, as it says: *And all your children will be learned of Hashem, and great will be the peace of your children* (*Yeshayahu* 54:13) – do not read *banayikh* [your children], but rather *bonayikh* [your builders]."
>
> (*Berakhot* 64a)

According to our translation above, the gemara midrashically applies this verse to *talmidei hakhamim* by replacing "children" with "builders"; as scholarship is a constructive act, *talmidei hakhamim* can be viewed as builders. Professor Zvi Groner once made a different suggestion to me that I subsequently found in the *Rif* of Rav Yoshiyahu Pinto (*Ein Yaakov, Berakhot*). Perhaps *bonayikh* is not from the root of *binyan* ("building") but from *bina* ("understanding"): those who learn Torah and achieve greater understanding bring peace to the world. This clearly refers to the scholars.

R. Hanina's aggadic statement appears at the conclusion of several talmudic tractates. These exact words bring *Yevamot, Nazir,* and *Kareitot* to a close, and are the penultimate words of *Berakhot* (which concludes by quoting a number of verses about peace). On one level, this reflects a desire to end each tractate with an aggadic flourish. Similarly, the Rambam ends each most of the books of his *Mishneh Torah* with a broader ethical or philosophical idea, and he probably learned to do so from the Talmud. The specific choice of this aggada as a conclusion to so many tractates reflects the immense value Judaism attributes to peace. Peace is also the theme of the closing blessing of the *Amida*, the last of the priestly blessings, and the last request of *birkat ha'mazon*. Peace usually appears at the end of a long list, as the crescendo of all blessings.

Beyond the general points outlined above, there may be some specific reasons why these four tractates end with the theme of peace. Maharsha (*Yevamot* 122b) explains that *Yevamot* includes many unusual leniencies to prevent cases of *agunot*. For example, the sages allow the testimony of one witness – even from among those who would normally be considered invalid – in order to establish the death of a husband at sea (*Yevamot* 88a). This will prevent his wife from becoming an *aguna*, having to wait a lifetime for further evidence that never materializes. A reader of this tractate might view these leniencies as a deviation from halakhic responsibility, so it is imperative to point out that promoting human welfare is a crucial goal of the halakhic system. The concluding quotations about the value of *shalom* are intended to explain the internal halakhic ideals that motivate the legal rulings that enable women to remarry. The sages ruled correctly when they utilized the resources of the halakhic system for the promotion of peace.

Maharsha offers a different reason for the placement of our aggadic statement at the end of *Berakhot*. Tractate *Berakhot* deals mainly with prayers and blessings. These religious utterances enable the Jewish people to maintain a positive relationship with the *Ribbono shel Olam* after the destruction of the Temple. Thus, the concluding message about peace refers to *shalom* between the Jewish people and Hashem; the sages facilitated such *shalom* by instituting *tefillot* and *berakhot*.

For many of us, though, the term *talmid hakham* essentially conjures up the endeavor of learning Torah. If the gemara indeed refers to this aspect of the sages' work, an obvious question arises. Every talmudic page records a constant stream of debate and argument. Indeed, rabbinic scholars debating halakhic and hashkafic points continue unabated in our own day. If *talmidei hakhamim* constantly argue, then in what sense do they promote peace?

R. Avraham Yizhak Kook (*Ein Aya, Berakhot*) explains that this question derives from a false assumption about the nature of peace. Peace is not achieved when all opinions but one are obliterated; rather, it emerges when the valid aspects of a myriad of positions are acknowledged. The variety of positions enables us to see that each one has its time and place. Thus, the verse utilizes the phrase *rav shelom banayikh* instead of *gadol shelom banayikh*, because peace stems more from multiplicity than from sameness.

This idea should not be identified with the relativistic claim that all positions are equally valid. Any such claim is patently false and not a realistic or helpful approach to promoting peace. Instead, Rav Kook argues, the complexity of so many issues means that each side has something of value to contribute. My argument may be essentially right, but debate makes it apparent that one of my opponent's critiques hits the mark. When my ideas are under attack, I should not cut off constructive discourse by telling my opponent that we are both right or by blithely assuming that everything he says is ridiculous. I must argue with my opponent, but voicing our differences will lead me to recognize the truth of some of his contentions.

R. Kook himself practiced what he preached. He believed firmly that the religious community was more correct than the secular Zionists, but he also believed, and taught, that the secular Zionist critique of the religious had elements of truth. For example, he felt that they were justified in claiming that some distorted conceptions of fear of heaven constrict life and inhibit vitality (*Orot haKodesh* 3, p. 34). Along similar lines, the secular Jewish rejection of halakhic observance may reflect a failure of the religious to show that the many halakhic details reflect a sweeping poetic vision of the good (*Orot*, p. 121).

Rav Kook did the same with non-Jewish philosophies that seem antithetical to Judaism. Arthur Schopenhauer's pessimistic thought is usually not seen as congenial to the religious person, but Rav Kook located the element of truth in Schopenhauer's vision (*Orot haKodesh* 2, p. 448). The problem of Schopenhauer's doctrine of the will is not that it is completely false, but that its adherents see it as the totality of existence when it is only a portion of the truth.

Rav Kook's approach remains powerful today, especially for those of us who identify with what might be termed Centrist Orthodoxy, a position subjected to strong criticism from both the right and the left. Are all of the critiques of this community from its liberal and haredi brethren invalid? The haredim claim that Centrist Orthodox Jews lack intense commitment; the secularists attribute ethical shortcomings to Orthodox Jews. Neither of these claims is completely false.

Acknowledging that one's rival or opponent in argument has something positive to contribute is an important step toward authentic Jewish unity. Communal peace will not come from all Jews adopting the same position or from asserting that all positions are equally valid. Nonetheless, we can and should appreciate the value of other voices without relinquishing our essential ideals.

CHAPTER 7

Character Traits

A Talmudic Joke and the Nature of Humility

> When R. Yohanan ben Zakkai died, the splendor of wisdom ceased. When R. Gamliel the Elder died, the honor of Torah ceased, as did purity and abstinence. When R. Yishmael ben Pavi died, the splendor of the priesthood ceased. When Rabbi [Yehuda haNasi] died, humility and fear of sin ceased.
>
> (Mishna, *Sota* 9:15)

> Rav Yosef said to the *tanna* [the person who recites mishnaic texts]: "Do not include [the line about] humility, because there is [still] me."
>
> (*Sota* 49b)

The compilers of the Talmud certainly understood the humor of Rav Yosef's statement when they placed it at the very end of the tractate. Indeed, the vast corpus of the Talmud incorporates more than a few jokes. Some of them combine real wisdom with humor. Perhaps R. Yosef means to teach us something important, in addition to giving us a chuckle.

It is a commonplace that religion prizes the character trait of humility, but precise definitions of humility are more elusive. One view identifies humility with total self-abnegation. Such feelings might derive from a strong sense of human sinfulness or from a contrast between limited man and infinite God. From this perspective, those who are truly humble conclude that they have no traits worthy of admiration.

The famed *rosh yeshiva* of Volozhin, R. Naftali Zvi Yehuda Berlin (known as Neziv), rejects this view in his *Ha'amek Davar* (*Bemidbar* 12:3, note 2). He argues that humility and a healthy awareness of personal accomplishments are not mutually exclusive. According to Neziv, we express humility when we do not focus on receiving public honors or recognition. The paradigm is reflected by people who are aware of their own achievements but do not demand to be honored at the shul dinner and do not care about when they are called up to the Torah.

Neziv cites R. Yosef's statement as support. In his view, R. Yosef's quip indicates that those who are humble may be fully cognizant of their own fine qualities. R. Yosef is not just making a joke, he says, but is telling us that those who are humble may sometimes call attention to their own abilities. Their humility finds expression in an overall disinterest in honors and communal recognition.

Neziv's reading of R. Yosef's comment finds support in another talmudic story about this illustrious sage. R. Yosef and Rabba were once both candidates to become *rosh yeshiva* in Pumbedita (*Horayot* 14a). The sages select R. Yosef, but he relinquishes the title to Rabba. During the more than two decades of Rabba's tenure, R. Yosef refuses to let the bloodletter make house calls for him, because he does not want to receive any special honors that might detract from Rabba's authority. This works beautifully with Neziv's vision of humility as the eschewing of honors. R. Yosef recognizes his own positive traits and humorously indicates that such recognition is not a problem, but he does not demand acclaim and shows great humility when it comes to public honors in Pumbedita.

It is worth pointing out that Neziv cites *Mesillat Yesharim* (presumably referring to chapters 21 and 22) as the foil to his own view. In that work, R. Moshe Hayyim Luzzatto identifies *anivut*, humility, with a *shefal berekh* (see *Sanhedrin* 88b), one who is lowly. Rabbi Berlin forcefully argues that we should not identify these traits. As *Mesillat Yesharim* has become the most prominent work of *mussar*, Jewish ethics, recent authorities do not very often explicitly take issue with it. Nevertheless, Neziv thinks that this mistaken perspective on humility must be contested.

The linguistic difference between *anav* and *shefal ruach* appears in other sources as well. Rabbi Levitas, head of Yavneh, teaches (*Avot* 4:4) that a person should be "very lowly of spirit." *Tiferet Yisrael* (R. Yisrael Lipshutz), in his explanatory comment there, echoes Neziv's idea. He explains that humble people recognize their own value but do not act in an aggrandizing fashion. Those who are lowly of spirit, on the other hand, constantly focus on their own shortcomings.

Moshe Rabbeinu and King David represent these two approaches. In the Torah, Moshe quite well understands his own significance and worth. As *Tiferet Yisrael* points out, "Can we imagine that Moshe Rabbeinu was unaware that he was the chosen one of mankind whom God spoke to face-to-face?" Yet Moshe does not demand acclaim or honor; therefore, the Torah (*Bemidbar* 12:3) applies the term *anav* to him. David describes himself as *shafel* (*Tehillim* 138:6), and several chapters of *Tehillim* illustrate a "broken spirit." These Psalms may reflect David's feelings after the sin of Bat Sheva (see *Tehillim* 51).

Tiferet Yisrael does not state a preference for either of these two models and apparently sees them both as legitimate. In contrast, Neziv's analysis prefers the *anav* to the *shefal ruach*. Perhaps he has good reason reasons for doing so. As an educator, I find Neziv's idea quite powerful. Without denying the negative impact of arrogance on the religious personality, we should understand that lack of confidence and a sense of self-worth can undermine us – the surest way to fail in any endeavor is to decide from the outset that we cannot possibly succeed. Many aspects of religious life, such as beseeching God in prayer and asking solid questions on a commentary, depend upon a certain sense of self-worth. Neziv reminds us to not identify humility with self-abnegation.

Perhaps R. Yosef intends one additional lesson. The following line of the gemara has Rav Nahman telling the *tanna* not to include fear of sin in the list of lost traits because he is still around. I submit that R. Nahman and R. Yosef are not bragging; rather, they worry that a reader of the list found toward the end of *Sota* might conclude that greatness in all respects came to a close with the conclusion of the mishnaic period. It is true that Judaism teaches that earlier generations have greater authority than more recent ones. If this idea leads us to conclude, however, that we cannot aspire to more than benign mediocrity, we will find ourselves unable to meet the challenges of our day. As Alfred Tennyson wrote in "Ulysses":

> Tho' much is taken, much abides; and tho'
> We are not now that strength which in the old days
> Moved earth and heaven; that which we are, we are;
> One equal-temper of heroic hearts,
> Made weak by time and fate, but strong in will
> To strive, to seek, to find, and not to yield.

May we appreciate our strengths as well as our shortcomings, yet not demand the honor due those strengths.

When Does Insincere Humility Have Value?

This *shiur* examines a legal discussion that lies on the border between the halakhic and aggadic realms.

R. Yehuda the son of R. Shimon asked of R. Shimon ben Pazi: "Which is preferable: rebuking for the sake of heaven, or humility not for the sake of heaven?"

He [R. Shimon] said to him: "Don't you agree that humility for the sake of heaven is preferable? As the master said, 'Humility is greater than all of them.' Humility not for the sake of heaven is also preferable, as R. Yehuda said in the name of Rav: 'A person should always involve himself in Torah and *mizvot*, even if for ulterior motives, because performing *mizvot* not for the sake of heaven will lead to fulfilling them for the sake of heaven.'"

(*Arakhin* 16b)

What precisely is the case under discussion in the gemara, in which a person must choose either to rebuke out of the best motivations or to express humility for an ulterior motive? Rashi explains that a falsely humble individual who justifies refraining from rebuking another with the claim "Who am I to rebuke" is really refraining out of fear of being disliked. Let us remember that the gemara concludes in favor of insincere humility. Tosafot challenge Rashi's interpretation: refraining from rebuking those who need rebuke is simply wrong and an abdication of an explicit biblical command! It cannot be that the gemara means to grant every phony a lifetime exemption from this *mizva*.

R. Yehuda Leib of Gur, in his *Sefat Emet*, provides a worthy explanation of Rashi. He suggests that our falsely humble fellow does, in fact, offer rebuke when necessary and thus fulfills the biblical mandate. However, he avoids looking too closely at the behavior of his friends and acquaintances, in order not to find himself in a position where he will have to rebuke them. A lack of interest in finding causes for rebuke can be an expression either of authentic humility or of ersatz humility. R. Shimon concludes that lack of interest in uncovering the religious shortcomings of others is worthwhile even when it stems from motivations of personal benefit.

Apparently, there are certain *mizvot* that must be fulfilled when they come up, but which should not be searched out. We would undoubtedly find something religiously objectionable about a person whose favorite *mizva* was rebuke, and who constantly searched for new opportunities to rebuke with great enthusiasm. Our reluctance to rebuke others finds expression in this talmudic decision that refraining from delving too closely into the religious backsliding of others has value, even when the motivations are not the purest.

Humility and Wisdom

> Our Rabbis taught: "A person should always be humble like Hillel and not impatient like Shammai." There was a story in which two people made a wager, saying: He who goes and makes Hillel angry shall receive four hundred *zuz*. Said one: "I will go and incense him." That day was Friday afternoon, and Hillel was washing his head. He went, passed by the door of his house, and called out: "Is Hillel here, is Hillel here?" Thereupon he robed and went out to him, saying: "My son, what do you require?" "I have a question to ask," he said. "Ask, my son," he prompted. Thereupon he asked: "Why are the heads of the Babylonians round?" He responded: "My son, you have asked a great question. It is because they do not have skillful midwives." He departed, tarried a while, returned, and called out: "Is Hillel here; is Hillel here?" He robed and went out to him, saying: "My son, what do you require?" "I have a question to ask," he said. "Ask, my son," he prompted. Thereupon he asked: "Why are the eyes of the Tadmurians bleary?" He replied: "My son, you have asked a great question. It is because they live in sandy places." He departed, tarried a while, returned, and called out: "Is Hillel here; is Hillel here?" He robed and went out to him, saying: "My son, what do you require?" "I have a question to ask," he said. "Ask, my son," he prompted. He asked: "Why are the feet of the Africans wide?" He said: "My son, you have

asked a great question. It is because they live in watery marshes."
He said: "I have many questions to ask but fear that you may
become angry." Thereupon he robed, sat before him, and said:
"Ask all the questions you have to ask." "Are you the Hillel who
is called the *nasi* of Israel?" "Yes," he replied. He retorted: "If
that is you, may there not be many like you in Israel." "Why, my
son?" he asked. "Because I have lost four hundred *zuz* through
you," he answered. "Be careful of your moods," he answered.
"Hillel is worth it that you should lose four hundred *zuz* and
yet another four hundred *zuz* through him, yet Hillel shall not
lose his temper."

(*Shabbat* 30b–31a)

This famous story is a long-time favorite of Jewish youth. It cel-
ebrates the sterling character of Hillel, who knew how to not lose
his temper even when bombarded with a series of silly questions
at the most inconvenient time possible. The opening line indicates
that humility is the secret for becoming like Hillel. A healthy sense
of one's own limitations helps one handle such trying situations
with equanimity. A look at some commentaries reveals further
insight into the humble personality.

Rav Kook points out that Hillel is *nitatef* ("he robes himself")
before greeting the questioner. I had always taken this as showing
how much Hillel could have been irritated, because he keeps getting back into the bath, only to have to dress again in response to
each knock on the door. R. Kook (*Ein Aya*) understands this verb
as referring to clothing oneself in a garment of honor, as when the
gemara (*Shabbat* 119a) employs it to describe R. Hanina's robing
himself to go out and greet the Sabbath queen. If so, this element
of the tale conveys that humility and the need to dress in a dignified fashion need not be at odds with each other.

Humility requires us to accurately evaluated ourselves, both
our good and our bad characteristics. Most people find it difficult
to admit their own faults, but those who are humble see their
faults clearly, even as they also note their more positive traits.

Hillel admits his own shortcomings but recognizes that he merits dignified clothing. Furthermore, if humility involves complete self-abnegation, it is impossible for a humble person to honor others – what honor can come from total nullity? Therefore, Hillel robes appropriately before he goes out to meet the questioner.

In addition to the points raised by R. Kook, I would add that Hillel represents an important institution, the patriarchate. Humble individuals in a communal leadership role must truly understand their faults and yet be able to perform the duties of their office with dignity.

Hillel also manifests humility in his responses to the questions. Rav Kook points out that arrogance can get in the way of intellectual pursuits. The arrogant person is often quick to dismiss a question as nonsense. The haughty person may eschew a simple explanation in the pursuit of a complex one that befits his self-image as a great thinker. However, some seemingly foolish questions contain bits of wisdom, and sometimes the simplest answer is the right one. Hillel's humility enables him to think seriously about the three questions and to find an answer that is both simple and worth knowing.

This brings us to the question of just what Hillel answers. R. Zvi Hirsch Hayes, in his commentary printed in the back of the Vilna *Shas*, understands the answer in scientific terms. Whether it be through Lamarckian adaptation or Darwinian survival of the fittest, the people of a given environment have adapted or evolved to whatever best survives in that environment. Hillel takes the question seriously and offers a scientific answer. Alternatively, R. Kook suggests that Hillel refers to divine providence. Hashem has so arranged the world that people in every different place are able to thrive. While an intellectual puffed up with pride would find the three questions beneath him, or only worthwhile if the answer involves a long and drawn out theory, Hillel's humility leads him to think seriously about the questions and to offer answers that are simple, elegant, and educational.

In this context, it is worth noting that several commentators wonder why Hillel bothers to answer such foolish questions. *Sefat Emet* (in his commentary on Shabbat) says that the questioner purposely asked what he thought were nonsense questions that would anger Hillel. To the questioner's chagrin, Hillel found real substance in them. In Rav Kook's view, this ironic twist emerges because of Hillel's humility.

Finally, Rav Kook sees one more aspect of the truly humble in this tale. As the *baalei mussar* were well aware, humble people always have one last test: are they arrogant about their humility? We can easily imagine people who are humble, self-effacing, but overly proud of their ability to face their own faults squarely. The questioner tried to use this trait against Hillel. When he said: "I have many questions to ask you but fear you will get angry," he was implicitly challenging Hillel's patience. He thought that the challenge would be the last straw. Hillel's calm response revealed that the great sage had overcome this final temptation of the humble.

If so, this story serves as an important paradigm: ideal humility is not self-abnegation, but the quite difficult endeavor of seeing oneself accurately, warts and all. When exercised correctly, such humility enables more sympathetic interaction with others, as well as the ability to analyze ideas more successfully.

Don't Despair

> There was an elderly woman who came before Rav Nahman. She said to him: "The *reish galuta* [exilarch] and all the rabbis of the *reish galuta*'s court are sitting in a stolen *sukka*." She cried out, but R. Nahman paid no attention to her.
>
> She said to him: "A woman whose ancestor had three hundred and eighteen slaves [i.e., Avraham Avinu] is crying out before you, and you pay no attention?"
>
> R. Nahman said to [his students]: "She is a complainer, and she shall receive only monetary compensation for the wood."
>
> (*Sukka* 31a)

This story raises several questions. Why did Rav Nahman ignore the poor woman's plight if the *reish galuta*'s staff had taken her wood? Why should she only receive compensation and not the return of the stolen items? Why does the woman make reference to Avraham and the three hundred and eighteen slaves with which he vanquished the four kings? Is this point somehow relevant to her case?

I once taught this gemara on a college campus, and one of the students suggested a highly intelligent explanation. Avraham utilizes three hundred and eighteen men in his battle against the four kings. After emerging victorious in battle, Avraham refuses to take the spoils of war from the King of Sodom, thus demonstrating that he will not exploit his stature to obtain money. The elderly woman held up Avraham as a counterexample to the behavior of the *reish galuta*'s circle.

R. Zadok haKohen of Lublin offers a beautiful interpretation of this story in his *Divrei Soferim* (16). According to Rav Zadok, Avraham is a crucial symbol of a particular component of Judaism. Avraham and Sarah had already despaired of having children when the angels came to tell them that they would have a son. Thus, the continuity of the Jewish people was assured only after complete despair had set in. God arranged for Jewish peoplehood to begin in this fashion so that it would become an entrenched principle that Jews should never despair.

Avraham displays a refusal to despair when he courageously engages the four kings in battle. After all, they had just defeated the five kings and were presumably a fearsome enemy. When Avraham assembles his three hundred and eighteen men, they too become a symbol of not giving up. R. Zadok then presents a *gematria* that even those not enthusiastic about *gematriot* should love. The numerical value of the word *ye'ush*, "despair," is three hundred and seventeen. Relying on the rule that a *gematria* can be off by one, R. Zadok argues that though the number of men numerically equals despair, their achievement in fact demonstrates man's ability to transcend despair. I would slightly alter

R. Zadok's insight. Since the three hundred and eighteen men represent moving beyond despair, they add up to one more than the numerical value of *ye'ush*.

According to Halakha, a thief is allowed to keep a stolen item and merely pay its value if it has changed possession (*shinui reshut*) and the original owner despairs of ever getting it back. If so, we can understand R. Nahman and the elderly woman. R. Nahman assumed that she must have given up hope once the powerful forces of the exilarch took her wood. Therefore, she was legally entitled only to financial compensation. The woman responded that she was a daughter of Avraham, with his three hundred and eighteen men. In other words, despite the odds, she had not given up, and was legally entitled to the wood.

Of course, this leaves open the question of why R. Nahman still did not listen to her. Rashi explains that there was a rabbinic edict allowing thieves who had stolen materials and used them in a building to keep the building standing and merely reimburse the owner. This edict was intended to make it easier for thieves to repent. According to Rashi, R. Nahman may have conceded that the woman had not despaired but denied her the wood on other grounds.

R. Zadok's reading should have deep resonance for students of Jewish history. He is not claiming that any unrealistic plan devised by Jews will succeed just because they are descendants of Avraham. At the same time, when historical forces place us in a precarious situation, we should remember Avraham and his three hundred and eighteen men.

Honor, Friendship, and Pursuing Ideals

> R. Abba said: "The Holy One, blessed be He, seized Yeravam by his garment and said to him: 'Repent, and I, you, and [King David] the son of Yishai will walk together in Gan Eden.' Yeravam asked: 'Who will be first?' [God answered:] 'The son

of Yishai will be first.' [Yeravam responded:] 'Then I am not interested.'"

(Sanhedrin 102a)

This story certainly conveys the destructive potential of human egotism. Yeravam turns down a portion in the world-to-come simply because David *haMelekh* will have a more prominent position. R. Yaakov Ettlinger, in his *Arukh laNer*, finds an additional element in this tale. He notes that God's original offer was "I, you, and the son of Yishai"; the ordering of the three parties implies that Hashem was giving Yeravam the opportunity to come before David. R. Ettlinger suggests that the original offer envisioned Yeravam coming first, based on his repenting out of the purest idealism. Once Yeravam responded by asking who would be first, however, it became clear that he was only capable of a much less refined type of *teshuva*, motivated by reward, and the divine offer changed.

If R. Ettlinger is correct, this story reminds us that the ravenous desire for honor ironically often prevents the hungry individual from satiating his appetite. Those who strive to achieve other ideals may end up admired by others, but those who shamelessly pursue admiration will only find themselves the object of ridicule. Honor falls into a broad category of achievements that one can only attain only through the pursuit of a different goal. Happiness and friendship may also depend on an indirect approach.

C. S. Lewis says it beautifully in *The Four Loves*:

> That is why those pathetic people who simply "want friends" can never make any. The very condition of having Friends is that we should want something else besides Friends. Where the truthful answer to the question *Do you see the same truth?* would be "I see nothing and I don't care about the truth; I only want a Friend," no Friendship can arise – though Affection of course may. There would be nothing for the Friendship to be about and Friendship must be about something, even if it were

only an enthusiasm for dominoes or white mice. Those who
have nothing can share nothing; those who are going nowhere
can have no fellow-travelers.

I am certainly not suggesting that choosing the right ideals leads
to a life in which every desire and aspiration is achieved and all
problems go away; this is patently false. Nonetheless, I think that
the degree to which achieving honor, happiness, and friendship
truly depend upon the pursuit of other ideals and are not achieved
directly is striking. Of course, we cannot pretend to want other
ideals and only act for the sake of honor; the indirect method
only works when we feel a genuine desire to strive for the noble.

Rav Avraham Yizhak Kook offers a different reading of this
aggada in his eulogy for Theodor Herzl (*Maʾamarei haRaʾaya*, pp.
94–99). He sees Yeravam as representing *Malkhut Yisrael*, and
therefore the gemara refers to the relationship between *Malkhut
Yehuda* (David) and *Malkhut Yisrael* (Yeravam). Rav Kook outlines
his perspective on the goals of Am Yisrael in order to clarify the
relationship between these two monarchies.

In R. Kook's view, the Jewish nation must strive to achieve
both material and spiritual success. While the former works
primarily on the universal plane that we share with non-Jews,
the latter depends more on our particularistic vision. Material
success is unquestionably the means, and spiritual success the
ultimate goal. Just we try as individuals to stay healthy in order
to accomplish our spiritual aspirations, so too the nation requires
robustness in order to realize its spiritual vision.

Why do we need the material component? Material poverty
often gets in the way of spiritual achievement, both individual and
communal. The individual who cannot find a steady job may find
it difficult to concentrate on study and prayer. A national collective
suffering the torments of persecution and exile may face comparable problems. There is a second factor as well. In *Orot* (p. 104),
Rav Kook argues that the full flourishing of Torah depends upon a
national political entity because Torah is not restricted to hermits

and ascetics; it relates to every political, economic, and social issue in a polity. Note how the modern state of Israel has spawned a host of halakhic discussions about military issues, national economics, the rights of minorities, and so on. Thus, material success does not simply allow breathing space for the spiritual – it expands the playing field on which the spiritual is active.

Yehuda and Yosef, the two leaders among Yaakov's children, already embody these twin themes at the end of *Sefer Bereishit*. Yosef provides material comfort in Egypt and excels on the universal plane in his interaction with the broader environment. Yehuda provides the unique spiritual message of Torah. The Davidic dynasty initially united the material and the spiritual. However, a rupture occurred, and the kingdom split in two. For R. Kook, this split was not just a political dispute but also a divide between our two themes. Yeravam, a descendant of Yosef from the tribe of Efrayim, stood for the material success of the Jewish people; the descendents of David, on the other hand, passed on an idealized vision of our spiritual heritage.

While R. Kook views the split as problematic, he argues that the two kingdoms could still have engaged in mutually beneficial interaction if not for Yeravam's pride. In our aggada from *Sanhedrin*, God's offer means that each kingdom can provide what it is able to, and the joint effort will enable the partners to walk with God. When Yeravam asks who will be first, God answers that the material flourishing represented by Yeravam must take a backseat to the essential goal of spiritual striving represented by David. Yeravam refuses to accept such a hierarchy, and the partnership crumbles. The rest of Jewish history reflects the problems deriving from the split between the two realms.

Finally, Rav Kook sees these two themes as emerging from the idea of a Mashiah ben Yosef and a Mashiah ben David. The former reflects the material efforts of Yosef, whereas the latter represents the spiritual ideals of Yehuda. According to *Hazal*, Mashiah ben Yosef dies because it ultimately becomes clear that the spiritual goal is paramount.

R. Kook is not simply referring here to Herzl the man, he is speaking in broader terms about secular Zionism in general. In keeping with his fundamental orientation, R. Kook grants secular Zionism significant value, but he sees it as lacking something crucial. We must respect its desire to give the Jewish people a state and a homeland as crucial elements of our vision. At the same time, we must foster an understanding that nationalism, when not animated by a spiritual perspective, misses out on the most significant element of the Jewish worldview.

The Problem of Sinful Thoughts and How to Prevent Them

> Thoughts of sin (*hirhurei aveira*) are worse than sin, and the illustration of this is the smell of meat.
>
> (*Yoma* 29a)

Some commentaries question this statement in light of other talmudic sources (e.g., *Kiddushin* 39b) indicating that sinful thoughts are not punishable. Others discuss in what sense sinful thoughts might prove more harmful than sinful behavior. Rambam (*Moreh Nevukhim* 3:8) maintains that sinful thoughts are more problematic because they relate to the essence of what it means to be a human being. Animals and humans share the realm of action, but only human beings utilize their minds to think, analyze, and ponder. In this sense, sinful thoughts corrupt the most significant part of a person. Interestingly, Rambam argues in this context that sinful speech should be classified together with sinful thoughts, because the power of speech is also exclusive to human beings.

A different approach identifies sinful thoughts with heretical thoughts. R. Yosef Albo (*Sefer haIkkarim* 4:29) points out that sins often stem from the denial of one of the three fundamental principles: God's existence, divine providence, or divine revelation. Thus, the term *hirhurei aveira* actually refers to heresy. If so, we can understand why the gemara regards thoughts that reject the fundamentals of our faith as worse than individual acts of sin.

R. Meir Simha haKohen of Dvinsk (*Meshekh Hokhma, Bereishit* 18:28) bases his explanation on a famous distinction made by R. Eliyahu of Vilna, the Gra. R. Eliyahu argues that the terms *din* and *heshbon* (see *Avot* 3:1) refer to two different modes of divine judgment for wrongdoing: the former relates to the actual transgressions, the latter to the wasted opportunity to do *mizvot*. From the perspective of *din*, sinful acts may be worse than sinful thoughts. From the perspective of *heshbon*, however, sinful thoughts are worse, because every moment of constructive thinking is considered a *mizva*, and thus the realm of thought invites a much greater sense of missed opportunity.

Rabbeinu Nissim (*Derashot haRan*, p. 72) says that this quotation from *Hazal* indicates the essential role of inwardness in religious life. He contends that positive *mizvot* share the significance of the internal component emphasized in *Yoma* with regard to transgressions. While Halakha clearly cares greatly about external action, the internal state is indispensable. Rabbeinu Nissim argues for the centrality of the inner state when it comes to *mizvot* relating to beliefs, *mizvot* of an interpersonal nature, and *mizvot* that demand a certain awareness of God acting in history. With regard to all three categories, physical performance absent the internal awareness would miss the essence of the *mizvot* in question. In the same way, sinful thoughts can relate to the essential internal component of certain types of evil.

All of the approaches described above assume that when the gemara says that sinful thoughts are worse, it means worse in the sense of greater culpability and a more weighty transgression. Alternatively, worse may refer to the measure of frustration and difficulty involved. That is how Tosafot Yeshanim explain our text. They illustrate the point utilizing the gemara's example. The smell of a juicy piece of meat is much harder on the one who has not partaken from it than on the one who has. Thoughts of sin are far more difficult to counteract precisely because they remain unfulfilled. The sin remains an ever-beckoning goal seemingly full of delight and splendor.

Presumably, Tosafot Yeshanim are not suggesting that we purposely sin so as to lessen the level of frustration. I see three possible practical implications of their interpretation. First, we should be understanding and sympathetic toward those who are frustrated by temptations. Second, we should not put ourselves in situations that encourage sinful thoughts. Finally, we should realize that forbidden fruit often loses its luster once one has taken a bite. Perhaps this thought will cool our ardor for the cheeseburger that seems so inviting.

As noted, the gemara's evaluation refers either to the degree of blame or to the level of frustration. Either way, we cannot escape the question of whether we can really prevent sinful thoughts from occurring. Such thoughts seem to come to us from a part of the personality that precedes reflection. Is there a practical method to avoid the pitfall of sinful thoughts?

Anaf Yosef, cited in *Ein Yaakov*, offers two suggestions. He first mentions the possibility that we cannot prevent sinful thoughts. Some temptations afflict even the most righteous of souls. However, we can control what happens after sinful thoughts arrive. Do we enthusiastically dwell on the sinful possibilities, or do we distract ourselves by thinking about other things? When thoughts of revenge emerge, do we relish the fantasy of publicly embarrassing our rivals, or do we dissipate our vengeful thoughts by diverting our attention elsewhere? *Anaf Yosef* suggests that the *hirhurei aveira* evaluated negatively by the gemara denote prolonged dwelling on the possibilities of sin and not fleeting thoughts of wrongdoing.

In his second interpretation, *Anaf Yosef* argues that we can prevent sinful thoughts, but not by attacking them directly. He recommends filling one's day with Torah study and other positive endeavors so that dreams of iniquity have little room to enter. It is well known that bored adolescents hanging out on street corners are prone to destructive behavior; less well-known is that the same phenomenon occurs with adults. Adults whose lives are filled with religiously significant activity will simply have less time for thoughts of sin; they will also, hopefully, find their lives meaningful enough to lessen the need to look beyond the bounds of religiously acceptable behavior for excitement.

One final approach comes from a famous passage in the Torah commentary of Ibn Ezra (*Peirush haArukh, Shemot* 20:13). He asks how the Torah could require people not to covet houses or animals belonging to their neighbors, since coveting of this kind seems natural and immediate. (Parenthetically, some authorities maintain that the prohibition "Do not covet" is only violated if one takes action to acquire the item.) Ibn Ezra answers his question with a parable: A poor villager does not desire to marry the princess, because he knows very well that she is out of his league. Similarly, humans are not jealous of the flying powers of birds, because personal aviation is simply not part of our universe of possibilities. Apparently, our orientation toward various possibilities influences which desires we have. Many of us are not tempted to steal or cheat on an exam even when we know we could get away with it and would benefit from the cheating or stealing. We recoil morally from such behavior and thus are less tempted by it. Ibn Ezra challenges us to so internalize the wrongness of problematic practices that they lose their allure.

None of the above is meant to suggest that resisting temptation is easy. We can understand the difficulty of the endeavor even as we recognize its importance and proceed with the three strategies outlined above.

CHAPTER 8

Speech

Limitations on Lying

> Rav was vexed by his wife. If he asked her to make lentils, she
> made peas. If he asked her to make peas, she made lentils.
> When his son Hiyya got older, he [Hiyya] would reverse the
> request [and then his mother would make what the father
> wanted].
>
> Rav said to his son: "Things are going better with your
> mother."
>
> Hiyya said: "I am reversing it for her."
>
> Rav said: "This is what people say [a talmudic expression
> for a popular adage]: 'The one who comes from you teaches
> you good sense.' You should not do this, as the verse says: *They
> have taught their tongue to speak lies and weary themselves to
> commit iniquity* (Yirmiyahu 9:5)."
>
> (*Yevamot* 63a)

Rav admires his son's clever strategy, as shown by his quoting the
adage about learning wisdom from children. At the same time,

he instructs his son not to continue misreporting to his mother. Several commentators wonder why Rav tells Hiyya to stop. After all, it is a well-accepted halakhic principle that one is permitted to lie for the sake of preserving peace. A few pages later in the very same tractate (*Yevamot* 65b), we learn that God Himself deviated from the strict truth to preserve harmony between Avraham and Sarah. Why shouldn't Hiyya employ the same principle?

R. Shemuel Edels (Maharsha) sees the verse cited from *Yirmiyahu* as the key to the answer. The prophet there speaks about learning to prevaricate. A situation in which Hiyya constantly lied to his mother would train him for a life of deceit. While the occasional lie to protect someone's feelings will not have a negative educational impact, an ongoing pattern of falsehood will. Therefore, Rav directs Hiyya to stop.

Iyyun Yaakov (R. Yaakov Reisher's commentary, found in the *Ein Yaakov*) makes a different suggestion. He argues that we should not lie in situations where the truth will invariably come to light. In such cases, the lie will only bring temporary relief until the full truth emerges, and the deceived person will be angry. R. Reisher is not merely telling us to lie only when we can get away with it. He is pointing out that those who engage in falsehood become entrapped in webs of their own making and ultimately cannot keep the falsehood going. In light of this, it behooves us to think carefully about lying, even when we do so for a good cause.

R. Shelomo Luria (*Yam Shel Shelomo*) says that lying for the sake of peace is permitted only for the occasional lie, but not for a consistent policy of lying. While his position seems to be the same as Maharsha's, R. Luria says nothing about training the child in deceit. Perhaps he intends to make a different point. If a relationship depends upon an ongoing pattern of falsehood, then the falsehood is not truly repairing the relationship, but is only covering up the fact that something in the relationship is rotten. An occasional lie can be reconciled with a healthy and meaningful relationship, but not a lifetime of falsehood. Rav understands that Hiyya's strategy does not address the tension between him and his wife, and he tells Hiyya to desist.

R. Yosef Hayyim (*Ben Yehoyada*) adds a point that works well with our understanding in the previous paragraph. He asks: Why did Hiyya tell his father the truth, and not lie to him as well? We might answer that in situations of tension between spouses, the children often feel responsible for the problem, attempt to bring reconciliation, and sometimes end up choosing sides. R. Hayyim explains that not telling Rav would lead to calamity. Rav would think the rift was repaired and would return to the former intimacy with his wife, including revealing his innermost secrets. If his wife remains angry with him, she will use those secrets to hurt Rav. Hiyya understands that Rav must know the truth if the strategy he has adopted is not to harm his father.

This explanation strengthens our interpretation of *Yam Shel Shelomo*'s position, namely, that false solutions often cause more harm than good. Although not every rift can be healed, falsehood is no substitute for true resolution.

Thus, the halakhic permission to lie for the sake of peace is governed by significant restrictions. One should not lie if it will train a person in falsehood, bring only temporary relief, or gloss over real issues that need to be addressed.

The Problem of Profanity

> R. Hana the son of Rav said: "Everyone knows why a bride enters a bridal chamber, but whoever disgraces his mouth and utters a word of folly – even if a decree of seventy years of happiness were sealed and granted unto him, it is turned for him into evil."
>
> (*Ketuvot* 8b)

What does R. Hana wish to highlight when he emphasizes that even though everyone knows what a bride and groom do on the wedding night, one should not mention it? According to Maharal, R. Hana's statement reveals the true problem with profanity and coarse chatter. When we try to explain the problem of profanity in the context of harming others, the argument breaks down. The problematic nature of a speaker's profanity does not stem from the offense taken by the listener. Everyone knows what will occur between bride and groom behind closed doors, so those who hear the comment will not be shocked. The problem is located elsewhere.

Maharal focuses on the term "disgrace of the mouth" (*nivul peh*). The problem of profanity is not what it does to the listener but what it reveals about the speaker. The need to speak rudely about coarse topics reveals the speaker's lack of dignity and gentleness. The gemara speaks about disgracing "his mouth" because it is an internal problem more than an interpersonal difficulty. Maharal broadens the point by developing the idea that in addition to the classic categories of *mizvot* between a person and God and *mizvot* between one person and another, there is a third category of *mizvot* – between man and himself. Refraining from coarse talk belongs in this third category.

Imagine someone we particularly respect telling dirty jokes. We would be troubled because this behavior would not coincide with a more dignified and exalted expression of humanity. R. Hana's statement represents a call for each of us to move from coarseness to refinement.

A Remedy for Slander

> R. Hama b. Hanina said: "What is the remedy for slander? If he is a scholar, let him engage in Torah…. But if he is unlearned, let him humble himself."
>
> (*Arakhin* 15b)

The second piece of advice seems straightforward enough. Some badmouthing stems from arrogance (although some stems from underconfidence too), and the humbled individual will not be so quick to point out the faults of others. But how does Torah study help curb a person's tongue? Maharsha relates this point to the general notion that Torah study protects us from sin. If so, R. Hama could just as easily have been talking about theft or eating non-kosher food. Another explanation might suggest a reason why Torah effectively aids against *lashon ha'ra* in particular.

R. Yisrael Meir haKohen, the *Hafez Hayyim*, offers such an explanation in his celebrated *Shmirat haLashon (Sha'ar haTorah*, chap. 1). Human nature being what it is, he argues, people will invariably talk about something, so the central question is what the content of their conversation will be. Those with matters of substance to discuss will have quality conversations. Those lacking the wherewithal for meaningful dialogue will invariably lapse into talking about others. The gemara's advice to study Torah means finding ideas worth discussing, thereby rendering the need for idle chatter inoperative.

Depart from Evil and Do Good

> R. Alexanderi declared: "Who wants life? Who wants life?"
> Everyone gathered around him. They said: "Give us life."
> He said to them: *Who is the person who desires life?…Keep your tongue from evil and your lips from speaking deceit. Depart from evil and do good (Tehillim* 34:12–14).
> Perhaps a person will say: "I have kept my tongue from falsehood, my lips from speaking deceit. I will go and indulge in sleep." The Torah teaches me [otherwise when it says]: *Depart from evil and do good*. Good refers to nothing other than Torah, as it says: *For I give you a good doctrine, do not abandon my Torah (Mishlei* 4:2).
> (*Avoda Zara* 19b)

This gemara lends itself to two possible interpretations. A person who says "I have kept my tongue from falsehood" may have succeeded at not using speech negatively, but may think that this is a sign of great righteousness. Therefore, the gemara points out that it is not enough to avoid the negative; one must also try to accomplish something positive. Many think that they are ethical paragons if they avoid murder, theft, slander, and the like. They must also confront the question of what acts of positive benevolence they have performed for others. "Depart from evil" but also "do good."

Another reading is possible. R. Alexanderi taught the people that the key to achieving life was to desist from utilizing the power of speech for evil purposes. The power of this idea might motivate some of his auditors to minimize their speaking altogether. With the dangers of talebearing, profanity, lying, and foolish chatter lurking every time one opens one's mouth, they might decide that silence is the best policy. According to this reading, the individual in question has not yet succeeded in avoiding evil speech and eschews talking altogether as a precaution.

The gemara felt the need to combat this attitude. Giving up speech is not the answer. While silence may preclude the possibility of negative speech, it prevents the myriad of positive endeavors that depend upon speech. Every aspect of the human condition lends itself to both positive and negative manifestations. A decision to cut something off invariably leads to cutting off some positive potential. Rav Kook (*Orot haKodesh*, introduction, p. 30) warns about a "fear of heaven" that saps energy for positive and negative endeavors. Indeed, some people are so nervous about not sinning that they practically stop functioning. Without minimizing the dangers of sin, we must recall that risks and opportunities go together. We must strive both to "depart from evil" and to "do good."

CHAPTER 9

Halakhic Observance

Of Roses and Prohibitions

> *A hedge of roses* (*Shir haShirim* 7:4). That even a hedge like roses is not breached. And this is what a heretic said to R. Kahana: "You say that a husband can be secluded with his wife when she is a *nida*. Is it possible that fire will be with flax and it will not be kindled?"
>
> R. Kahana answered: "The Torah testified about us when it employs the phrase *a hedge of roses*. Even if the hedge is like roses, it will not be breached."
>
> (*Sanhedrin* 37a)

What is the symbolism of the hedge of roses? A fence made of flowers certainly seems insubstantial when compared with an iron gate or a stone wall. A bystander noticing such a hedge around a field would probably regard it as a complete failure at preventing outsiders from coming in. In the same way, the human conscience would seem to be a paltry defense of halakhic observance against the temptation of antinomian behavior. Nonetheless, despite appearances, our halakhic hedge of roses does motivate people to stay out of the garden. Ideals can be more effective barriers than stone walls.

The preceding interpretation explains the symbolism of a wall of flowers, but not the specific choice of roses. The simplest explanation, offered by Rashi on *Shir haShirim*, relates the redness of the rose to the color of menstrual blood. Since the heretic employed the example of *nida*, it makes sense for Rav Kahana to utilize this imagery. Maharsha (on *Sanhedrin*) suggests that Rav Kahana mentions a beautiful fence to convey a desire to uproot the fence and smell the flowers. Despite the attraction of doing so, committed Jews are capable of restraint.

I would build upon the idea that the rose represents a thing of beauty but move the symbolism in a different direction. We often think of restrictions and prohibitions as ugly restraints on happiness, accomplishment, and creativity. William Blake eloquently expresses this assumption in his poem "The Garden of Love": "And Priests in black gowns were walking their rounds/ And binding with briars my joys and desires." The gemara makes roses the symbol of the prohibition to indicate that, contrary to our initial assumption, the restriction itself can often be a source of joy and self-expression. This is true on a number of levels.

First, restrictions prevent the overindulgence that ruins any enjoyment. Parents who prevent a child from gorging on too many candy bars are actually enabling the child to enjoy the noshing experience without becoming sick.

Second, barriers ensure that moral ugliness does not accompany the pleasure. Gluttony and sexual promiscuity can destroy people and families; halakhic restrictions help prevent that from happening.

Finally, absolute freedom sometimes leaves us standing still, whereas a structured life enables us to express ourselves within that structure. The orchestral conductor does not want freedom to choose the notes the musicians play. Rather, the conductor wants to express a personal style in the context of a particular score. In much the same way, the details of Halakha need not contradict individuality and self-expression. For example, the words of the *Amida* provide a context in which we all find our own paths to communicating with Hashem.

G. K. Chesterton (*Orthodoxy*, p. 145) offers a wonderful image for the idea that restrictions and structure can enhance joy, playfulness, and vitality. Imagine that children are playing a game on a steep hill on an island in the sea. If there is a danger of falling off the cliff, their movements will be hesitant and cautious, and the game will be ruined. However, if there is a fence around the top of the hill, their concern is removed, and they can play with abandon. So, too, our halakhic hedge of roses allows for, and sometimes is precisely what enables, a life that includes delight and joy.

Novelty and the Evil Inclination

> R. Yizhak said: "A person's evil inclination tries to renew itself against him daily, as it says *And all the inclinations of the thoughts of his heart are only evil all day (Bereishit 6:5)*."
> R. Shimon ben Lakish said: "A person's inclination tries to overpower him daily and tries to kill him, as it says: *The wicked waits for the righteous and seeks to slay him (Tehillim 37:32).* And if not for God's help, a person could not succeed against it, as it says: *And God does not abandon him in his hand* (ibid. 37:33).
> (*Sukka* 52a–b, *Kiddushin* 30b)

It would seem that the *yezer hara* has two distinct strategies: *mitgaber* ("overpowering") and *mithadesh* ("renewing"), that is, force and novelty. (Parenthetically, I believe that the term *yezer hara* as used in the gemara does not refer to a figure in red tights holding a pitchfork but to an element of the human personality.) What is the significance of novelty as a strategy for provoking sin?

Maharal explains in his *Hiddushei Aggadot* that the inclination adjusts in tandem with the person. Our personalities change over the course of time, and the religious and moral temptations we face change as well. For example, an adolescent might think of temptation in purely sexual terms, whereas an older person might well be more tempted by honor. Reish Lakish is instructing us to be aware of the changing temptations at different stages of life and to conduct ourselves accordingly.

R. Hanokh Zundel ben Yosef, a nineteenth-century commentator on midrash and aggada from Bialystok, cites a terrific reading of this gemara in his *Anaf Yosef* (found in the *Ein Yaakov*). He begins by distinguishing between two types of sins. There are sins that people have a natural inclination for, such as sins of the flesh. There also are sins for which we do not have an inherent inclination, such as the prohibition not to wear clothing of mixed linen and wool. With regard to the latter, the evil inclination can only get us to transgress with an act of *hitgabrut*, or strong force.

With regard to the more obviously tempting sins, the evil inclination does not require such effort. Here it faces a different challenge. Hedonism begins in a state of great excitement but usually leads to an acute sense of boredom. A life dedicated to tasting the finest steaks, for example, can retain one's interest for only so long before the choicest meats cease to look appealing. The evil inclination must employ the strategy of novelty in an attempt to persuade us that the next steak will be a qualitatively different experience. That inclination is *mithadesh* each day.

Søren Kierkegaard understood this point, for he describes boredom as the challenge to the hedonist in his book *Either/Or* (see the section entitled "Diapsalmata").

> Once pleasure had but to beckon me and I rose, light of foot, sound and unafraid. When I rode slowly through the woods, it was as if I flew; now when the horse is covered with lather and ready to drop, it seems to me that I do not move. I am solitary as always; forsaken, not by men, which could not hurt me, but by the happy fairies of joy, who used to encircle me in countless

multitude…. My soul has lost its potentiality. If I were to wish for anything, I should not wish for wealth and power, but for the passionate sense of the potential, for the eye which, ever young and ardent, sees the possible.

Pleasure disappoints, possibility never.

These considerations suggest a strategy for educating the hedonistically inclined. We might point out to them that the freshness and visceral delight that now seem so attractive will ultimately not last. While I would not deny that observant Jews can find themselves bored with religion, I confidently assert that the ongoing opportunity for spiritual growth and deeper understanding of Torah provides the continuing sense of the potential and the possible spoken of by Kierkegaard.

One last insight on this gemara appears in the *Shem miShemuel* (*Parashat Nizavim* 5675) of the Sohachover Rebbe. He argues that there exists a power of novelty and innovation in this world. If we do not employ this power in a religious setting, it will find expression in more problematic contexts. In other words, innovation and freshness is a basic aspect of being human and should not be rejected or ignored. If we do so, the need for novelty will emerge in an uglier fashion. Without downplaying the strong sense of tradition and structure in Orthodox Judaism, we should feel challenged to provide our students with a sense of potential freshness. This may involve encouraging new Torah insights, adding personal supplications to the fixed text of prayer, or other such strategies. Resisting the evil inclination depends upon fostering a strong sense of vitality and potentiality within the bounds of traditional Judaism.

The Significance of Ubiquitous Crimes

Rav Amram said in the name of Rav: "From three sins a man cannot escape every day: sinful [lustful] thoughts, *iyyun tefilla*, and *lashon ha'ra* [speaking ill of others]." Do we truly think this about *lashon ha'ra*? Rather, it refers to the dust of *lashon ha'ra* [but not to *lashon ha'ra* proper]. Rav Yehuda said in the name of Rav: "Most people are involved in theft, a few in sexual crimes, and all in *lashon ha'ra*."

(*Bava Batra* 164b)

I have not translated *iyyun tefilla* because there is no neutral way to render it in English. Every translation of this term reflects a different specific interpretation. Rashbam explains it as referring to the belief that one's prayers, if performed perfectly, cannot fail to bring the desired result. This is religiously problematic, because it makes prayer into a ritual guaranteed to manipulate God. Authentic prayer works with a healthy sense of humility before the inscrutable divine will.

Tosafot object to this interpretation, because the gemara refers to common sins, and one who approaches *tefilla* in this fashion is unusual. In fact, many people pray without assuming that their prayers will be answered. Instead, Tosafot explain that the gemara refers to lack of *kavana* (intent) during davening. This certainly reflects a constant problem. We can well understand a talmudic suggestion that this fault applies to everyone.

Why does the gemara feel compelled to point out the most commonly found transgressions, as if it were keeping score in some kind of competitive sport between sins? On one level, it warns us to take these challenges seriously and to take the time to struggle with such thorny issues. Knowing that a certain issue poses a great challenge can inspire diligent preparation for confronting it.

On another level, this gemara instructs us not to become overwrought when we fail. Understanding that almost everyone struggles with these issues helps put our own moments of weakness in perspective. Treating every uninspired *minha*, or each bit of gossip spoken, as a religious failure of terrifying proportions often leads to intense depression, not religious growth.

Maharal (*Hiddushei Aggadot*) sees the three frequent problems as reflecting three areas of religious endeavor. *Iyyun tefilla* refers to our relationship with God. *Lashon ha'ra* relates to our relationship with fellow humans. Lustful thoughts belong in the category of our relationship with ourselves, because these thoughts assault the dignity of the person having them.

We have already seen how Maharal utilizes the third category to explain the problem of profanity. I believe that the inclusion of this third category describes an important area of religious life that often goes unnoticed. Certain actions are fundamentally wrong because of their impact on the actor, and what they reflect about the actor, irrespective of whether or not they harm others. It may be a mistake to criticize profanity or looking at dirty magazines as interpersonal crimes. Perhaps what is essentially wrong with these actions is that they degrade the human being performing them.

While Rav Amram does not distinguish among his three ubiquitous crimes, Rav Yehuda underlines the contrasting frequency of three significant transgressions. Rashbam explains that most people become entangled in theft when they withhold someone else's profits in business dealings. They would not enter someone else's property and steal what they find there. Yet the same people fail to understand that one can steal in the absence of a dramatic act of taking. Any business involves temptations to more subtle forms of theft.

According to Rav Yehuda, *lashon ha'ra* is more common than theft and sexual immorality. The Maharal offers a novel explanation for this phenomenon. He points out that both theft and sexual immorality come with a certain degrading quality that embarrasses the sinner. It is hard to work up much self-righteousness about committing theft or adultery. *Lashon ha'ra*, on the other hand, often involves an element of self-righteousness. The speaker implicitly adopts an air of superiority in talking about the misdeeds of others. The Maharal sees this hidden self-congratulation as the root of the frequency of *lashon ha'ra*.

A host of themes emerge from this brief aggada. These few lines animate our thinking about prayer, theft, *lashon ha'ra*, lustful thoughts, and the problems of the most common transgressions. The challenge is to seriously confront our most difficult religious duties and not to see every failure as proof of our utter wickedness.

Joy and Dedication

It was taught in a *beraita*: "Rabban Shimon ben Gamliel said: 'Any *mizva* that [the Jews] accepted joyously – such as circumcision (*mila*), as it says (*Tehillim* 119:162): *I rejoice at your word as one who finds great spoil* – they still perform joyously. However, any *mizva* that they accepted with quarreling – such as *arayot* [sexual prohibitions], as it says (*Bemidbar* 11:10): *And Moshe heard the people crying to their families*, namely, about the matter of families – they still perform with quarreling, as there is no *ketuba* that does not involve some strife.'"

It was taught in a *beraita*: "R. Shimon ben Elazar said: 'Any *mizva* that the Jews were willing to commit martyrdom for at a time of governmental edicts, such as idolatry and circumcision, is still adhered to strongly. However, any *mizva* that the Jews were not willing to commit martyrdom for at a time of governmental edicts, such as *tefillin*, is still adhered to weakly.'"

It is as Rav Yannai taught: "*Tefillin* require a clean body like that of Elisha *Baal Kenafayim* [the Master of the Wings]."

Why was he called Elisha *Baal Kenafayim*? Once, the evil government decreed that whoever put on *tefillin* would have his brain cut out. Elisha put on *tefillin* and went to the market, where a quaestor saw him. Elisha ran and the quaestor ran after him. When the quaestor reached him, Elisha removed the *tefillin* from his head and held them in his hands.

He said to him: "What is that in your hands?"

He said to him: "The wings of a dove." He opened his

hands and the wings of a dove were in them. Therefore, they
called him Elisha *Baal Kenafayim*. Why did he specifically say
the wings of a dove and not another bird? He did so because
the Jewish people are compared to a dove.

(Shabbat 130a)

According to this gemara, circumcision is a *mizva* that the Jews
both accepted joyously and were willing to risk their lives for. Before discussing the relationship between these two facts, let us look
at each one individually. The gemara cites a verse from *Tehillim* to
illustrate that the Jewish people accepted circumcision with joy.
The verse does not explicitly mention circumcision, but the proof
stems from the usage of the singular *imrateha*, "your word." Since
the first *mizva* the Jewish people received, in the time of Avraham,
was circumcision, the singular word refers to this *mizva*. Having
accepted this *mizva* joyously, the Jews continue to perform it joyously, for every *mila* is accompanied by a festive meal.

Arayot serve as a contrast to *mila*. Although the Jewish people
in the desert ostensibly complained about the lack of meat, *Hazal*
understand their complaints to really have been about the many
restrictions imposed by Halakha. In addition to the proof-text
cited in our gemara, *Hazal* explain that the people's fond memo-
ries of free fish in Egypt (*Bemidbar* 11:5, *Sifri* and Rashi ad loc.)
refer to freedom from the commandments. The people are embarrassed to openly complain about the restrictions, so they couch
their complaints in other words, but the text of the Torah reveals
the truth. Some of the Jews are particularly perturbed about the
new sexual prohibitions, and their initial resistance to these halakhot has long-term repercussions.

In the next section, the gemara lists circumcision and the
prohibition against idolatry as two commandments for which the
Jewish people are willing to give up their lives. Indeed, many of
the heroic martyrs in our tradition were trying to preserve these
very *mizvot*. By contrast, the gemara depicts tefillin as a *mizva*
that does not inspire a person's willingness to give up one's life

and cites the Elisha story to illustrate this lack of dedication. Yet the story seems to indicate that Elisha was quite dedicated to the *mizva* of *tefillin*. Did he not put them on at great personal risk?

Rashi and Tosafot offer different explanations of how this story shows reluctance to be martyred for *tefillin*. Rashi explains that Elisha stands out because he is the only Jew who was willing to risk his life to preserve this important *mizva*; Elisha is the exception who proves the rule. Tosafot disagree and argue that Elisha was not adequately committed, because he does not tell the Roman official the truth about the *tefillin*. Instead of making a public stand for a Jewish ideal, Elisha declares that he is not holding *tefillin* but something else altogether.

The two interpretations raise the question of the obligation for martyrdom in the realm of *mizvot aseh* (positive commands). As is well known, in times of religious persecution, Jews are expected to give up their lives to preserve any *mizva* outlawed by the authorities (*Sanhedrin* 74a). Ramban (Shabbat 49a) mentions two explanations of why this ruling would not apply to *mizvot aseh*. Avoiding a *mizva* involves a passive act, unlike the active transgression of a negative prohibition; only the latter, the active violation, generates a demand for martyrdom. Furthermore, the authorities always have the ability to prevent us from fulfilling positive *mizvot*. They could simply put us in jail without access to *tefillin*. Martyrdom to avoid a transgression makes sense, but martyrdom to fulfill a positive *mizva* would be a fruitless endeavor.

Of course, this calls into question Elisha's putting on *tefillin* altogether. Perhaps he was recklessly endangering himself when Halakha does not call for such action. Ramban suggests that Elisha originally thought that he could put them on without being caught. Additionally, Ramban states that in some circumstances, a Jew has the right to risk his life as an act of extra piety, even when Halakha does not command it. Rambam (*Hilkhot Yesodei haTorah* 5:4) vociferously rejects this option. Rambam would have to say either that Elisha was obligated to risk his life (he may think that *mizvot aseh* are not legally different from negative commandments) or that Elisha thought that he could get away with it without being seen.

Are the conversations about accepting *mizvot* joyously and the willingness to commit martyrdom for *mizvot* related? We could answer in the negative, contending that the talmudic chapter about circumcision, the nineteenth chapter of *Shabbat*, begins with two distinct points about how the Jewish people have historically related to this commandment. However, I want to answer in the affirmative.

We associate martyrdom with difficulty, dedication, perseverance, and suffering. Many of us associate joy with lightheartedness, frivolity, and fun. From these starting points, it would seem that these two themes should not overlap, as they reflect totally different states of mind. A deeper understanding reveals that the most authentic joys of life also emerge from perseverance and dedication. Without denying the pleasures of the palate, we can conclude that they pale beside the pleasures of mastering a difficult but beautiful section of Torah or of engaging in an act of *hessed* sorely needed by the recipient. Thus, the gemara may have purposely juxtaposed these two ideas about *mila*. The joy of the *mizva* and the passionate commitment to it are naturally interwoven: joy engenders commitment, and commitment helps to produce joy.

Inadvertent Crimes

> The Rabbis taught: "Moshe had set apart three cities [of refuge] on the other side of the Jordan, and corresponding to them, Yehoshua set apart [others] in the land of Canaan.... Did Trans-Jordan need [the same number of cities] as the whole land of Israel [i.e., as there were many more tribes in Canaan, why would both areas require the same number of cities of refuge]?

Abbaye said: "Because murder was common in Gilead."
(*Makkot* 9b)

Many commentators object that Abbaye's answer misses the mark. The cities of refuge are intended as a home for those who inadvertently kill someone, so the fact that the inhabitants of one city are more murderous than the norm does not in itself create a greater need for cities of refuge. Intentional murder is a capital crime; its frequency should have no bearing on the number of people who need to settle in the cities of refuge. Thus, Abbaye's focus on intentional murder seems beside the point. Various solutions to this problem have been offered. Ritva suggests that the intentional murderers pretended that their acts were committed accidentally and fled to cities of refuge until the courts could sort out who belonged where, and thus a more murderous society does require more cities of refuge.

Maharal (*Gur Aryeh Bemidbar* 35:14) suggests a more powerful answer. A society with many murders does not value human life or recoil at the idea of causing a person's death. The higher murder rate reflects a lack of concern for human life and generates a cheapening of the value of human life. A society of this kind will also have more inadvertent murders because it will not take the precautions that would limit such occurrences. Trans-Jordan needs more cities of refuge not because the intentional criminals will find their way there, but because crimes of intentionality and crimes of negligence stem from the same root, and a society with more of one will have more of the other.

Moral and religious success mandates an understanding that "I didn't mean it" is often not a satisfactory excuse. The example of driving a bit recklessly comes readily to mind. If we truly valued human life, we would not take any chances behind the wheel. The close relationship between intentional and inadvertent crimes should make us more sensitive about the seriousness of the latter.

Jewish Sexual Ethics

Once a man who was very zealous about the *mizva* of *zizit* heard of a harlot across the ocean who took four hundred gold coins as her wages. He sent her four hundred gold coins and arranged a time. When the time came, he went and sat at her door. Her maid went in and said: "The man who sent you four hundred gold coins has arrived and he is sitting at the door."

She said: "Let him enter."

He entered. She spread out for him seven beds, six of silver and one of gold. In between each bed was a silver ladder and the uppermost one was of gold. She went up to the top bed and lay there naked. He also went up and sat naked opposite her. His four *zizit* came and slapped him across the face. He slipped off and sat on the ground. She too slipped off and sat on the ground.

She said: " By the Roman Capitol, I will not let you go until you tell me what blemish you saw in me."

He said: "By the Temple, I never saw a woman as beautiful as you, but there is a *mizva* that God commanded us called *zizit*. With regard to it, the phrase *I am the Lord, your God* is written twice, [signifying] 'I am the one who will exact punishment in the future, and I am the one who will give reward in the future.' Now they [the *zizit*] have appeared to me as four witnesses."

She said: "I will not let you go until you tell me your name, the name of your city, the name of your teacher, and the name of the study hall in which you learn Torah."

He wrote this down and gave it to her.

She arose and divided her estate; a third for the government, a third for the poor, and a third she took in her hand, not including the bedspreads. She came to the study hall of R. Hiyya.

She said to him: " Rebbe, instruct me and they will make me a convert."

He said to her: " My daughter, perhaps you have set your eyes upon one of the students."

She took out the document and gave it to him. He said to her: "Go and attain your acquisition."

The bedspreads that she had spread out for him for prohibited activity, she now spread out for him lawfully.

(*Menahot* 44a)

On one level, we have a story about how the *mizva* of *zizit* prevents sin. One might suggest that the fringes strike at the man's conscience more than they physically smite him. On another level, the story emphasizes both the heroic ability to desist at the height of temptation, and how such heroism can inspire others to repair their ways. Rabbi Eliezer Berkovits (*Crisis and Faith*, pp. 64–70) finds another level of meaning that helps in the formation of a Jewish sexual ethic. The key lies in noticing a shift in the interaction between the two protagonists after the man has chosen to desist. In the first part of the story, they never communicate directly. Each one speaks to the maid, but no words pass between the customer and the harlot. As soon as the man leaves the bed, the woman speaks directly to him. Second, they do not inquire about each other's identity in the first section. Only after it becomes clear that they will not lie together does she ask his name, as well as the names of his teacher and school.

These two shifts convey the essence of Jewish sexual ethics. Prostitution represents the height of impersonal lust. In such a relationship, each party views the other as a commodity. The harlot views the customer as a source of money, and the customer sees the harlot as a source of pleasure. From this vantage point, there is no point to communicating or to learning the other's identity. When the relationship shifts from I–It to I–Thou, and the two parties become interested in each other as people, then the union can be sanctified. Various halakhic restrictions on the interaction between the sexes can be understood from this perspective. Halakha strives to prevent the dehumanizing impact of a relationship that reduces human beings to material goods.

When I first read this story, the happy ending troubled me. I thought that the fact that they end up together destroys the heroism of the man's gesture and conveys the mistaken notion that the righteous will always receive the very pleasure they renounce. R. Berkovits points out that the story's conclusion adds a crucial element. The importance of the I–Thou relationship should not obscure the fact that physical enjoyment remains part of a healthy marriage. Thus, our two protagonists ultimately form a deeper relationship that includes a physical component.

CHAPTER 10

Jewish Philosophy

Afflictions of Love: The Relationship Between Suffering and Sin

> Rava, and some say Rav Hisda, said: "If a person sees that suffering (*yissurin*) comes upon him, let him examine his conduct, as it says: *We will search our ways and return to Hashem* (*Eikha* 3:40). If he searches and finds nothing [objectionable], let him attribute [the suffering] to neglect of Torah study, as it says: *Happy is the man whom You cause to suffer, Hashem, and teach him from your Torah* (*Tehillim* 94:12). If he attributes it [to neglecting Torah study] and still finds nothing, it is clearly afflictions of love (*yissurin shel ahava*), as it says: *For God chastises whom He loves* (*Mishlei* 3:12)."
>
> (*Berakhot* 5a)

The question of the relationship between sin and suffering has been a constant in the history of Western religious thought. The preceding gemara suggests that not all suffering in this world can be assumed to be punishment for sin. At the same time, it suggests that repentance should be the sufferer's first response. Let us examine the three stages of the gemara's response to suffering before concentrating on that mysterious term, "afflictions of love."

As mentioned, the suffering individual begins by searching for the sins that might be the cause of his suffering. If he cannot find any such sins, he attributes the suffering to neglect of Torah study (*bittul Torah*). Why didn't he locate the problematic *bittul Torah* in the original stage of spiritual stock-taking (*heshbon ha'nefesh*)? Ramban explains (*Sha'ar haGemul*, p. 180) that the initial search looks for violations of negative prohibitions. It turns up nothing, the suffering person looks for a possible deficiency in the area of positive *mizvot*, such as insufficient Torah study. For the Ramban, *bittul Torah* is not a unique problem; it represents the broader category of not adequately fulfilling positive *mizvot*.

By contrast, *Yismah Moshe* (cited in *Likkutei Batar Likkutei* on *Berakhot*) explains that *bittul Torah* is meant in a specific way. As people can always utilize their time more productively and free up more of it for Torah study, an intensive religious evaluation will find *bittul Torah* even when the basic search for sins identifies nothing. The first investigation finds no sinful cause of the pain, but the second and more probing look at how the person uses his or her time does find some problematic behavior.

The Vilna Gaon (Gra) offers a third perspective in his commentary on *Berakhot*. He suggests that neglect of Torah study explains why the first search turns up empty. A person who does not truly understand the manifold religious responsibilities of the Torah may find no sins when doing *heshbon ha'nefesh*, whereas someone who learns Torah thoroughly would know which areas are deficient. For the Gra, the second stage, looking for *bittul Torah*, rectifies the poor application of the first stage, the fruitless search for sin.

Yet the gemara does go on to talk of individuals who do not find that *bittul Torah* adequately explains their suffering. Some suffering cannot be explained by claiming that victim did not fulfill positive commandments, did not use time well, or did not fully understand the broad nature of religious responsibility. If we do sometimes break the nexus between sin and punishment, what other explanations for suffering exist?

Rashi (ibid.) says that God gives us undeserved suffering in this world in order to compensate us with reward in the world-to-come. While the terse quality of Rashi's writing precludes a precise understanding, he may be referring to an idea mentioned by the Rambam in the name of the Mutazalite Kalam (*Moreh Nevukhim* 3:17). According to this school of Islamic thought, we can "cash in" our suffering "chips" from this world for greater rewards in the next world. Rav Sa'adia Gaon endorses this possibility in *Emunot veDeot* 5:3.

Rambam rejects this approach; indeed, it does seem odd that God would inflict pointless suffering just so as to give the victim a greater reward in the next world. If God wants to give reward beyond our merit, He can certainly do so without increasing our afflictions. Rambam apparently identifies the Mutazalite position with the concept of "afflictions of love," and he goes so far as to claim that this concept may appear in the Talmud, but only as a rejected, minority position.

Ramban (cited above) refuses to accept that God punishes the innocent out of love. He explains that afflictions of love come upon those who have sinned inadvertently. When the gemara mentions a person whose self-search cannot find any sins that would have brought about the given punishment, it refers to a search for purposeful iniquities. Although inadvertent transgressions are far less serious than willful crimes, they too deserve punishment, both because the sinner could have been more careful and because the sin leaves a mark that taints the soul. These afflictions are "of love" because they repair the soul and ready it for the world-to-come.

Maharsha suggests that "afflictions of love" refer to vicarious atonement. He cites the famous verses in *Yeshayahu* 53 in which a righteous person apparently suffers for the sins of others. Of course, this reading of *Yeshayahu* 53 immediately calls to mind the Christian reading of the chapter, and we tend to think that Judaism does not endorse the Christian concept of vicarious atonement. However, are we correct in assuming that there is a divide between Christianity and Judaism on this issue? On the one hand, some sources (e.g., *Moed Katan* 28a) speak of the death of the righteous being an atonement, and *Yeshayahu* 53 can be read along the same lines. On the other hand, many passages in *Yehezkel* (e.g., chap. 18) and other places emphasize individual responsibility and reject the concept of suffering for the sins of others. Radak (*Yeshayahu* 53:4) states that the verses in *Yeshayahu* reflect an erroneous popular belief, but that in reality we each suffer only for our own transgressions. Perhaps we can say that Judaism is far more conflicted about vicarious atonement than Christianity.

Rabbi Shalom Carmy once suggested to me a different dividing line on this matter. Some Christians believe that man is so depraved that only vicarious atonement can pave the way toward salvation. Our tradition may include some form of vicarious atonement, but it is not based on the view that human lowliness is so extreme that help from the suffering of the righteous is the only possible route to salvation.

Both Maharal (*Netivot Olam, Netiv haYissurin* 1) and Ran (*Derashot haRan*, p. 174) explain that afflictions sometimes promote personal religious growth. For Maharal, suffering helps break our attachment to the material; for the Ran, suffering helps free us from the snare of wild imagination. Either way, afflictions help us focus our attention on the most important things in life. Whereas Ran and Maharal write about suffering moving us away from certain potentially harmful aspects of the human personality, we can broaden the point to a much wider range of religious growth. Struggling with frustrations and difficulties often brings out new reservoirs of strength and helps us realize aspects of our humanity that we would not have found otherwise.

This last approach differs from that of the Mutazalite Kalam because, according to Ran and Maharal, the suffering is not spiritually pointless. Rather, it provides an avenue of growth for the human religious personality. Of course, some kinds of suffering might be too crushing to have so positive a effect, and I am not suggesting that this model will explain every difficult case of unjustified suffering.

John Hick, a contemporary Christian theologian, builds a similar theodicy in his *Evil and the God of Love* (see pp. 256–259). He contrasts a pet owner with a parent. The former is solely interested in providing a life of comfort for the pet. The latter is interested in the personal growth and development of the child. This will sometimes include decisions that make life more taxing for the child because in those struggles, the child achieves religious, ethical, and personal maturity.

Note that we have discussed various understandings that break the easy causal connection between sin and punishment. Yaakov Elman has written a number of articles showing the many other talmudic models that also sever this link (see his "The Contribution of Rabbinic Thought to a Theology of Misfortune"). Apparently we can believe in divine, providential justice and still understand that the pain of others and even our own difficulties need not always be traced back to sin. Suffering should make us think of *teshuva*, but several different models explain why we suffer.

Optimism and the Song of Songs

> On another occasion, [R. Gamliel, R. Elazar ben Azarya, R. Yehoshua, and R. Akiva] were going to Jerusalem, and when they came to Mount Scopus, they rent their clothes. When they came to the Temple Mount, they saw a fox coming out of the Holy of Holies; [the others] wept, but R. Akiva laughed.
> (*Makkot* 24b)

Before we can understand this aggada, we need to consider another source, which requires some background knowledge. In mishnaic times, people kept their *teruma* produce alongside the Torah scrolls, and mice seeking to reach the food often damaged the scrolls. The sages ended this desecration by decreeing that touching the scrolls is *metamei yadayim* ("ritually defiles the hands"). This decree ended the practice of keeping *teruma* with the scrolls because defiled *teruma* had to be destroyed. A question then arose regarding whether certain of the *Ketuvim*, such as *Kohelet* and *Shir haShirim*, were included in the edict. If they were, their sacred status would be recognized, and thus in this instance causing defilement would actually be a sign of sanctity.

> R. Akiva said: "God forbid! No one in Israel ever claimed that *Shir haShirim* does not defile the hands. After all, the universe in its entirety was never as worthwhile as the day that *Shir haShirim* was given to Israel; all Scriptures are holy, but *Shir haShirim* is the holiest of the holy. If there was ever a debate, it was only about *Kohelet*."
>
> (*Yadayim* 3:5)

Why was there a question about the ritual status of *Shir haShirim*, and what was R. Akiva's argument that it surely defiles hands? One possibility is that R. Akiva is strongly contesting the view that the parable of *Shir haShirim* could mistakenly be taken for a secular love song. Another gemara (*Sanhedrin* 101a) indicates very strong opposition to treating the Song of Songs as a human love song. Perhaps R. Akiva seeks to affirm the metaphorical reading of the book as a song of love between God and the Jewish people.

Rabbi Moshe Avigdor Amiel, former Chief Rabbi of Antwerp and Tel Aviv (*Derashot El Ami* 2:15), understands the tension about this work differently. He links R. Akiva's statement about *Shir haShirim* with his reaction to the Temple ruins. *Shir haShirim*, a powerful love song between God and the Jewish people, represents the spirit of optimism and hope. Some of the sages questioned the continuing significance of the *Shir* now that the Temple had been destroyed and the Jews had been exiled, asking whether optimism still had a place in the now fragmented world? When R. Akiva contends that *Shir haShirim* does generate *tumat yadayim*, he is forcefully asserting that our aspirations and hopes are no less relevant in our broken world.

The same spirit enables R. Akiva to laugh when he encounters foxes roaming the Temple Mount. He sees them as the confirmation of a biblical prophecy, and this fills him with hope that more positive prophecies of consolation will also be fulfilled. The same optimistic spirit enables R. Akiva to maintain that *Shir haShirim*, the great love song between God and the Jewish people, remains the holy of holies even when we are confronted with destruction.

According to R. Amiel, Judaism incorporates more of the optimism of *Shir haShirim* than the pessimism of *Kohelet*. *Kohelet* is read once a year on Sukkot, but *Shir haShirim* appears in the *Siddur* to be recited every Friday night. Of course, this optimism should not be confused with the notion that religion readily solves all human problems and that religious life consists of resting by still waters in a green pasture. (R. Joseph Soloveitchik attacks this Pollyannaish view of religion in the majestic fourth footnote of *Halakhic Man*.) Authentic religion understands the unfortunate truth that life includes tragedies, difficulties, and frustrations, and that we cannot easily deal with them or confidently understand their place in the cosmic scheme. At the same time, our faith in the divine promise and in a life of Torah and *mizvot* does enable a certain optimism even as we acknowledge the existence of suffering. R. Akiva certainly mourns the loss of the Temple, but he continues to look forward to a better future.

The preceding analysis may affect our reading of a fascinating midrash:

> R. Hiyya taught that only in his elder years did the Holy Spirit reside in Shelomo, enabling him to write the three works of *Mishlei*, *Kohelet*, and *Shir haShirim*. R. Yonatan maintained that he wrote *Shir haShirim* first and then *Mishlei* and then *Kohelet*. He brought a proof from the way of the world: the

young sing, middle-aged people tell parables, and the elderly
see the vanity of the world.

(*Shir haShirim Rabba* 1:10)

The correct relationship between optimism and pessimism emerges from this discussion. R. Yonatan identifies the time of composition of each of Shelomo's works based on the stages of life.
This seems eminently reasonable: youthful ardor dominates in
the mornings of our lifetime, and experienced cynicism comes
to dominate as evening falls. Why does R. Hiyya argue with an
approach that seems true to much of human experience and
instead claim that all three works were penned at the same time
in Shelomo's life?

R. Amiel suggests that all of life should include elements of
both the optimism of *Shir haShirim* and the pessimism of *Kohelet*.
In fact, it is only *Kohelet*'s ability to balance the youthful ardor of
song with an authentic understanding of the difficulty of human
existence that enables the song to continue through the ripeness
of advancing years. Cheaply acquired optimism is quickly shat-
tered on the rocks of human suffering; an equally easy despairing
cynicism also misses the mark, for it indicates blindness to the
many wonderful aspects of human existence.

It is only a more realistic optimism that sees effort and difficulty as unavoidable but still finds cause for hope that we will
survive the vicissitudes of human life. May we all merit to share in
this more complex optimism and experience the love and rapture
of a genuine relationship with the divine.

Human Initiative and the Divine Hand

The Rabbis taught: "King Hizkiyahu initiated six actions, three
of which the sages endorsed and three they did not endorse. He
dragged his father's bones on a bier of ropes, and they endorsed
him; he pulverized the Copper Snake, and they endorsed him;

he hid away the Book of Cures and they endorsed him. He cut off the doors to the Sanctuary and sent them to the Assyrian king, and they did not endorse him; he sealed up the waters of the Upper Gihon, and they did not endorse him; he made a leap year during Nissan, and they did not endorse him."

(Pesahim 56a)

What was the Book of Cures, and why was hiding it praiseworthy? Rashi explains that this book enabled people to cure any ailment instantaneously. Such a book needed to be hidden because sickness has its place in the divine scheme of things – ill health reminds us of our human frailty and turns our attention back to Hashem. Therefore, when the ability to instantly restore good health counteracted the religious benefits of sickness, Hizkiyahu removed the Book of Cures.

In his commentary on the Mishna (*Pesahim* 4:9), Rambam offers two other interpretations. Perhaps the book described healing based on pagan practices, which would violate a biblical prohibition. The Jews had such a book because one is allowed to study this type of material in a purely theoretical way; once some of them began to actually use the practices in the book to treat illnesses, it needed to be taken away. Alternatively, Rambam suggests, the book may have been an encyclopedia of poisons and antidotes, and the problem was that people began to make extensive use of the sections describing poisons. According to both of Rambam's views, the problem has nothing to do with human medicinal success getting in the way of the divine plan.

Indeed, the Rambam cites such an idea only to vociferously denounce it. He draws a powerful analogy to human attempts to combat hunger. Just as turning wheat into bread does not violate any religious ideal, so too curing the sick is in no way religiously problematic. Not only does the human initiative not contradict a sense of dependence on the divine, it enhances it. Rambam points out that just as we thank God when we eat food, we can thank God for creating the cure developed by human hands.

Interestingly, although the six actions of Hizkiyahu are found in our contemporary editions of the Mishna, they are not part of the mishnaic text in the Gemara (both Talmud Bavli and Yerushalmi), and Rambam seems to follow the Gemara. The fact that the Rambam comments on a non-mishnaic text in a commentary on the Mishna reveals how strongly he felt about this idea. He begins his comment with the words: "This halakha is a *tosefta*, but I saw fit to explain it as well because it is beneficial." The Rambam only rarely uses his commentary on the Mishna to discuss texts other than a given mishna. He apparently felt that endorsing human initiative in the world of medicine was so important that he departed from his usual procedure in order to highlight this point.

Hazon Ish (*Emuna uBitahon* 5:5) refutes the Rambam's analogy between procuring food and searching for cures, arguing that seeking food is the norm of human existence, while sickness is a deviation from the norm. Unlike hunger, illness reflects divine punishment. Therefore, only illness constitutes a divine message to repent. We respond to hunger by harvesting wheat, but ideally we should respond to illness with prayer and repentance.

My sympathy in this debate lies fully with Rambam, but I should mention a solid argument advanced by Hazon Ish. He points out that the gemara (*Bava Kama* 85a) needs the scriptural phrase Ve'rapo yerapei ("He shall certainly cure," *Shemot* 21:19) to allow the doctor to cure. No parallel gemara requires a source to allow the hungry person to take steps to alleviate his hunger. Apparently, Hazon Ish argues, healing involves more religious questions than preparing food. Of course, the Rambam might counter that it was only a theoretical possibility that healing might be problematic; once we have the derivation, we discover that seeking remedies does not truly differ from seeking food. On a theological plane, Rambam clearly sees no distinction between hunger and sickness; illness may be less frequent than hunger, but it is very much a part of the natural order. God set up that order for us to function within as we utilize the best of our human resources.

These two approaches reflect broad differences in religious understanding. I shall paint the two perspectives in broad strokes that will admittedly leave out some nuances. One approach denies or minimizes the natural order, tending to see all difficulties as divine punishments and playing down the significance of human initiative within the natural order; the other approach maximizes the natural order, viewing many difficulties as the normal functioning of nature and granting great value to human naturalistic efforts to alleviate those difficulties. (See David Shatz's fine article in the *Torah u'Madda Journal*, vol. 3, for a discussion of these issues.)

Rav Yosef Dov Soloveitchik firmly identifies with Rambam on this issue. He sees human scientific efforts in general, and the realm of medicine in particular, as the fulfillment of a religious duty:

> To live, and to defy death, is a sublime moral achievement. That is why Judaism has displayed so much sympathy for scientific medicine and commanded the sick person to seek medical help. Curing, healing the sick is a divine attribute reflecting an activity (*rofe holim*) in which man ought to engage."
> ("Majesty and Humility," p. 34)

R. Yisrael Lipshutz also strongly endorses human science and medicine. In his commentary on the Mishna (*Tiferet Yisrael*), he discusses, in the eighth chapter of *Yoma*, how to treat both scurvy and rabid dog bites. The same attitude is reflected in his commentary on the source about Hizkiyahu (*Pesahim* 4:10). R. Lifshitz assumes an interpretation similar to the Rambam's first explanation. He suggests that the Book of Cures discussed amulets with images and constellations, but he does not think that using such a book, in and of itself, constitutes idolatry. Therefore, when people were led to idolatry by the book, Hizkiyahu hid it but did not destroy it (as he destroyed the Copper Snake). This enabled people to use the Book of Cures in times of real danger. Apparently, even a work that might lead to idolatry must be preserved if it can heal serious human illness.

We see that religious people who believe in the stability of the natural order and endorse human initiative within that order must be careful not to set up a theology that removes God's providence from the world. We must achieve a certain balance between the human and the divine. Religious ideals should not inhibit human efforts to alleviate human suffering; on the contrary, they should inspire such efforts. Still, at the same time, that effort must be seen as part of the scheme of divine providence.

Fear, Freedom, and the Goodness of Creation

> The Rabbis taught: For two and a half years, the house of Hillel and the house of Shammai argued. One said that it was pleasant (*noah*) for man to be created, and the other said that it would have been more pleasant for man to not have been created. They voted and determined that it would have been more pleasant not to have been created, but now that he had been created, he should investigate his deeds.
>
> (*Eruvin* 13b)

> Everything is in the hands of heaven except the fear of heaven.
>
> (*Berakhot* 33b)

The pessimism about the creation of humanity reflected in the gemara in *Eruvin* seems to contradict an explicit biblical verse. After God creates Adam and completes the creation of the world, the Torah tells us that "*God saw all that He had created, and it was very good*" (*Bereishit* 1:31). Given the fact that the Torah clearly endorses the value of humanity and the entirety of creation, how could the schools of Shammai and Hillel raise the possibility that it might have been better for man not to have been created?

In truth, it is not clear that the biblical phrase "very good" refers to the creation of man. It may refer to the totality of the created order, and not specifically to the impact that the addition of people had on that order. R. Yosef Albo argues (*Sefer haIkkarim* 3:2) that every aspect of the created order except mankind received the *ki tov* evaluation. This stems from the fact that only humanity has free will. Every other creature fulfills the goodness of its purpose immediately upon coming into existence. Only humanity, with its freedom to corrupt its mission, cannot be called good until its goals are achieved. The drama of human freedom suspends the declaration of *ki tov*.

We can accept R. Albo's interpretation of the first chapter of *Bereishit* and still think that the creation of mankind was a positive event. The goodness of mankind may come after time rather than immediately, but it is nonetheless considered to be "very good." Why does the gemara offer an apparently negative evaluation?

The answer may depend upon precise translation of the gemara. As the text presented above reflected, the gemara employs the term *noah* and not *tov*. In other words, the gemara refers to the "pleasantness" of creation and not to its "goodness." Some things in this world are both good and unpleasant. Nonetheless, even if the gemara is evaluating only pleasantness, the conclusion in favor of nonexistence seems surprising.

In his *Pahad Yizhak* (*Rosh haShana* 7), Rav Yizhak Hutner offers an insightful analysis that begins with the second gemara cited above. This gemara affirms the existence of human freedom, for it asserts that "fear of heaven" is not subject to divine control. While we could understand the phrase "Everything is in the hands of heaven except for the fear of heaven" as conveying that God controls everything with only one exception, that is not the way Rambam understood it. In his letter to Ovadia the Proselyte, Rambam explains that "Everything is in the hands of heaven" refers to the natural order, while "except for the fear of heaven" refers to the totality of human endeavor. This leads Rambam to deny the idea of *bashert*. Finding the right spouse falls within the province of human endeavors, and is therefore subject to human freedom, and not divine decision.

This talmudic endorsement of free will raises a question. As serving God out of love represents a higher level than serving God out of fear, why does the gemara utilize the term "fear of heaven" to describe our human choices? It should have said, "Everything is in the hands of heaven except for love of heaven." R. Hutner explains that there is an important difference between fear of heaven and love of heaven. The *ohev* ("lover") desires the opportunity to freely choose service of God. The *yarei* ("fearer"), terrified of religious failure, starts by wishing the onus of choice would go away, thus removing the possibility of sin. Only after expressing this fear does the *yarei* come to terms with human choice, in order to select the good. The gemara selects the term "fear of heaven" because it wants to emphasize this initially frightening aspect of human freedom.

Rav Hutner tells the story of a scholar who was afraid to take a seat on a religious court, out of fear of making the wrong ruling. His teacher said to him: "Who should be a judge? A person not concerned about making incorrect rulings?" As this story illustrates, there are times when the healthy thing is to have an impulse to avoid a certain situation. The successful person, however, can express that impulse and then proceed to confront the challenging situation.

According to R. Hutner's analysis, the fearful rejection of choice is a crucial prerequisite for moving to the higher level of embracing the chance to make the right choice. Only those who truly understand the burden of responsibility can ably take on that responsibility. We can now explain that the pessimistic gemara in *Eruvin* refers to a stage that precedes "And God saw all that he had created, and it was very good." Mankind must first experience the weighty responsibility of free choice and declare that it would have been more pleasant to not have been created, and then move on to the loving fulfillment of responsible decision-making. Once humans internalize the serious nature of their responsibility, and begin to make the right choices, they can say that it was better to have been created, and that the world in which they participate is indeed "very good."

(For another approach to the gemara in *Eruvin*, see *Sefer haIkkarim* 4:29.)

Of Rivers and Men

> R. Pinhas ben Yair was going to redeem captives. He came to the Ginnai River. He said: "Ginnai, divide your water for me and I will pass."
>
> The river said to him: " You are going to do the will of your Maker, and I am going to do the will of my Maker. It is doubtful whether you will accomplish your goal, but I certainly will."
>
> He said: "If you do not divide, I will decree that water never pass through you." It divided for him.
>
> There was a man carrying wheat for Pesah. R. Pinhas said: "Divide for this person as well, as he is engaged in a *mizva*." It divided for him.
>
> There was an Arab merchant accompanying him. R. Pinhas said: "Divide for him as well, so that people will not say: 'This is how they treat those that accompany them.'" It divided for him.
>
> R. Yosef said: "This man is even greater than Moshe and the six hundred thousand, as there it only divided once, and here it divided three times."
>
> Perhaps here too it was only once? Rather say that he is equal to Moshe and the six hundred thousand.
>
> (*Hullin* 7a)

R. Menahem Meiri's only comment on this story relates to the final section. For Meiri, the story tells us how to treat those who accompany us on a journey, even if they are strangers or gentiles. We should show them friendship and not leave them to the world of accidents. While this theme is certainly part of the story, it does not explain the greater part of our tale. What did our sages want to teach us with this episode?

We might extract from the story that we should appreciate the power of the sages. When confronted with an obstacle from within the natural order, R. Pinhas had enough metaphysical clout to force the river to split. According to this approach, R. Pinhas never truly answers the river's argument. In the debate with the river, he emerges victorious because he threatens the river into doing his bidding.

Yet perhaps the story is not about the power and influence of the sages. Let us recall that the river argues that it is more success-ful at fulfilling its mission. Indeed, it succeeds in performing its mission every day. R. Pinhas, on the other hand, represents flawed and limited humanity, which often fails. What could R. Pinhas re-spond to this argument? Maharsha explains his counter-argument. R. Pinhas responds that only humans have free will. The river always succeeds because it has no choice. If he could prevent its water from coming, the river could not choose to respond. The reason human success is not guaranteed is precisely because they are always subject to the variables and dynamism of free will. Thus, the river's argument runs backwards. It is precisely the lack of guarantees that makes humanity great. We do the best we can to struggle with decision-making and the vicissitudes of human life. No other part of the natural order can compete with that. When faced with the greatness of humanity, the river gives way.

My student Gavin Berger noticed an interesting literary tech-nique in the story. The story repeatedly alludes to the exodus from Egypt. R. Pinhas goes to redeem captives, that is, to take people out of bondage. A body of water splits, a Jew carries wheat for Pesah, and R. Yosef compares R. Pinhas to Moshe and the six hundred thousand. According to Maharsha's reading, the story highlights an aspect of the exodus. A slave does not have the freedom to make the choices that matter, and in this respect *ye-ziat mizraim* enabled the Jewish people to more fully realize their human greatness. The twin themes of free will and the exodus naturally intertwine.

Authority, Heavenly Voices, and the Interpretation of Torah

> It was taught there: "If you cut it [an earthenware oven] into sections and put sand between the sections, R. Eliezer says it is pure, and the sages say it is impure. And this is the oven of Akhinai." What is Akhinai? R. Yehuda said in the name of Shemuel: "They surrounded him with words like an *akhna* [snake] and made it impure." It was taught: "On that day, R. Eliezer responded to them with all the arguments in the world and they did not accept them from him."
>
> He said to them: "If I am right, this carob tree will prove it." The carob tree was uprooted from its place and moved one hundred cubits; some say, four hundred cubits.
>
> They said to him: "We do not bring proofs from carob trees."
>
> He said to them: "If I am right, this stream of water will prove it." The stream started to flow backwards.
>
> They said to him: "We do not bring proof from streams."
>
> He said to them: "If I am right, the walls of the study hall will prove it." The walls of the study hall inclined to fall.
>
> R. Yehoshua rebuked them [the walls]. He said to them: "If talmudic scholars contest one another in matters of Halakha, why does this concern you?" They did not fall, out of respect for R. Yehoshua, but they did not straighten, out of respect for R. Eliezer, and they are still inclined there.
>
> He said to them: "If the halakha is as I say, let it be proved from the heavens." A heavenly voice came forth and proclaimed: "Why are you contesting R. Eliezer, when Halakha follows him in every area?"
>
> R. Yehoshua arose and said: "It is not in heaven (*Devarim* 30:12)." What does this mean? R. Yirmiyah said: "The Torah has already been give at Sinai. We pay no heed to heavenly voices,

since it has already been written in the Torah at Sinai, *follow the majority (Shemot* 23:2).''

R. Natan came upon Eliyahu. He said to him: "What is the Holy One, blessed be He, doing at this time?"

Eliyahu said to him: "He is laughing and saying, 'My children have defeated Me; My children have defeated Me.'"

(*Bava Mezia* 59a–59b)

This famous story continues and subsequently moves in some important directions, but we will stop at this point and provide some interim analysis. Many cite this gemara as an example of the individual's freedom to interpret without conceding to authority. As Walter Kaufmann notes, however, this conclusion misreads the tale entirely (*Critique of Religion and Philosophy*, pp. 336–337). The gemara here does suggest that humans are to interpret the Torah without explicit divine assistance, but this incident involved a majority forcing its decision upon a minority, dissenting view. Thus, whatever the story says about the relationship between the human and the divine, it most certainly does not call for the standpoint, so popular nowadays, of personal freedom from religious authority structures.

How can the sages ignore a heavenly voice and knowingly continue to teach an incorrect religious ruling? Tosafot suggest that in reality they did no such thing. According to Tosafot, the heavenly voice came forth only to defend the honor of R. Eliezer, but did not truly reflect a divine judgment in the case at hand. Perhaps Tosafot could not imagine a conscious decision to ignore what one knows to be correct. Furthermore, a different gemara, in *Masekhet Yevamot* (14a), relates that the sages chose to follow the rulings of Beit Hillel based on the guidance offered by a heavenly voice. This source certainly suggests that a heavenly voice can influence the process of determining Halakha.

Despite this implications of the gemara in *Yevamot*, Rabbenu Nissim (*Derashot haRan, Derush* 3, pp. 44–45) disagrees with Tosafot's interpretation. He explains that the heavenly voice

In fact reflected the absolute truth of the matter; R Eliezer was indeed correct, while the majority erred. However, the nature of the halakhic system is such that the sages are supposed to arrive at their conclusions based solely on human effort and intelligence. Information received from heavenly supplements has no place in their mode of operation. Therefore, in order to maintain the integrity of the system, R. Yehoshua and his colleagues were forced to adhere to their ruling, even though they now knew it to be in error. It is Rabbenu Nissim's approach that has become more famous, partly because R. Aryeh Leib Heller cites it in the introduction to his celebrated work, *Kezot haHoshen*. To fully understand this position, we must first examine why the system makes halakhic rulings depend on human reasoning rather than on ongoing prophetic revelations. Rabbenu Nissim attributes the dependence on logical deduction to the inherent limitations of prophecy. Prophets are not empowered to receive prophecy on demand; furthermore, prophecy itself will not remain a constant of Jewish history. Therefore, a more enduring approach to halakhic rulings was necessary. There will not always be a prophet, but there will always be a sage; halakhic decision-making is in the hands of the latter.

However, this explanation only clarifies the need for sages; it does not justify ignoring prophetically conveyed information. Abravanel (commentary on *Devarim*, p. 162) therefore adds another reason for why Halakha depends on the sage rather than the prophet. If we allowed prophetic messages to carry halakhic weight, even in an interpretive mode, this would ultimately erode our sense of the Mosaic prophecy at Sinai as a unique revelation that could never be supplanted. Once people turn to later prophets to elucidate the covenant, they will also turn to those prophets for new direction and, potentially, even for abdication of the old covenant. The eternality of Torah requires that we ignore any prophetic message that seeks to impact the halakhic system.

This idea works beautifully with a clever remark about the story of R. Eliezer's dispute with the rabbis found in Rav Zvi

Hirsch Chajes's commentary (printed in the back of the standard Vilna edition of the Talmud). Our quotation of the gemara ended with the words *Nizhuni banai* – "My children have defeated me." R. Chajes argues that the word *nizhuni* derives from the term *nezah*, "eternity," rather than *nizahon*, "victory." Hashem's expression of joy here pertains to the sages' decision to reject heavenly voices, thereby ensuring the Torah's eternality. According to this reading, God laughs, so to speak, and proclaims: "My children have made My Torah eternal."

Why does R. Eliezer enlist certain specific items to miraculously prove his stance? Do they have any particular symbolic significance? Maharsha answers in the affirmative. He sees each miraculous manifestation as a specific challenge R. Eliezer poses to the majority. The carob tree, which takes a very long time to bear fruit, is a symbol through which he questions the productivity of the other sages. He concedes that the majority generally wins – but only when it shows itself capable of thinking productively. A majority made up of intellectually barren scholars must be discounted.

Hazal often compare Torah to water because water runs downhill, just as Torah scholarship is reserved for the humble individual who lowers himself. Maharsha suggests that the stream indicates that R. Eliezer is questioning the other sages' sincerity. Perhaps, he contends, it is arrogance that prevents them from conceding that he is right. Finally, R. Eliezer asks them if it is their desire to triumph, as if they were engaged in some schoolboy competition, that prevents them from admitting their error. The collapsing walls of the study hall represent the inevitable destruction of Torah institutions when childish competitiveness prevails.

R. Eliezer's accusations were apparently off the mark, and the other sages were sincerely motivated by a desire to maintain the integrity of the legal system. At the same time, however, Maharsha's symbolic reading of R. Eliezer's claims is an instructive model for our own approach to Torah scholarship. Judaism indeed gives primary significance to human reasoning in the process of halakhic decision making. However, this does not mean that *Yahadut* is a kind of silly-putty, adjustable in whatever way each individual sees fit to mold it. Those who interpret Torah must meet three criteria. First, they must be wise and knowledgeable, or in R. Eliezer's words, more productive than the carob tree. Second, they must not be motivated by arrogance. Third, they must not be driven by a competitive desire to win talmudic contests. Only those who meet these criteria can utilize their human intellects and decision-making faculties to interpret the Torah.

Rabbi Eliezer's Excommunication

This section analyzes the next part of the gemara narrative presented in the preceding section.

> It was taught: On that day, they brought all the *taharot* that R. Eliezer had ruled pure and they burned them in fire, and they voted and excommunicated R. Eliezer. They said: "Who will go and inform him?"
>
> R. Akiva said: "I will go, lest the wrong person go and inform him in a way that destroys the world."
>
> What did R. Akiva do? He wore black and wrapped himself in black and sat at a distance of four meters from R. Eliezer.
>
> R. Eliezer said to him: "R. Akiva, why is today different from other days?"
>
> He answered: "Rebbe, It seems to me that your colleagues are separating from you."
>
> He [R. Eliezer] also tore his garment, removed his shoes and sat upon the ground. Tears poured from his eyes....
>
> It was taught: There was great anger in the world on that day, and everyplace where R. Eliezer turned his eye was burned. R. Gamliel was traveling on a boat and a wave threatened to sink the boat. He said: "It seems to me that this is only because of R. Eliezer ben Hyrcanus." He stood up and said: "Master of the universe! It is revealed and known before You that I did

not do this for my own honor or for the honor of my father's house, but for Your honor, so that disputes will not proliferate in Israel!" The sea calmed from its anger.

Ima Shalom, R. Eliezer's wife, was the sister of R. Gamliel. From the time of this episode, she would not allow her husband to fall on his face [while reciting *Tahanun*]. One Rosh Hodesh day, she became confused as to whether the previous month was full [30 days] or not full [29 days]. Some say that a pauper came to the door and she brought him bread. She found R. Eliezer fallen on his face [in prayer]. She said: "Arise, for you have killed my brother." Meanwhile, a voice came from the house of R. Gamliel that he had died.

R. Eliezer said to her: "How did you know [that this would happen]?"

She said: "I have a tradition from my grandfather's house that all gates are closed except for the gate of *ona'a* [verbal abuse]."

(*Bava Mezia* 59b)

This story conveys a good deal of halakhic information. For example, we learn from it that one omits *Tahanun* from the prayer service on Rosh Hodesh: on the day Ima Shalom mistakenly thought was Rosh Hodesh, she felt no need to actively prevent her husband from *nefilat apayim*, assuming that he would omit it on his own. In addition, Ritva derives from our tale that ideally, *Tahanun* should immediately follow the *Amida*. He reasons that Ima Shalom could not have prevented her husband from reciting *Tahanun* all day, but she could have delayed her husband each day by displacing *Tahanun* from its optimum time, thereby minimizing its effectiveness.

Another halakhic issue centers around the ban placed on R. Eliezer. Tosafot and Ritva understand that it was the type of ban known as *nidduy*, and they must therefore reconcile R. Eliezer's conduct while under excommunication with the halakhic guidelines of *nidduy* found in *Moed Katan*. Ramban disagrees, claiming that the sages employed the harsher form of excommunication, *herem*, and this explains the tearing of garments, removal of shoes, and some other aspects of R. Eliezer's conduct. Despite the importance of these two legal issues, the essence of the story clearly belongs to the aggadic realm.

What was the wisdom in R. Akiva's method of informing his teacher of his excommunication? First, he conveys the news indirectly. We often relate bad tidings in an indirect fashion in the hope that the recipient's gradual realization of the sad development will lessen the blow. Maharsha notes an additional element. By dressing in black, R. Akiva implies that all the other scholars, himself included, are excommunicated. Maharsha argues that the same point emerges from the formulation "your colleagues are separating from you" – as if they are the ones being pushed away from the place of importance. According to Maharsha, this method communicates the tension of the entire incident. The sages find it necessary to excommunicate R. Eliezer but also have a sense of the problematic nature of this drastic measure.

We have to ask who was right in this episode. On the one hand, R. Eliezer's grievance carries heavenly weight, and R. Gamliel, the head of the rabbinical court, suffers the consequences. The broader talmudic context of the story, dealing with *ona'at devarim* (verbal oppression), suggests that the other sages had wronged R. Eliezer. On the other hand, Hashem accepted R. Gamliel's contention on the boat that he acted for the good of Am Yisrael. Furthermore, let us recall that God smiled approvingly when the sages refused to accept the heavenly voice calling upon them to side with R. Eliezer. Thus we seem to have conflicting pieces of evidence as to where God's sympathies lie.

One resolution might differentiate between the halakhic decision to reject R. Eliezer's position and the ban consequently placed upon him. Perhaps the former was justified, but not the latter. Therefore, Hashem approved of their ruling against R. Eliezer but punished them for excommunicating him. R. Yaakov Emden (in his commentary, printed in the back of the Vilna *Shas*) offers a somewhat different version of this explanation. He says that the other sages had the right to excommunicate R. Eliezer, but were punished for the pain they inflicted upon him. Since R. Eliezer was a great man who found favor in heaven, the sages should have emulated the favorable heavenly judgment and not caused him grief. R. Emden draws a parallel to a gemara in *Ta'anit* (23a), which records Shimon ben Shetah's remark that he would excommunicate Honi haMe'agel (Honi the Circle Drawer) if not for the fact that Honi's deeds find favor in heaven. If we take the parallel to Honi seriously, R. Emden is suggesting that the miracles performed on behalf of R. Eliezer indicate divine favor that should have stifled any thought of excommunication.

We can propose an alternative reading. Indeed, the sages were justified in banning R. Eliezer despite the heavenly approval manifested in the miraculous support for his position. In fact, since R. Eliezer refused to accept the normal halakhic methodology, the miracles may even have provided additional justification for the ban. Nevertheless, even justifiable actions have repercussions and implications. In situations where competing values are at stake, even doing the right thing often comes with a cost. R. Meir Simha haKohen (*Meshekh Hokhmah Bemidbar* 6:14) suggests that the Nazarite may do something quite positive when he separates from wine and from becoming defiled by a corpse. Yet the same Nazarite brings a sin offering because his decision prevents him from going to a relative's funeral or from utilizing wine for *kiddush*. Preserving some modicum of halakhic unity may have mandated banning R. Eliezer, but hurting a great man must leave a mark of some kind. The sages needed to internalize this point and find ways to maintain R. Eliezer's honor even as they continued to promote the ban.

I believe this point to be of major significance. We often make choices among competing ideals and probably often make the right choice (assuming that the situation allows a right choice). Nonetheless, we should not make the mistake of thinking that the right choice frees us from any further follow-up. The right choice may have forced us to temporarily relinquish a competing ideal for which we must find ways to compensate. If we choose *aliya* over remaining in the Diaspora to care for our parents, we must find a way to enhance our *kibbud av va'em* while living in a different country. Conversely, if our family responsibilities lead us to stay in the Diaspora, we must increase our support for Israel from abroad. In this incident, the sages choose the ideal of preventing halakhic anarchy over the ideal of preserving R. Eliezer's honor. The choice may have been perfectly acceptable, but the neglected ideal had to be respected. If this is not done successfully, the implications can be very grave, and indeed R. Gamliel, who, as head of the court, bore responsibility for this shortcoming, paid the ultimate price for R. Eliezer's humiliation.

R. Akiva's Classroom and the Nature of the Oral Law

> R. Yehuda said in the name of Rav: When Moshe went up to the heavens, he found the Holy one, blessed be He, sitting and placing crowns on the letters [of the Torah].
>
> He said: "Master of the universe, who prevents you" [from giving the Torah without the crowns]?
>
> He said to him: "There is a person many generations in the future named Akiva ben Yosef who will expound piles of laws from each tittle."
>
> He said: "Master of the universe, show him to me."
>
> He said to him: "Turn around."
>
> He went and sat in the eighth row [of R. Akiva's classroom], and he did not understand what the lecture was saying. He became depressed. When the lecture arrived at a certain point, the students said: "Rebbe, what is your source for this?"
>
> He said to them: "It is a law transmitted to Moshe at Sinai." Moshe was placated.
>
> (*Menahot* 29b)

This fascinating story raises an immediate question. How could Moshe Rabbenu, the greatest of the prophets and the recipient of the Torah, not understand the class taught by R. Akiva? Rashi says that Moshe had not yet received the Torah at the time of this incident. Thus, he does not understand what R. Akiva is saying for the simple reason that he had not yet stood at Sinai and received the Torah. According to this reading, if Moshe had attended the lecture after having received the Torah, he surely would have understood every word.

As an alternative, we might suggest that this story indicates something quite significant about the nature of the Oral Law. Perhaps Moshe did not understand the *shiur* because the development of Halakha in the centuries from Sinai to the time of the *tannaim* had opened up some ideas that he was not aware of and had not considered. The differences between the two interpretations go to the heart of an essential question about the Oral Law.

There are two basic approaches to the Oral Law. One approach sees Moshe as having received the answers to all subsequent halakhic questions. The advantage of this approach is that by removing the human element, it ensures that the sages have the right answers. The other approach argues that Moshe received much information and a system for working out Jewish law, but that it was then the job of the sages to utilize their human intelligence in interpreting the law. This approach might view human involvement in the formation of Torah, though always within the framework divinely given, as a good thing. The human element may bring out important aspects of the religious personality and may help forge a connection between the people and the Torah. Moreover, this approach gives the sages a method for dealing with new halakhic cases, such as the question of electricity on Shabbat.

In classic Jewish fashion, a debate emerges regarding the historical cause of debates. According to the first approach, halakhic debates represent a breakdown in transmission. Had we been more diligent in transmitting the traditions of Moshe, there would have been no arguments. Due to our weakness, debates crept in. For the second position, on the other hand, debates reflect the natural functioning of the system. Different people will analyze halakhic ideas within the framework and come to different conclusions. The many talmudic debates are not a breakdown of the system but its flowering.

In his introduction to his commentary on the Mishna, Rambam cites the *gaonim* as holding the first position, while he endorses the latter position. Rambam mentions a talmudic source that apparently confirms the position of the Gaonim.

> When the students of Shammai and Hillel increased and they did not serve their masters sufficiently, debates increased in Israel and the Torah became like two *Torot*.
>
> (*Sanhedrin* 88b)

This passage suggests that lack of student diligence caused debate, the position of the Gaonim. Rambam offers an alternative reading. He points out that when weak intellects approach a subject, the range of potentially wild conclusions immediately increases. Strong intellects may not always agree, but the range of possible interpretations is limited by their intelligence. Thus, the diminishing quality of students did lead to an increase in the number of debates, but not because debates per se mean a breakdown of the system. Rambam's reading highlights an important part of this latter theory. Valuing a human element in the Oral Law does not mean that all interpretations are valid and that there is no such thing as an erroneous opinion or an opinion outside the appropriate halakhic methodology. When poor students use weak arguments or erroneous methods to raise new possibilities, Torah suffers.

Moshe did not understand R. Akiva because the Oral Law had developed over time. However, God specifically took him to the classroom of R. Akiva, a man of great intelligence and dedication to study, and a scholar working within the parameters of the halakhic system. This story teaches the glorious balance between human and divine in the Oral Law.

Demons in The Talmud

> "A person should not have less than four cups of wine [on the *Seder* night]." How could the Rabbis institute something dangerous? Didn't we learn that a person should not eat or drink in even quantities?...R. Nahman said: "It is a *leil shimurim*, a night when we are guarded from harmful forces." Rava said: "A cup of blessing can combine to produce good results but not bad results." Ravina said: "The Rabbis instituted four cups in the manner of a free person. Each one is a *mizva* in its own right."
>
> (*Pesahim* 109b)

> In the West [Israel], they are not cautious about having things in pairs. Rav Dimi from Naharda'ah was cautious even about the markings on a barrel. There was a story in which the barrel burst. The rule of the matter is that for those who take note of the *zuggot* [pairs], the *zuggot* take note of them. Those who do not take note of the *zuggot* are not bothered by the *zuggot*. Nonetheless, it is good to show a modicum of concern.
>
> (*Pesahim* 110b)

The gemara apparently thinks that it is dangerous to eat or drink an even number of items. It would seem that certain demonic forces descend upon even numbers, so that only eating an odd number of items keeps us safe. Even more surprisingly, the danger recedes greatly if we do not give these forces undue attention. Perhaps based on this line of thinking, the scholars in Israel took the route of relative indifference to *zuggot*. Clearly, this gemara calls for some explanation.

There is a well-known debate about how to understand talmudic references to demons. Some commentators took such *gemarot* at face value, whereas Rambam denied that demonic beings exist. For example, one gemara (*Makkot* 6b) explicitly mentions the possibility of a criminal receiving warning from a demon. Rambam (*Hilkhot Sanhedrin* 12:2) cites this case as a scenario in which a person hears the warning but cannot identify the source. Rambam offers a naturalistic reading in which demonic beings do not exist and the term *shed* refers to a natural phenomenon whose source we have not yet discovered.

How would Rambam interpret our gemara about the danger of even numbers? Fortunately, R. Menahem Meiri, a follower of Rambam's school of thought, provides an explanation in his commentary on *Pesahim*. Meiri argues that in talmudic times, the masses were influenced by popular beliefs and superstitions. The sages fought against these beliefs when they were linked to idolatrous practices, but if the beliefs were simply foolish and not idolatrous, the sages did not reject them directly and instead took steps to limit their impact.

In the case of *zuggot*, no demonic forces exist in even numbers, but the popular belief that they do sometimes created that very reality. People who ate an even number of a given food became convinced that they would become sick, and this resulted in a psychosomatic illness. The gemara provides an excellent proof for Meiri's theory. The gemara suggests that only those who show excessive interest in the *zuggot* are affected by them. According to Meiri, those who show little interest in *zuggot* will not experience the psychosomatic impact. Of course, Meiri would still have to explain why the gemara advises a modicum of caution.

Why did our sages not simply tell the masses that these beliefs were false? Perhaps because they knew that such a campaign would require great energy and had little chance of success. Once people internalize certain beliefs, it is quite difficult to convince them otherwise. The sages took on this difficult project to combat the remnants of idolatry, but not to combat mere stupidity. However, the sages did not despair of educating the masses. Instead, they adopted the clever strategy of limiting the impact of *zuggot*. They affirmed their belief in *zuggot* but added many categories in which the dangers of even numbers do not apply (such as the answers of the three *amoraim* given above), thereby slowly weaning the people away from this incorrect belief. At the end of the day, this more subtle method worked, and *zuggot* stopped troubling the Jewish masses.

I believe that Meiri presents us with a broader pedagogical question. On the one hand, educators should teach their students the truth and not condescendingly and cynically assume that they cannot handle the truth and need to be fed various fabrications to keep them *frum*. On the other hand, it is not helpful to teach an idea that the teacher knows the student will not understand. In this latter situation, a good teacher must eschew the approach of immediately aiming for the full truth and instead try to slowly bring the student closer to the truth. Rather than always directly taking on the overly superstitious student, it is sometimes more effective to attempt to minimize the influence of superstitious belief in the student's life. Finding the correct method in these situations is no easy matter. Indeed, the balance of the ideal and the real represents the central challenge of every educational endeavor.

> It was taught: Abba Binyamin said: "If the eye had been given the ability to [fully] see, no creature would be able to stand before the *mazikim*."…
>
> If you want to see them, bring the tail of a first-born black cat, that is the daughter of a first-born black cat. Burn it in fire, grind it up, fill your eyes with the ashes and then you will see them.
>
> (*Berakhot* 6b)

I am not aware of Rav Kook's general position on demons, but his commentary on the aggadot in *Berakhot* finds metaphorical meaning in the cited *gemarot*. Abba Binyamin teaches us something about the basic human curiosity for knowledge. For the most part, we should look favorably upon intellectual inquisitiveness. However, there are people who are so frustrated by any form of ignorance that they fail to appreciate that ignorance can sometimes be a boon to humanity. Abba Binyamin instructs us that knowing everything can sometimes have destructive consequences. One example quickly comes to mind. It has become quite common for expectant parents to read books from the "What to Expect When Expecting" genre. These books are often quite helpful, and they supply much good information. At the same time, it is not a favor to nervous parents to teach them about all the possible illnesses that could accost the fetus. Such knowledge mostly causes harm and illustrates that sometimes ignorance is bliss.

With regard to the talmudic method for seeing demons, Rav Kook also finds metaphoric significance. Blackness is a ubiquitous symbol for the darker and more problematic aspects of life. In terms of the choice of animal, R. Kook mentions a gemara in *Horayot* (13a) that contrasts the dog's gratitude to its master with the cat's indifference to its master. Those who have pets testify to the difference in feedback owners receive from cats and dogs. The cat symbolizes the ability to forget our Maker. Rav Kook argues that the damaging and demonic aspects of our existence stem from forgetting the *Ribbono Shel Olam*.

I would argue that Rav Kook does not offer a metaphoric reading because he definitively adheres to Rambam's position that demons do not exist. Perhaps he believes in demons, and perhaps he has no position on the matter. The vigorously held belief that motivates his interpretation has nothing to do with the existence of demons. Rather, it stems from the conviction that the gemara is not a collection of superhero stories. If we search the gemara for demon stories as we would eagerly anticipate the next *Superman* comic book, then we have missed the point. The gemara is not an action and adventure story, but a work of religious and ethical instruction. R. Kook found deeper meaning in this gemara because he was convinced that the gemara would not have mentioned the "cat method" for viewing demons if it did not contain some message of religious import. Those who are attracted to talmudic stories bordering on the occult would do well to internalize Rav Kook's approach.

CHAPTER 11

A Balanced Religious Life

Integration and the Tale of a Lifetime

> R. Illai said: "A man is known in three ways: by how he drinks
> (*be'koso*), how he is with his money (*be'kiso*), and in his anger
> (*be'ka'aso*)." And some say: Also in his play.
>
> (*Eruvin* 65b)

Although the play on words of *be'koso*, *be'kiso*, and *be'ka'aso* certainly appealed to R. Illai, we can assume that the three items he
selected reflect a substantive point. One the one hand, they have a
common denominator. In all three, a corrupt aspect of personality
that is normally hidden is suddenly revealed. Drunkenness and
anger certainly reveal normally hidden aspects of a personality,
and many people show a new side of themselves when asked to
open their wallets. *Ben Yehoyada* adds that R. Illai lists the items
in order of increasing applicability. Many people do not drink,

but everyone deals with money. Some parts of life, such as Shabbat, exclude monetary discourse, but the danger of anger always applies. Alternatively, we can view each item as representing an independent category.

R. Shemuel Edels, Maharsha, adopts this second approach in his commentary on *Eruvin*. Although I find his categorization of anger to be somewhat forced, his essential idea is quite profound and important. R. Edels argues that a person's traits relate to three aspects of life: being good to others, being good to Hashem, and being good to oneself. The challenge of money belongs to the interpersonal realm. As a talmudic statement compares anger to idolatry, Maharsha understands the challenge of anger as belonging to the sphere of relations between a person and God. The temptation to drink relates to how a one treats oneself.

Maharsha's third category represents the innovative idea. It is a commonplace that religion challenges us in the realms both of interpersonal behavior and with regard to our relationship with Hashem. According to Maharsha (and Maharal, whose parallel ideas we encountered earlier), it also challenges us to think about how we treat ourselves. Imagine a person with a drinking problem who claims that his drinking binges do not interfere in any way with his interpersonal responsibilities or religious duties. We could try to convince such a person that alcoholism will invariably cause harm in these areas. Alternatively, we could point out that he is not being fair to himself. Maharsha teaches us that this too constitutes a religious sentiment.

Let us turn our attention to the final item in the gemara. Why does "play" reveal the truth about a person in a way that more serious pursuits do not? The answer may have to do with the religious call to live an integrated life. Most observant Jews realize that *mizva* performance demands a certain religious orientation and seriousness of purpose. While in the *beit midrash* or *beit haknesset*, they would not dream of consciously excluding religious values. At the same time, they may think of their leisure time as divorced from religious demands. They fail to realize that while certain areas of life are indeed *devar reshut*, neither forbidden nor commanded, religious ideals are not irrelevant to those areas. Halakha has nothing against playing basketball, but it does have something to say about how one plays. Halakha's voice in this area is not to be found in a section of the *Shulhan Arukh* called *Hilkhot Basketball* but in the more general command to live a life of holiness, service, and morality. The individual whose play exhibits religious ideals (e.g., playing without selfishness, laziness, or anger) has moved to a more profound level of commitment. Sometimes it is precisely our conduct while engaged in a leisure activity that reveals our true quality.

Another gemara helps to develop this idea:

> King Ptolemy gathered seventy-two sages and put them in separate rooms without revealing to them why he had gathered them. He went into each room and asked each sage to translate the Torah [in Greek]. The Holy One, blessed be He, placed good counsel in the heart of each one, and they all translated in an identical fashion. They wrote for him…*And God finished on the sixth day.* (*Megilla* 9a)

In this gemara, the many sages choose not to offer a literal translation in passages where literalness might lead the readers astray. In the original, the verse actually says *"And God completed his work on the seventh day"* (*Bereishit* 2:2). An innocent reader might mistakenly understand that Hashem also created something on the seventh day. Therefore, they took liberties with the translation. Yet we must still ask how to explain a verse that superficially indicates that God did create on the seventh day. Commentators suggest various solutions, but we will focus on Rashi's. He explains that the six days of physical creation did not encompass everything needed, because the world still lacked rest. Hashem completed the created order on the seventh day by adding the element of rest.

Rashi's answer is satisfying, but it brings us to a different question. If this problem can be resolved so easily, why didn't the sages just translate the verse literally and explain it to the Greeks using Rashi's interpretation? Rabbi Norman Lamm provides an excellent answer in "A Jewish Ethic of Leisure" (in *Faith and Doubt*, pp. 193–194). Rabbi Lamm explains that there are two possible conceptions of rest. One approach thinks of rest as pure passivity, a time to get away from it all and not think about ideals and accomplishments. The other conception sees rest as something with creative potential.

Shabbat is the finest example of the latter model. We keep Shabbat by abstaining from work, but we experience Shabbat as something positive and creative. According to Rabbi Lamm, the Greeks thought of rest in purely negative and passive terms, and so could not view it as part of the positive created order. The seventy-two sages decided that the Greeks need a non-literal translation because they did not understand the creative model of rest.

The attempt to practice a positive kind of rest should be expanded beyond Shabbat to all our leisure activities. This message should have special relevance for those who, like the author, think that Judaism grants value to many activities that are not concrete *mizvot*. In an excellent essay entitled "Rejoinder: Synthesis and the Unification of Human Existence," Rabbi Shalom Carmy writes of the challenge facing Modern Orthodox Jews to live a unified existence. R. Carmy utilizes the image of the human life as a story. In discussing our adherence to our core ideals, he writes:

> A life is integrated if it tells a coherent story in the light of those principles and ideals; it is dis-integrated to the degree that the individual's experience, thoughts, and deeds fail to cohere with them, or insofar as the principles and ideals are internally inconsistent.
>
> ("Rejoinder," p. 41)

When thinking about the quality of our recreational activities, it behooves us to ask whether they fit into the same story as our learning, davening, and *zedaka*. Just as a good author strives to craft a unified story, each of us is constantly engaged in writing the most important tale there is, our own life story, and therefore we must certainly work to attain coherence of meaning in the wholeness of a human life.

Torah and Seeing Ugliness

The Rabbis taught: "A person should always be soft like a reed and not hard like a cedar."

Once R. Elazar the son of R. Shimon was coming from his teacher's house in Migdal Gedor, riding on a donkey. He was traveling along the bank of the river with a feeling of great joy and a sense of arrogance, because he had learned a great deal of Torah.

A very ugly person happened upon him. The ugly person said: "How are you, Rebbe?"

R. Elazar did not reply. [Instead,] he said: "Empty one – how ugly this fellow is! Are all the people of your town as ugly as you?"

The ugly person responded: "I don't know, but you should go to the craftsman who made me and tell him how ugly is the vessel he made."

R. Elazar knew that he had sinned. He got off the donkey, prostrated himself before the other fellow, and said: "I have pained you. Forgive me."

The man said: "I will not forgive you until you go to the craftsman who made me and tell him how ugly is the vessel he made."

R. Elazar followed him until they came to his town. All the townspeople came out to greet R. Elazar and they said: "Welcome, our Rabbi, our Rabbi, our teacher, our teacher."

The ugly fellow said: "Who are you referring to as your rabbi?"

They said: "The one who is walking behind you."

He said to them: "If this is a rabbi, let there not be more like him in Israel."

They said: "Why?"

He said to them: "This is what he did to me."

They said to him: "Nevertheless, forgive him because he is a great Torah scholar."

He said to them: "For your sake I forgive him, but on condition that he not become accustomed to act this way."

R. Elazar immediately entered [the study hall] and taught: "A person should always be soft like a reed and not hard like a cedar."

(*Ta'anit* 20a–20b)

The story ends rather ambiguously – to whom was R. Elazar referring when he discouraged harshness? He may have been criticizing his own harsh response at the beginning of the story. If so, his teaching reveals that he has internalized the lesson.

Alternatively, he may have been referring to the ugly person's refusal to forgive him. After all, the man refused to forgive R. Elazar, even after he had trailed after him all the way to town. Furthermore, the ugly person tried to publicly embarrass R. Elazar when the townspeople came out to greet the visiting rabbi. R. Yoshiyahu Pinto, *Rif* in the *Ein Yaakov*, notes this ambiguous ending.

Leaving aside the ambiguity, we could ask what the point of the tale is. On the simplest level, it cautions against arrogance and cruel speech. Furthermore, it reveals that great scholars are capable of improper behavior. We cannot help but contrast this type of talmudic story with contemporary rabbinic biographies in which great rabbis are portrayed as flawless. However, the story bears further exploration.

R. Yizhak of Karlin, brother of the *Mishkenot Yaakov*, suggests a metaphorical meaning (see his *Keren Ora* on *Ta'anit*). He notes that this incident occurs when R. Elazar is returning from learning in yeshiva, and that R. Elazar's transgression stems from an arrogance based upon extensive Torah knowledge. According to *Keren Ora*, this story examines the relationship of Torah to the world around it. A Torah scholar can look upon the world beyond the *beit midrash* as unredeemable, full of unmitigated ugliness. R. Elazar chooses this route, and this choice inspires his cruel comment. What he sees is not so much aesthetic ugliness as spiritual and moral ugliness.

A comment of Maharal enhances this interpretation. Maharal (*Netivot Olam, Netiv haAnavah* 7) notes that no other talmudic story mentions a place called Migdal Gedor. This suggests that the place-name here has symbolic import. As Maharal notes, it is made up of terms referring to towers and fences. The tower symbolizes a high point, from which those on top can look down on others, while the fence connotes rigid boundaries. The bank of the river might also represent such a boundary. The scholar who chooses to follow R. Elazar's path draws a sharp dividing line between the *beit midrash* and the outside world.

Of course, a *talmid hakham* can choose a different path. He can see the outside world for the mixed bag it is, and use the Torah to sanctify the broader realm of human experience. From this perspective, the ideals and values of Torah should permeate the full range of human endeavors, including work, leisure time, family life, and secular academic pursuits. R. Elazar needed to learn to see this world as full of potential, and not just full of ugliness.

Keren Ora offers an interesting argument for this approach. He cites several verses (*Devarim* 7:6, 14:2, and 26:18) that describe the Jews as an *am segula*, a "treasured nation." This language indicates that God in fact cares about all the nations of the world – after all, a precious item is only special when its owner has other items of worth that are outshone by the precious item. Thus, the Jews' special quality indicates that the rest of humanity also has significant value. According to R. Yizhak, "It is well known that the main aspect of the giving of the Torah was not just to mend Israel, but to mend all His creations so that all their actions would be pleasing before God." The traveling scholar must see more than ugliness in the broader Jewish and non-Jewish worlds. These worlds include precious materials that can be mined successfully with the tools of Torah.

Avot deRabbi Natan (41:1) has a different version of our story, in which the protagonist is R. Shimon ben Elazar. The fact that the version in our talmudic texts tells this story about the son of R. Shimon bar Yohai certainly works well with our theme. As we know from the famous episode of the cave (*Shabbat* 33b), R. Elazar ben R. Shimon was prone to see all endeavors other than prayer, Torah study, and *mizva* performance as worthless. In our story, this tendency gets him into trouble.

It should be noted that *Keren Ora*'s point differs from the point frequently emphasized in *Torah u'Madda* literature. He speaks not about the help Torah can get from the outside world, but rather about the help Torah can give to the outside world. As David Shatz has pointed out, Rav Kook employed the halakhic terminology of *hoza'a* and *hakhnasa* to convey the dual nature of the mutually beneficial relationship between Torah and other endeavors. According to the *hoza'a* model, Jews need not "be creative *within* the realm of secular disciplines; their creativity lies, rather, in the process of infusing these disciplines with religious significance." (See Shatz's "Integration of Torah and Culture," p. 554. Also see his essay on Rav Kook in *Engaging Modernity*.)

Without claiming there is an exact affinity between the thought of *Keren Ora* and that of R. Kook, we can still discern a common theme. Torah was never meant to hide from the world, calling it ugly from behind a high fence. Torah was meant to transform the world.

Dealing with Contradictions

> Rav Yehuda said in the name of Rav: "Remember this man positively, and Hanania ben Hizkiya is his name. For if not for his efforts the book of *Yehezkel* would have been hidden away, as its words contradict the words of Torah. What did he do? He took three hundred bottles of oil up to his attic, and

he sat there until he expounded [in a way that resolved the contradictions]."

(Shabbat 13b)

Rav Yehuda the son of Rav Shemuel bar Shilat said in the name of Rav: "The sages wanted to hide away the book of *Kohelet* because its words contradict each other. Why did they not do so? Because it begins with words of Torah and ends with words of Torah.".…

And they also wanted to hide away the book of *Mishlei* because its words contradict each other. Why did they not do so? They said: "Did we not look into the book of *Kohelet* and find a way to explain it? Here too let us delve into it."

(Shabbat 30b)

Three different canonical works were candidates for *geniza* because of the problem of contradictions. In all three cases, the problems were successfully resolved. A number of commentaries note that the resolutions differed in the three cases. Hanania solved the contradictions between *Yehezkel* and *Humash* by reconciling these two sources and showing that they complement each other. In contrast, the internal contradictions in *Kohelet* are initially addressed by pointing out that the book opens and closes on an important religious note. The same gemara proceeds to resolve the contradictions in *Kohelet*, but implies that it was the religious messages at the book's twin poles that enabled it to get past the censor. If so, how did two good sections overcome the problem of contradictions?

Maharsha (on fol. 30b) explains that the sages knew that *Yehezkel* was an established prophet and that his written words were prophetic. This was sufficient motivation to try to resolve any problems in that work. *Kohelet*, on the other hand, was the product of Shelomo's human wisdom. The sages might not have expended great effort to make this work part of Tanakh were it not for the fact that it begins and ends with significant themes.

These two parts of *Kohelet* inspired the sages to work out its contradictions and include it in the canon.

R. Yaakov Reisher raises similar questions in his *Iyyun Yaakov* (found in *Ein Yaakov,* on fol. 30a). He also asks how two good parts compensated for the internal inconsistencies. He answers that contradictions are not sufficient reason to hide away a work. Only heretical themes would justify this. According to R. Reisher, it was not the contradictions that worried the sages but the possible heretical interpretations that would follow from them. Once the sages saw the pure religious impulses of the book's opening and closing themes, they felt assured that the middle sections did not border on the heretical.

In support of this idea, note that the version of this aggada in *Vayikra Rabba* (28:1) explicitly says that the problem of *Kohelet* was that its words seem to incline toward the heretical. I would add that R. Reisher might be making a more far-reaching point. Conflicting themes are no reason to reject a work, because the conflicts may simply reflect the fact that reality is complex, and that sometimes only the tension of opposition conveys the truth of the matter. As *Kohelet* notes, some forms of joy deserve approval and others do not. However, when the complexity gives way to heresy, the time has come to protest.

Let us now turn to the example of *Mishlei*. The sages did not point to specific outstanding *pesukim* in this work but mentioned the example of *Kohelet*. Their success at resolving the problems of *Kohelet* apparently filled them with confidence about their ability to do so for *Mishlei*. I suggest that this can serve as a broader model for both our personal thinking about religion and our educational endeavors. We need not try to resolve each and every challenging religious question. This would lead us to offer poor answers when a humble confession of ignorance would be far better. What we do need to accomplish is to explain enough of Torah in a profound and reasonable fashion that a certain presumption of reasonableness spreads to the entirety of Torah. When the bulk of Torah shines forth in all its splendor, we can learn to live with the sections whose light we find ourselves currently incapable of seeing.

Youthful Exuberance and the Wisdom of Experience

> What appeared on the coin of Avraham Avinu? An elderly
> man and woman on one side, and a young boy and girl on
> the other.
>
> (*Bava Kama* 97b)

It seems obvious that the gemara refers not to an actual coin but to some symbolic image of Avraham's accomplishments. Avraham did not have a kingdom with its own currency, but he did initiate a spiritual revolution of awesome proportions. If so, what is the symbolic meaning of age and youth? According to Rashi, the coin symbolizes Avrahram and Sarah, the older couple, passing on their spiritual message to the next generation, Yizhak and Rivka. In contrast, Maharsha understands both sides of the coin as referring to Avraham and Sarah, because even in their old age they were granted the youthful ability to have a child.

R. Yehiel Yaakov Weinberg, in his *LiFrakim* (p. 375), agrees that both sides of the coin depict Avraham and Sarah. The two of them were able to combine the best of youth with the best of experience. The young are filled with energy, enthusiasm, and a revolutionary spirit. Indeed, the first Jewish couple energetically changed the world's concept of religion. On the other hand, older people tend to be more thoughtful, settled, and steady. Avraham and Sarah excelled in this area as well. They were able to combine the burning idealism of youth with the wisdom and consistency of age.

R. Yosef Dov Soloveitchik writes that several notable Rabbonim – his father, his grandfather, and R. Hayyim Heller – exhibited this trait. In his eulogy for R. Heller, R. Soloveitchik writes of the religious scholar:

On the one hand, he is knowledgeable-sated, strong of intellect, rich in experience, sober-sighted, crowned with age, great of spirit. On the other hand, he remains the young and playful child; naive curiosity, natural enthusiasm, eagerness and spiritual restlessness, have not abandoned him.

(Shiurei HaRav, p. 63)

May we succeed in not letting our wisdom dull our enthusiasm, and in not letting our energy overrun our wisdom.

The Man of Eternity and the Man of the Moment

R. Hamnuna said: "*Who is like the wise man, and who knows the interpretation of a matter (pesher davar)* (*Kohelet* 8:1). Who is like the Holy One, blessed be He, who knows how to make a compromise (*peshara*) between two righteous people!"

Hizkiyahu said: "Let Yeshayahu come to me, just as we find that Eliyahu went to Ahav."

Yeshayahu said: "Let Hizkiyahu come to me, just as we find that Yehoram, son of Ahav, went to Elisha."

What did the Holy One, blessed be He, do? He brought afflictions upon Hizkiyahu and said to Yeshayahu: "Go visit the sick," as it is written: *In those days, Hizkiyahu became deathly ill, and Yeshayahu son of Amotz came to him and said, "Thus said God: Set your house in order, because you will die and not live* (*ii Melakhim* 20:1)."

What does the verse *you will die and not live* mean? You will die in this world and not live in the world-to-come.

Hizkiyahu said to Yeshayahu: "What is all this [why do I deserve such harsh punishment]?"

Yeshayahu said to him: "Because you did not engage in procreation."

He answered: "Because I saw through the holy spirit that I would have unworthy children."

Yeshayahu said to him: "What do you have to do with the

secrets of the Merciful One? You should do what is incumbent upon you, and the things that are up to the Holy One, let Him do."

(*Berakhot* 10a)

Maharsha points out that this aggada builds upon a close reading of the relevant passages in Tanakh. After Hizkiyahu beseeches God to restore his health, the prophet reports that Hashem has accepted the king's prayers and will add fifteen years onto his life. When Hizkiyahu dies, however, Menashe, his son, is only twelve years old. Thus we see that the king bore children only after his illness and the resulting exchange with the prophet. As with many aggadot, the midrashic impulse takes off based on an exegetical issue that arises from the *pesukim*.

At first glance, it would seem that this story has two distinct components. The first part addresses the clash between prophecy and the monarchy. Who represents the office whose honor demands that the other pay him a visit? The second part of the gemara then moves to a much different issue – the question of functioning according to semi-prophetic visions. Hizkiyahu argues that such a vision about the fate of his children is sufficient grounds for not having offspring. Yeshayahu counters that we must fulfill the *mizvot* incumbent upon us regardless, rather than reach important decisions based upon secrets revealed in dreams and visions. We will begin with the assumption that these sections really do reflect two distinct issues, and then later return to a more integrated reading.

Who was victorious in the clash between the honor of monarchy and that of prophecy? On the one hand, Yeshayahu eventually does go to visit the king. On the other hand, it is Hizkiyahu who falls ill, and thus the visit assumes the different character of *bikkur holim*. The commentators differ on this point. R. Yaakov ibn Habib, the *Kotev* in the *Ein Yaakov*, argues that the prophet's honor took precedence; after all, the king suffered terribly, whereas the prophet remained healthy. Conversely, R. Yaakov Reisher (*Iyyun Yaakov*) suggests that the prophet was ultimately forced to travel because a king's honor takes precedence. He draws evidence from the gemara's ruling in *Horayot* (13a) that a bystander should save the king's life before that of the prophet.

Of course, Hizkiyahu's illness might have nothing to do with the clash of honor, and may only have been a punishment for not having children. According to our gemara, the prophet informs the king that he lacks a portion in the world-to-come. At first glance, this seems unduly drastic. Choosing not to have children is certainly wrong, but we do not usually view it as rendering someone worthy of perdition. Maharsha appears to have understood that Hizkiyahu did not truly lose his *olam haba*. Without fully explaining the reference, he mentions a gemara in *Bava Batra* (116a) which states that the term *shekhiva* applies to those with righteous offspring, while the term *mita* is appropriate for those without such children. In Maharsha's reading of the gemara, those with problematic children are not denied entry into the world-to-come, but they die in the sense that their work is not perpetuated in this world. Perhaps Maharsha understands Yeshayahu's remark to mean that Hizkiyahu would not see his work continued, not that he was denied entry into the world-to-come. Alternatively, R. Yaakov Reisher mentions the possibility that refraining from procreation is a far more grievous sin when one belongs to the Davidic line, so much so that the king would indeed forfeit his share in the world-to-come.

Hizkiyahu's choice to not have children might relate to a famous rishonic debate about the Yosef story. Why does Yosef act harshly toward his brothers when they first come down to Egypt? Ramban (*Bereishit* 42:9) suggests that Yosef bore the responsibility of ensuring that his dreams would be actualized and thus had to manipulate matters such that Binyamin and then Yaakov would bow before him in Egypt. Abravanel (*Bereishit*, p. 398) disagrees, arguing that mistreating others for the purpose of ensuring a dream's fulfillment is unjustified. The debate between Hizkiyahu and Yeshayahu may reflect this issue, the king siding with Ramban, and the prophet with Abravanel.

In his *Ein Aya*, Rav Kook gives us a harmonious reading of the two parts of the gemara. According to R. Kook, priest and king represent two different world perspectives. The prophet works in the realm of eternal ideals and attempts to ready the people to achieve immortality. The king, on the other hand, works in the world of immediacy. He focuses on strengthening the people in the here-and-now. These two perspectives often clash, and what proves beneficial for the moment may not help from the perspective of eternity. Rav Kook cautions against an exclusive and extremist focus on either of these perspectives.

From this perspective, Hizkiyahu stood for the current needs of the people, while Yeshayahu demanded that the broader vision of eternity take pride of place. Hashem engineered the compromise that ensued. From an external perspective, it seemed as if the king had triumphed, in that the prophet made the trip to the king's palace. However, those with a more penetrating outlook understand that it was the prophet who emerged victorious, because he traveled only to visit an ailing monarch. The surface view served the necessary function of maintaining the honor of the kingship in the eyes of the people. The deeper level underscores that the needs of the moment should often take a backseat to our eternal vision.

R. Kook views the later debate between priest and prophet as a manifestation of the same split that gave rise to the earlier debate. Hizkiyahu foresees his children's unworthiness and imagines the immense national trauma of an evil king. From this point of view, it seems preferable to avoid having children. But Yeshayahu, representing the totality of history, argues that discontinuing the Davidic line will have tragic long-term implications for Am Yisrael. From this perspective, we should overlook the problems of the moment in order to maintain eternal ideals.

The clash between the needs of the moment and the needs of eternity challenge any communal leader and educator. Finding the proper balance demands deep thought and hard work, and we should be reluctant to apply Rav Kook's insight too easily to our current problems. At the same time, his insight can provide a framework for our thinking when we approach the pressing issues of the day.

Prolonging Life, Shortening Life, and the Well-Balanced Life

> Rav Yehuda said: "Three things prolong a person's days and years: One who extends his prayers, one who extends his table, and one who extends his time in the lavatory."
>
> Rav Yehuda said: "Three things shorten a person's days and years: One who is given a Torah scroll to read and does not read, one who is given a cup of benediction to bless with and does not recite the blessing, and one who assumes authority."
>
> (*Berakhot* 54b–55a)

The talmudic explanation for the first list is straightforward. The first item refers to one who prays with great devotion. The second refers to someone who eats a lengthy meal in order to provide more time for poor guests to arrive. Both these people engage in religiously meritorious behavior and deserve reward. The third item, regarding the fellow in the bathroom, presumably refers to a health issue and not to reward for *mizva* performance. If so, the second list is structured as the mirror image of the first. Those who refuse the Torah scroll or the cup of benediction refuse *mizvot*. The one who assumes the mantle of leadership does not sin but does take on work that can shorten a life in a naturalistic way. Both lists include two items of divine reward and punishment and one item of naturalistic impact on a lifespan.

Rav Kook's *Ein Aya* finds deeper significance in Rav Yehuda's two statements. He suggests that the items on the first list complement each other and warn of the danger that a single positive ideal might crowd out other important ideals. A person who prays with great devotion runs the risk of focusing all his energies on achieving closeness to Hashem and forgetting about the needs of the poverty-stricken. Thus, Rav Yehuda supplements the long prayer with the long table that helps the poor. Another person might be so dedicated to *mizvot*, both of the *bein addam la'makom* and *bein adam le'havero* varieties, that he forgets to care for his basic physical needs. Thus, the first two items need to be complemented by the extended stay in the bathroom ensuring basic physical maintenance.

According to Rav Kook, R. Yehuda's second list portrays the opposite of the former list. The person who turns down the Torah will not achieve the knowledge necessary for extended prayer. As an aside, it is striking to note how Rav Kook assumes that true devotion in prayer cannot emerge from ignorance but only from serious learning and deep understanding. The person who turns down the cup of benediction, usually drunk at public festive celebrations, resents having to share his meal with others. Such a person diametrically opposes the extended table. Finally, the person tempted by public office is often a visionary motivated to change the world. That type of person is subject to the temptation to forget about more basic responsibilities, such as the extended time in the lavatory.

The continuation of the gemara cites a specific example of a life shortened by the onus of leadership. Yosef passes away before his brethren because he took on an important post in the Egyptian government. We have already mentioned a naturalistic account of the impact of assuming leadership. Rav Kook, on the other hand, reads it in light of the religious framework mentioned above. Yosef was indeed a visionary who sought to realize his youthful dreams. His chasing after that lofty ideal may have led him to forget about some more basic responsibilities to his father (some *rishonim* suggest that Yosef never contacted Yaakov from Egypt because he was trying to enable his dreams to come true). For this reason, he did not share the longevity of his brethren.

Many people need no reminder to take care of their physical needs or to feel responsible for basic ethical requirements. Such people must be exhorted to strive to attain closeness to divinity or to realize a grand vision. Yet precisely those people who hear the call of greatness and feel charged to change the world need a reminder to tend to basic responsibilities.

CHAPTER 12

The Goal of Life

Dynamism and Rest in the World-to-Come

> R. Hiyya bar Ashi said in the name of Rav: "*Talmidei hakhamim* have no rest in this world or in the next world, as it says: *They will go from strength to strength and appear before God in Zion* (*Tehillim* 84:7)*.*"
>
> (*Berakhot* 64a)

Let us begin by noting the part of the statement that seems easy to understand. We can well appreciate Rav Ashi's idea with regard to this world. We certainly do not envision the goal of this world as achieving an eternal siesta on the beach with a piña colada in hand. Rather, we view this world as a place for constant striving and accomplishment. The ubiquitous challenges of character refinement and depth of Torah knowledge ensure continuous potential for growth. Indeed, if we truly understood the potential worth and value of every day, we could not possibly aspire to years of serene laziness.

Søren Kierkegaard employs a clever parable for those who would like to finish their responsibilities in life early in order to free themselves up for fun and games.

> When in a written examination the youth are allotted four hours to develop a theme, then it is neither here nor there if an individual student happens to finish before the time is up, or uses the entire time. Here, therefore, the task is one thing, the time another. But when the time itself is the task, it becomes a fault to finish before the time has transpired. Suppose a man were assigned the task of entertaining himself for an entire day, and he finishes this task of self-entertainment as early as noon: then his celerity would not be meritorious. So also when life constitutes the task. To be finished with life before life has finished with one, is precisely not to have finished the task.
>
> (*Concluding Unscientific Postscript*, pp. 146–147)

The other half of R. Ashi's statement is more surprising. R. Ashi states that scholars will not know rest even in the world-to-come. Isn't the world-to-come about finding our well-deserved rest after a lifetime of toil and effort? Don't we refer to the future existence as a "day that is all rest and a tranquility for eternal life"? Or do we suddenly discover that we will also have to deal with pain, frustration, sweat, and tears in *olam haba*?

R. Shemuel Edels (Maharsha) explains that the righteous sit in the world-to-come and enjoy the splendor of the divine radiance that comes from intellectual comprehension. On the one hand, this means constant activity of mind and soul. On the other hand, the activity in question represents the greatest sense of delight and tranquility. Thus, there is no contradiction in saying both that the world-to-come represents the ultimate rest and that the righteous will not know rest in the world-to-come.

Maharal (*Netivot Olam, Netiv haTorah* 9) concurs with this line of interpretation, arguing that the *talmid hakham* will know rest but not completion because there is no end to understanding.

IIe adds that it is for this reason that the Torah was given on Shabbat. Everything pertaining to the six days of creation knows a cessation of activity on the seventh day. The Torah, which burst forth in its creative splendor on a Shabbat, knows nothing of its activity coming to rest; it does not belong to the physical world of the six days of work.

Lest the preceding thoughts about comprehending divinity focus too much on the intellectual, I feel confident in stating that these commentaries assume that only people of refined character will succeed in enjoying the comprehension of the divine radiance. We do not need to fully work out this interplay between character and intellect in order to understand that two lifetimes of activity constitute human destiny. Success, when the activity involves a good deal of difficulty and effort, enables the future, more serene activity of enjoying our closeness and comprehension of the divine.

Excuses, Responsibility, and Achievement

> The Rabbis taught: The poor, the rich, and the wicked come before the [heavenly] court. They say to the poor man, "Why did you not occupy yourself with Torah?" If he says, "I was poor and I was concerned about my sustenance," they say to him, "Were you any poorer than Hillel?"...
>
> They ask the rich man, "Why did you not occupy yourself with Torah?" If he says, "I was rich and preoccupied with my possessions," they say to him, "Were you any wealthier than R. Elazar?"...They ask the wicked man, "Why did you not occupy yourself with Torah?" If he says, "I was good-looking and preoccupied with my evil inclination," they say to him, "Were you better looking than Yosef?"...
>
> Thus Hillel obligates the poor, R. Elazar ben Harsom obligates the rich, and Yosef obligates the wicked.
>
> (*Yoma* 35b)

I have omitted those parts of the gemara that tell how these three individuals overcame their hardships to succeed in Torah. Although each of the stories merits analysis, a broader overview of the gemara will suffice for our purposes. A few questions immediately emerge. First, doesn't it seem odd to include our forefather Yosef, known traditionally as Yosef the Righteous, Yosef *haZaddik*, in the category of the wicked (*reshaim*)? Second, a glance at the overall narrative reveals that the gemara lumps together three individuals with very different excuses. Most of us would probably feel far more sympathetic to the poor man's defense than that of the rich fellow. Why does the gemara place side by side people with very different degrees of culpability for their inadequacy?

R. Yosef Hayyim of Baghdad writes in his *Ben Yehoyada* that each of these individuals actually has two excuses. The poor man says that he was too busy working long hours performing difficult, menial tasks to find time to engage in Torah. He is also claiming, in effect, that constant anxiety about providing for his family denied him the psychological equanimity required for meaningful learning. The rich man echoes the excuse of limited time. Managing estates and businesses can certainly fill up one's day. He is also claiming that in fact he increased Torah study by donating the new wing of the yeshiva, say, or supporting other educational programs. R. Yosef Hayyim's explanation teaches us that we can affirm the importance of financial contributions without concluding that such largesse exempts those who give generously from the responsibility of seeing to their own growth in learning and devotion.

The *rasha* similarly gives two excuses. Like the others, he too employs lack of time as a justification. The late-night bar scene does not leave much time for learning. Second, he is claiming that he does not belong in a *shiur* because of his evil ways. How could the holy Torah connect to a rotten personality like him? Herein lies a profoundly important insight and an answer to our first question. Those who evaluate themselves as irredeemably evil are often unable to repent, because they deem it pointless to try to bring sanctity into their evil lives. A healthier approach would be to acknowledge their need for improvement without adopting the self-referential identity of the *rasha*. Thus the third category actually refers to a person struggling with temptation, and not to an all-out *rasha*. That is why Yosef, as the paradigm of successful triumph over temptation, belongs in this category. The gemara refers to this category as that of the *rasha* precisely because it is his self-identification that perpetuates his sinful tendency.

Let us return to our second question. As mentioned, the gemara combines a range of excuses with varying degrees of cogency. For example, "I was occupied in supporting my poor family" is much more convincing than "I was busy enjoying the town nightlife." Why does the gemara juxtapose these three categories, apparently treating all of the excuses as equally valid? I believe that the answer emerges from a simple analogy. Imagine a sports team that loses its star player to injury midway through the year. In theory, the team could choose to lose the rest of their games content with the knowledge that they have a compelling excuse for losing. Quite obviously, however, coaches and teams do not react that way. They try to find a way to win despite the availability of an eminently reasonable excuse.

A basic distinction explains this reaction. On the one hand, we can evaluate a situation from the perspective of moral culpability. From this perspective, the quality of the excuse becomes central to the analysis. Alternatively, we can focus our attention on achieving the goal we deem important. From this second perspective, the quality of the excuse is entirely irrelevant. The members of the athletic team are interested not in acquitting themselves before the heavenly court of sports, but in winning every game. They will focus not on their justifiable grounds for absolution, but on how to win games even under the difficult conditions that have presented themselves.

The goal of becoming an educated Jew certainly demands more effort than athletic success. This gemara shifts our focus from the question of responsibility to that of achievement. In a discussion of culpability, the poor person would receive a higher grade than his wealthy peer. However, this gemara emphasizes the need to become learned even when reasonable excuses lie readily at hand. Within that framework, it is more productive to find models for overcoming hardships than to explore the relative worth of different excuses. Rather than rely on their respective excuses, Hillel, R. Elazar, and Yosef all demonstrated the ability to overcome obstacles in order to achieve the most important goals in life.

Hidden Blessings

> R. Yizhak said: "Blessing is found only in something that is hidden from the eye, as it says: *God will command the blessing to be with you in your silos (Devarim 28:8)."* [The word *ba-asamekha*, "your silos," is related to *samuy,* "hidden."] It was taught in the school of R. Yishmael: "Blessing is found only in something upon which the eye cannot gaze, as it says: *God will command the blessing to be with you in your silos."* The Rabbis taught: "He who goes to measure [the produce in] his silo should say, 'May it be your will, Lord, our God, that you send blessing in the work of our hands.' If he began to measure, he should say, 'Blessed be the One who sends blessing to this pile.' If he measured and afterward blessed, it is a wasted prayer, because blessing is not found in something measured or counted, but only in something hidden from the eye."
>
> (*Bava Mezia* 42a)

The clue to understanding the statements of R. Yizhak, the school of R. Yishmael, and the Rabbis may lie in the last of them. Apparently one can hope for blessing up until the point where he has counted his assets and arrived at a precise amount. Any subsequent request for blessing is a wasted prayer. Why can't the farmer measure and then pray? Maharsha mentions the possibility that this gemara builds upon the concept of *ayin hara.* Once the farmer gives his bounty a number, others grow jealous, and this has negative repercussions. One can explain *ayin hara* metaphysically or can maintain, naturalistically, that the jealousy of others often leads to harm without any metaphysical machinery playing a role.

R. Yaakov Reisher (*Iyyun Yaakov*) rejects the *ayin hara* explanation for this gemara. The Rabbis, he observes, seem to be describing a farmer who measures alone in his silo, with no one else present to give him the "evil eye." He argues that divine providence prefers to work with a hidden hand and not in an openly miraculous fashion. Once a measurement has been taken, any change in the number would mandate an overt miracle. Before the count has concluded, providence can step in to help without broadcasting its miraculous intervention.

R. Yizhak Arama, in his *Akeidat Yizhak* (*Emor* 113b), offers a terrific explanation of this passage. He says that life's most authentic blessings cannot be found in the quantifiable, such as wealth or possessions. True blessing is located in the realm of the spirit, a realm that does not lend itself to quantification. It is to this critical message, the *Akeidat Yizhak* contends, that this gemara refers. Marc Shapiro has translated an address of Rav Azriel Hildesheimer (*Torah u'Madda Journal*, vol. 9, p. 79) in which the same idea appears. Those of us fortunate enough to enjoy the wonders of friendship, child-rearing, acts of kindness, observance of Shabbat and festivals, powerful prayer experiences, and the depths of learning, understand this quite well. The ultimate blessings are not to be found in the measured or the numbered, but in the non-numerical realm of the spirit.

R. Arama's interpretation does not explain the difference between praying before measuring and praying after measuring. Either way, the blessing in question refers to produce, something inherently quantifiable. Perhaps R. Arama's explanation only works for the statements of R. Yizhak and the school of R. Yishmael. Note that the first two statements did not mention the issue of when to pray while measuring. If so, the final quotation from the Rabbis teaches us about the workings of providence or about the evil eye, but the earlier two citations tell us where life's blessings truly lie.

Two Types of Sacrifice

> Miracles were performed in connection with the Nikanor Gates [of the Temple], and his memory was praised.
>
> (*Yoma* 37a)

> What miracles were preformed in connection with his gates? Nikanor went to Alexandria in Egypt to bring the doors. On his return voyage, a huge wave threatened to capsize the boat, so they took one of the doors and cast it into the sea, but still the sea continued to rage. When they prepared to cast the other one into the sea, Nikanor rose and clung to it, declaring: "Cast me into the sea with it!" The sea immediately became calm. He was, however, deeply grieved about the first door. As they reached the harbor of Akko, it broke the surface and appeared from under the side of the boat; others say a sea monster swallowed it and spit it out onto dry land.... Subsequently, all the gates of the Sanctuary were exchanged for golden ones, except for the Nikanor Gates [which were bronze], because of the miracles done with them; others say that they remained because the bronze of which they were made had a golden hue.
>
> (Ibid. 38a)

I would like to briefly focus on two shorter themes before addressing the central idea of this aggada. Over the course of this story, Nikanor progresses from gift-giving to a more enduring dedication, illustrating how the authentic volunteer spirit ultimately demands more than writing a check and even more than creating a gift. It involves an ongoing commitment to make sure that the donation reaches its desired destination, that is to say, is used for its intended purpose. Nikanor's decision on the boat to save the second door represents this lasting dedication to a good cause.

The end of the story also steers us in a clear direction. Why were Nikanor's doors left in place as the sole Temple gates not refurbished with gold? The second explanation is technical, that the hue of the bronze meant that there was no great aesthetic difference between Nikanor's doors and the other doors. The other possibility, however, expresses an important idea: that an object's history often proves more powerful than the beauty of its appearance. Just as individuals zealously keep objects of personal significance even if ugly, the Gates of Nikanor generated a profound impression even when they could not match the beauty of the other doors.

Let us now turn to the story's dominant themes. The sensitive reader cannot help noticing several parallels with the story of Yona. There is a storm at sea, and something needs to be thrown overboard to save the ship. A sea creature swallows what was cast into the ocean and spits it out onto dry land. Clearly, this tale must either be compared to or contrasted with that of Yona.

To me, it seems that a sharp contrast emerges. Yona is passive during the early part of the storm, sleeping below deck as the other sailors pray. While he agrees to be cast into the sea, this seems to reflect a kind of apathy – a feeling that it doesn't matter what happens – more than an act of heroism. The fact that the literary parallel between the two stories equates Yona with the lifeless doors further indicates his passivity. Nikanor, by contrast, risks his life precisely because he cares deeply. One can make a sacrifice out of indifference or out of idealism, but only someone who fully appreciates the great worth of life has the capacity to truly sacrifice, because only that person understands what it means to give up something worth caring about. The challenge is to emulate Nikanor's sacrifice rather than Yona's.

After this idea was sent out via the Internet, two astute readers questioned me about Nikanor's heroism. They said that he seems to risk his life for a material object, albeit an object for the *Beit haMikdash*, and this seems to be anti-halakhic behavior. Why celebrate a person who seemingly makes the wrong choice? I found two commentaries that discuss this point. R. Yaakov Reisher, in his *Iyyun Yaakov*, suggests that Nikanor relies on the rule that *sheluhei mizva einan nizakin*, "messengers for a *mizva* are not harmed." This explanation is quite difficult, because the gemara (*Kiddushin* 39b) explicitly states that this principle does not apply in a situation of significant danger to life. Indeed, based on this principle, we would not choose to drive recklessly on the way to a *shiur*.

R. Hayim David Azulai (Hida) gives a different answer in his *Marit haAyin*. He explains that Nikanor did not really intend to cling to the door as the sailors tossed it into the ocean; he would have relented if they had decided to cast it in. He was simply asking them to wait and see if the sea would calm. Any case of rough seas involves balancing the degree of danger with the desire not to rashly toss important items overboard. According to Hida, Nikanor was balancing these factors differently from the sailors, not offering to give up his life for a door.

Lastly, we might investigate the possibility that he was willing to give up his life as an act of supererogation. Does Halakha allow for such acts? Rambam (*Yesodei haTorah* 5:1, 4) says that we are forbidden to give up our lives in any case where Jewish law does not command martyrdom. Other *rishonim* allow acts of martyrdom even when not obligatory, but they limit the possibility to situations in which the martyrdom enables the fulfillment of an obligation. It seems unlikely that they would allow such an act by Nikanor when it would not have accomplished this goal.

The Weight of Decisions

> *Fear no man* (*Devarim* 1:7). R. Hanin explained: "Do not gather in your words before any man." The pair of witnesses should know about Whom they testify, and before Whom they testify,

and Who will punish them in the future, as it says: *And the two men who have the quarrel will stand before God* (*Devarim* 19:17).

Furthermore, the judges should know Whom they judge, and before Whom they judge. and Who will punish them in the future, as it says: *God stands with the congregation of the mighty* [*in the midst of the judges He judges*] (*Tehillim* 82:1). Thus, with regard to Yehoshafat, it says: *And he said to the judges: "Take heed what you do, for you do not judge for man but for God"* (*ii Divrei haYamim* 19:6).

Perhaps the judge will say: "Why should I get involved in this trouble?" The verse (ibid.) teaches us: *And He is with you in the matter of judgment*: a judge has nothing more than what his eyes see.

(*Sanhedrin* 6b)

Witnesses and judges must feel the weight of the responsibility vested in them, for a decent society depends upon the ability of the courts to administer justice. According to the preceding gemara, God's intimate involvement in the judicial process means that both the witnesses and the judges should feel the eyes of divine providence watching them. It is God who oversees the court and who will punish those who fail to adhere to the requirements of honesty and integrity.

R. Yaakov Reisher (*Iyyun Yaakov*) asks: Since God punishes every type of transgression, how is a court case unique? He answers that the divine presence in the courtroom means that any sin done there is akin to sinning directly in front of our Maker. The heightened sense of divine interest in the court proceedings magnifies the sin involved if a person shows indifference to the responsibilities of the court.

In what sense do the witnesses testify about God and the judges judge Him? Rashi and others explain this idea based on a gemara in *Sanhedrin* (8a), where God complains that the wicked trouble Him to restore money to its rightful owners. If so, every false witness and dishonest judge also forces God to arrange compensation for his victims. In this sense, all judgments affect the *Ribbono shel Olam.*

Perhaps there is another sense in which we can say that any judgment is about God. Every ruling by a halakhic judge should ideally be built upon fundamental halakhic ideals and principles; the judge who follows these principles reveals his fealty to the divine law, while the dishonest judge chooses to ignore God's Torah. In that sense, he renders a negative verdict on Hashem and His Torah.

With all this focus on the awesomeness of judicial responsibility, the gemara is nervous that the prospective judge will abandon his bench in search of another profession. Why get involved in so grave a matter when it seems much safer to go into carpentry or shoemaking? Therefore, the gemara concludes with a reassuring note: "a judge has nothing more than what his eyes see"; that is to say, judges who do their best to arrive at the correct ruling will not be held responsible for erroneous decisions.

Although the gemara states this principle in reference to court cases, later rabbinic voices broaden the idea to the endeavor of learning and to publishing *seforim.* In the introduction to *Iggerot Moshe,* Rav Moshe Feinstein expresses the tension between a fear of mistaken rulings and the need for learned people to make decisions. Rav Moshe cites this gemara to indicate that the appropriate person can make valid decisions, even though the decisions may not reflect the absolute truth.

The principle may extend beyond the question of Torah learning. In a fascinating responsum, R. Ovadia Yosef (*Yabia Omer* 8, H.M. 12) permits plastic surgery despite the risk involved in any surgical procedure. He argues that the doctors have the right to rely upon their judgment that the risk is infinitesimal, and that even if they err, "a judge has nothing more than what his eyes see." Here, the quotation applies not only to halakhic rulings but to medical evaluations. Competent authorities in any field have the right to make weighty decisions, despite the risk of error.

When they carry out their task faithfully, they are not held liable for such errors.

Finally, we can extend this principle one more step. Until now, all our illustrations of this principle focused on authority figures of one kind or another. The same idea can apply to ordinary individuals. We all face major decisions that no one else can make for us. These decisions include choices of all kinds: which yeshiva to attend, what *hashkafa* to identify with, choosing a career, selecting a spouse, the many aspects of parenting, and figuring out where to buy a house and grow roots.

The first part of the gemara instructs us to take these decisions seriously. We must think hard about these issues, seek advice from the appropriate people, and become as educated as possible before making such decisions. We cannot relinquish responsibility by leaving such decisions to fate or to someone else. At the same time, the second part of the gemara instructs us not to feel crushed by the gravity of these decisions. We should have confidence that if we work on the issues seriously, we can arrive at reasonable decisions.

It is true that many areas of religious life depend on authority figures to make rulings. However, with regard to the personal issues we have mentioned, giving up choice reflects a loss of nerve and a lack of responsibility. We can appreciate the gravity of these decisions without shying away from the need to make them. In this sense, we are all judges, and indeed, "a judge has nothing more than what his eyes see."

CHAPTER 13

Modernity

From Criticism to Construction

> Someone who sees a place where a miracle was done for the
> Jewish people says: "Blessed is the One who performed a
> miracle for our forefathers in this place."
>
> (*Berakhot* 54a)

The Rabbis taught: Someone who sees the place where the Jews
crossed the Red Sea, the place where they crossed the Jordan,
the place where they crossed the River of Arnon, the stones of
Algavish in Morad Beit Horon, the stone that Og, King of the
Bashan, wanted to throw at the people of Israel, the stone that
Moshe sat upon when Yehoshua waged war with Amalek, Lot's
wife and the walls of Jericho swallowed in their place; on all of
these he must give praise and thanks before God....

All of these examples make sense, as they are miracles
[that saved the Jewish people], but Lot's wife is a punishment!
One should say [upon seeing Lot's wife], "Blessed is the True
Judge." But the source says "praise and thanks" [which suggest

215

a more joyous blessing]? We learned that on Lot and his wife one makes two blessings. On his wife, one says, "Blessed is the True Judge." On Lot, one says, "Blessed is the One who remembers the righteous."

(Berakhot 54a–b)

Before discussing the central issue, I must mention Rashi's point that "the righteous" mentioned in the blessing on seeing the place of Lot refers to Avraham and not to Lot. Aside from the fact that Tanakh does not depict Lot as particularly righteous, attributing the reference to Avraham helps resolve two different problems. The gemara explicitly states that the only case in which every Jew makes the blessing is when the miracle helped the Jewish people collectively. If the miracle merely saved a single individual, then only that person recites the blessing. Lot's salvation would not generate a blessing to be recited by others unless the salvation had more global implications because it revolved around the merits of our avot. Similarly, the Yerushalmi (Berakhot 9:1) discusses a case when a miracle for an individual generated a communal sanctifying of the divine name, such as Daniel's miraculous salvation from the den of lions.

Second, the blessing recited on remembering the salvation of Lot differs from the blessing cited in the mishna, namely, "Blessed is the One who performed a miracle for our forefathers in this place." Maharsha explains that the mishna's version is for all instances in which people were miraculously saved due to their own merits. As Lot was saved only because of Avraham's status, the blessing changes to "remembers the righteous" to convey that God recalls the righteous when giving out punishments to others, and that the merits of those righteous people can forestall such punishments.

A more precise understanding of this blessing allows us to move on to our fundamental question. Although this gemara does address the unlikely inclusion of the example of Lot's wife, one has to wonder whether the gemara has truly resolved the difficulty. If the gemara wants to discuss joyous blessings of thanks upon seeing locations of miraculous salvation, why mention Lot's wife at all? The gemara could describe the blessing regarding Lot's wife in a separate discussion. Why does the gemara artificially link the joyous blessing about Lot's salvation and the sober acceptance of justice for Lot's wife?

We could offer a technical answer. It may be that a person can recite these blessings only upon seeing a concrete physical reminder of the miracle. Someone could possibly see the pillar of salt that was once Lot's wife, but no one can encounter a physical remnant of Lot's escape (see Meiri, however, who writes that seeing the location of Sodom inspires the blessings, and not necessarily seeing the pillar of salt). If so, it is only the sight of Lot's wife that can generate both blessings. Indeed, *Arukh haShulhan* suggests (*Orah Hayim* 218:11) that the essential blessing is for Lot's wife, and that Lot's salvation arises only by association.

R. Kook offers an important alternative answer in his *Ein Aya*. He begins by pointing out that in ideological clashes, many people oppose a particular position because they see the negative results that will emerge from it. However, if they are unable or unwilling to promote a positive vision in place of the rejected view, then they have not truly completed the task. To fully appreciate Rav Kook's idea, I consider the image of a bright undergraduate philosophy major relishing the chance to poke holes in the theories of the great thinkers. He sits back in his chair and attacks Plato, Aristotle, and others, all the while taking great pride in his critical acumen. If we ask this student to articulate his own theory, he demurs, arguing that he is just a critic. He is taking the easy way out. It is always easier to be a critic, because anyone can challenge an opponent's premises, saying things like "How do you know that," "Define your terms more precisely," and "What are your standards of evidence," until the other side has to struggle to come up with answers. To actually argue for something takes much more work. Ultimately, not standing for anything renders the whole endeavor pointless.

Thomas Carlyle understood this point when he criticized Voltaire, in "The Everlasting Yea," for being purely negative about religion:

> What! That hast no faculty in that kind? Only a torch for burning, no hammer for building? Take our thanks, then, and – thyself away.
>
> (*Sartor Resartus*, p. 147)

John Stuart Mill also gave a low ranking to those he called destructive philosophers –

> those who can perceive what is false, but not what is true; who awaken the human mind to the inconsistencies and absurdities of time sanctioned-opinions and institutions, but substitute nothing in the place of what they take away.
>
> (*Mill on Bentham and Coleridge*, pp. 42–43)

If we turn back to the time of Sodom, we see that Avraham faced this challenge. Is he only going to criticize Sodom and its evils, or is he also going to articulate a vision of a more just and worthy society? Tanakh juxtaposes Avraham's hospitality with the hatred of guests exhibited in Sodom; in part, this is to demonstrate that Avraham moves beyond criticism to positive acts of construction and building. In the same vein, here is how God explains why He has decided to inform Avraham about the impending destruction of Sodom: "For I know him, that he will command his children and his household after him, that they shall keep the way of God, to do charity and justice" (*Bereishit* 18:19). Far from being just a critic, Avraham stands for a nobler dream. We now understand why the gemara feels the need to integrate the blessing for Lot with the blessing for Lot's wife. Lot's wife represents the destruction of corrupt Sodom. Lot's being saved in the merit of Avraham reflects the constructive vision of Avraham's life. These two themes must be interwoven in order to convey the need to move beyond the rejection of Sodom to the more positive endeavor of building a better world.

Although I singled out undergraduate philosophy majors as an example, the point has much broader scope. Observant Jews can also get caught up in the critical mode, pointing out the flaws in every Orthodox group but failing to explain just how we might do things better. R. Kook's insight reminds us to avoid this trap, which in many ways is the intellectually easy way out.

Rav Kook saw this as a significant theme worth repeating. In a celebrated passage in *Arpilei Tohar* (p. 39), he writes:

> The purely righteous do not complain about evil, but add righteousness; do not complain about heresy, but add faith; do not complain about ignorance, but add wisdom.

A Change of Environment and a Change of Heart

> R. Mani was frequently found before R. Yizhak ben Elyashiv. Once, R. Mani said to him: "The rich members of my father-in-law's household harass me."
>
> R. Yizhak ben Elyashiv said: "Let them become poor," and they became poor.
>
> After a while, R. Mani came back and said: "They now press me to support them."
>
> R. Yizhak ben Elyashiv said: "Let them become rich again," and they became rich again.
>
> R. Mani said: "The people of my household are not [i.e., my wife is not] satisfactory to me." R. Yizhak ben Elyashiv said: "What is her name?" R. Mani answered: "Hanna." R. Yizhak decreed: "Let Hanna become beautiful," and she became beautiful.
>
> R. Mani returned and said: "She has become overbearing to me." R. Yizhak ben Elyashiv said: "Let Hanna revert to her plainness," and she reverted to her plainness.
>
> There were two students before R. Yizhak ben Elyashiv.

> They said to him: "Let the master ask for mercy for us so that we will become very wise." He said to them: "It [the power to affect things by praying] was with me, but I sent it away."
>
> (*Ta'anit* 23b)

This story includes several different ideas. First, it says something about knowing what to ask for. We need to pray for divine help in the truly important matters, rather than becoming caught up in who has money or who has the best-looking spouse. The specific matters that *Hazal* included in the requests section of the *Amida* may educate us in this regard. Second, it points out that we sometimes desire things that are very much a mixed blessing. The petty jealousies and family squabbles that often come in tandem with having more wealth than one's friends and relatives should make us question our aspirations for great riches. We can certainly reject poverty as a religious ideal and still understand the pitfalls of wealth.

The third level of the story's meaning may be even more important. We often think that we can make our lives better by changing this or that external factor in our environment. This story teaches that an authentic approach to improvement demands that we look within more than without. It turns out that R. Mani's social and domestic problems were not a function of economics or physical appearance; only a genuine attempt to improve the relationships in question could have helped. Modern man tends to think of bettering society by means of political and social changes. However, the success of any political structure, any society, depends on the nature of the human beings who reside within it. As André Gide wrote in his critique of Communism, "Man cannot be reformed from the outside – a change of heart is necessary" (*The God That Failed*, p. 185).

In the final episode, the two students ask for something more worthwhile than riches or physical beauty, but they are still rebuffed. This brings us to the last layer of meaning. Even the things most worth asking for, or perhaps we should say especially the things worth asking for, cannot be achieved with a mystical utterance. R. Yizhak tells his students that he has sent the power away (my explanation follows Maharsha rather than Rashi) because he wanted them to understand that the route to becoming a *talmid hakham* runs through long hours of work in the study hall. Authentic achievement requires effort and intelligence, not magic.

Can We Kill the Evil Inclination?

And they cried out with a great voice to the Lord, God (*Nehemya* 9:4). What did they say? Said Rav – some say, R. Yohanan – "Woe, woe. It is the [inclination for idolatry] that destroyed the Temple, burned the Sanctuary, killed all the righteous, and exiled Israel from our land, and it is still dancing among us. Was it given to us for any reason other than to receive reward [for resisting it]? We want neither it nor the reward."

A note fell from heaven, upon which was written: "Truth." Rav Hanina said: "From here we can derive that the seal of the Holy One, blessed be He, is truth."

They sat fasting for three days and three nights, and it was handed over to them. It departed from the Holy of Holies as a fiery lion-cub. The prophet [Zekharya] said to Israel: "This is the inclination for idolatry, as it is written: *And he said: 'This is the wickedness'* (*Zekharya* 5:8)."

As they grabbed hold of it, one of its hairs fell out; it raised its voice and the sound carried four hundred parasangs [1,400 miles].

They said: "What should we do? Perhaps, God forbid, they might have mercy upon him from heaven."

The prophet said to them: "Cast it into a pot of lead and close its opening with lead – for lead muffles the sound, as it is written: *And he said: 'This is the wickedness.' And he cast it down into the basket, and he cast the lead weight upon its opening* (*Zekharya* 5:8)."

They said: "Since this is a time of grace, let us ask for mercy regarding the inclination for [sexual] sins." They asked for mercy, and it was handed over to them.

It said to them: "Realize that if you kill me, the world will be finished."

They imprisoned it for three days, but when they then looked in the entire land of Israel for a fresh egg, they could not find one.

They said: "What should we do? Should we kill it? The world will be finished. Should we ask for mercy on a portion? They do not grant halves in heaven."

They blinded its eyes and let it go. This helped, in that people are no longer tempted by their relatives.

(*Yoma* 69b)

On one level, this story points to a historical change. The scriptural narrative tells us that idolatry remained a constant threat during the First Temple period; as we proceed to the time of the Second Temple, the Jewish people seem to have ceased struggling with the temptation of idolatry. Many other sins are still a problem, but not idolatry. Thus, this gemara has prophets from the time of the return from the Babylonian exile, the beginning of the Second Temple era, seeking the termination of the inclination for idolatry.

Presumably, the gemara intends to convey some content beyond the historical. Perhaps a series of questions will point us in the right direction. We could ask why the embodiment of this inclination emerge from the Holy of Holies, Surely, the gemara does not want to associate something evil with the holiest chamber of our most sacred place? Several *aharonim* in the *Ein Yaakov* suggest answers, but their explanations leave us unsatisfied. *Ez Yosef* argues that God's two major creations are the world and the human being: just as the evil inclination resides in the innermost part of the human being, so the embodiment of that inclination comes from the center of the world, the Foundation Stone within the Holy of Holies. *Anaf Yosef* adds that the fire represents the arrogance in the heart that leads us to idolatry. Alternatively, the fire may simply reflect the power of a given urge. In other contexts (see *Kiddushin* 81a), the gemara utilizes the metaphor of fire to depict a burning temptation. The lion adds another image of power. Without denigrating the approaches of these *aharonim*, we will search for some other interpretation of the chosen location.

A few more questions emerge from this tale. What is the symbolism of the hair that falls from the idolatrous inclination? Why are they able to eradicate this temptation, but find it impossible to do away with the urge for sexual transgressions? The clue to solving these riddles lies in a comment by R. Meir Simha haKohen of Dvinsk. In the Vilna Gaon's commentary on *Seder Olam*, he connects the end of the inclination for idolatry with the termination of prophecy. Indeed, both seem to come to an end at the conclusion of the Babylonian exile. R. Meir Simha (*Meshekh Hokhma, Bemidbar* 11:17) contends that the Gra is commenting on a verse in *Zekharya* (13:2):

> And it will be on that day, says the Lord of hosts, I will cut off the names of the idols from the land and they will not be mentioned again, and I will also remove the prophets and the unclean spirits from the land.

Most commentaries assume that the prophets referred to in this verse are false prophets associated with pagan temples; they are removed together with the idols. According to R. Meir Simha, the verse refers to authentic prophets: they come to an end when the idols cease to tempt us. Why would the positive institution of prophecy and the negative institution of idolatry be linked? Perhaps this indicates that all the forces and energies in this world have the potential for positive and negative realization. Getting rid of any force, then, must have both negative and positive effects.

This idea finds support in the latter part of the gemara. The sages contemplate killing the sexual urge but discover that then the world would be destroyed, because the same force that leads many to sin also perpetuates the propagation of the world and helps forge loving relationships between husbands and wives. Recall that they consider asking for mercy on a portion; Rashi says this means that they wanted the sexual urge to be present only between spouses. The answer "They do not grant halves in heaven" now takes on deeper meaning; it means that there is no force in the world that cannot be utilized constructively, on the one hand, or perverted, on the other. Our job is not to eliminate our urges, but to figure out how they can be part of a dignified and holy existence.

The notion that removing any force from the world involves sacrificing something may have been understood on some level even earlier in the story. The sages offer to give up the reward for overcoming the temptation to idolatry; from that perspective, they lose something positive when that urge leaves the world. Yet the positive aspects eradicated are apparently far greater. The same urge to idolatry helps bring about the phenomenon of prophecy. Therefore, their decision to eradicate the temptation to idolatry comes at a significant spiritual cost.

R. Meir Simha does not explain the link between idolatry and prophecy. I would suggest that both involve an intense feeling of the divine presence. We may be disgusted by many elements of pagan ritual and nevertheless appreciate that child sacrifice stemmed from an awareness, however sordid, of the overwhelming divine presence. A similar awareness, but nobler and more refined, appertains to the prophetic experience. It follows that relinquishing one mandates a loss of the other as well.

This may be the very reason why the sages do not destroy this impulse entirely. Rav Yaakov Emden understands the hair that falls out as symbolizing that a bit of this inclination remains here on earth. We may have justifiably eliminated the inclination for idolatry, but the desire for a religious experience of grand intensity needs to remain part of our world, if only in a reduced form. As I have argued in the preceding aggada, modern man often tries to save the world by manipulating the political, economic, and technological forces around him. This approach frequently demonstrates a failure to realize that corrupt people can warp any system; the same technology that produces new cures also produces frightening weapons of mass destruction. Rather than looking for an external panacea, our essential efforts must be directed toward producing finer human beings who will know how to utilize the forces about them in the best way.

Honi Demands Rain

Once it happened that the greater part of Adar had passed and yet no rain had fallen. The people sent a message to Honi the Circle Drawer, "Pray for rain to fall." He prayed and no rain fell. He thereupon drew a circle and stood within it....

He exclaimed " Master of the Universe, Your children have turned to me because [they believe] me to be a member of Your house. I swear by Your great name that I will not move from here until You have mercy on your children."

Rain began to drip. His students said to him: "Rabbi, we look to you to save us from death. We think that this rain came only to release you from your oath."

He said before Him: " I did not request this but rather rain that fills the wells, cisterns, and caves."

The rain began to come down with great force, every drop being as big as the opening of a barrel.... The students said: "Rabbi, we look to you to save us from death. We think that this rain comes only to destroy the world."

He said before Him: "I did not request this but rain of blessing and bounty." Then rain fell normally until the people had to go up to the Temple Mount because of the rain....

Shimon ben Shetah sent to him: "If you were not Honi, I would have placed you under the ban; for were the years like the years of Eliyahu, in whose hands were the keys of rain, would not the name of heaven be profaned through you? But what can I do, for you act petulantly before God and He grants your desire."

R. Yohanan said: "This righteous man [Honi] was troubled all his days by the verse *A song of ascents, when God brought back those that returned to Zion, we were like dreamers* (*Tehillim* 126:1)." He said: "Is it possible for a person to sleep for seventy years?"

One day he [Honi] was journeying on a road and saw a man planting a carob tree. He asked him: "How long does it take for this tree to bear fruit?" He said: "seventy years."

He [Honi] said: "Are you certain that you will live another seventy years?"

He said: "I found carob trees in the world. Just as my forefathers planted for me, I plant for my children."

Honi sat down to have a meal and sleep overtook him. While he was sleeping, a rock formation enclosed around him and he slept for seventy years. When he awoke, he saw a man gathering fruit from the carob tree. He asked him: "Are you the man who planted the tree?"

He said: "I am his grandson."...

[Honi returns to his house, but they do not believe his claim to be Honi.] He went to the study hall. He heard the Rabbis saying: "The law is as clear as in the days of Honi the Circle Drawer, because when he came to the study hall, he would solve all the rabbis' difficulties."

He said to them: "I am he." They did not believe him and did not honor him as he deserved. He became depressed. They asked for mercy and he passed away.

Rava said: "It is as people say: Either companionship or death."

(*Ta'anit* 23a)

How should we evaluate the character of Honi? If results are the criteria, the first story indicates that his methods were successful. At the same time, Shimon ben Shetah doubts the appropriateness of Honi's approach from the perspective of possible profanation of the divine name. Shimon's concern focuses on the possibility that God might not respond to Honi, who would then be forced to violate his oath sworn in God's name. Rashi adds that Honi did not speak respectfully enough to God.

The second story indicates that Honi's method is problematic from another perspective. Aharon Agus (in *The Binding of Isaac and Messiah*, pp. 70–82) has developed an overarching theory about two personality types in the Talmud. There are those who look for immediate solutions in one great moment of heroism, such as martyrdom or a miracle. Others endure difficulties and patiently await the unfolding of history as they direct their energies toward guarding the law. Honi, who demands an instantaneous solution from God, represents the first approach. The obvious flaw in this approach is that solutions are not always immediate, and implementing them sometimes depends upon the ability to persist and endure.

From this perspective, the second story provides a critique of Honi in the first. Honi cannot understand why the psalmist lauds the return from Babylon because he feels that seventy years of exile is much too long to wait for redemption. Similarly, he fails to appreciate the planting of the carob tree when the payoff is so distant. Nonetheless, we need to eat carobs, and ancestors must plant with their grandchildren in mind. Moreover, we need to find solace, and can do so even in the possibility of a slow return from the exile. Honi's lack of understanding in the latter tale reflects poorly on his approach in the former.

Yonah Frankel's reading is similar to that of Agus except that Frankel emphasizes an egocentric element in Honi's personality (*Sippur haAggada – Ahdut Shel Tohen veZurah*, pp. 183–189). He bases this on the fact that Honi does not feel adequately honored upon his return to the study hall. I am inclined to reject Frankel's reading because R. Yohanan refers to Honi as a *zaddik*. Furthermore, lack of patience and selfishness are distinct character flaws. An altruistic person can alleviate the pain of others even without understanding the need for long-term solutions. Honi genuinely wants to help the people in the first story. His problem stems from his need for immediate resolutions.

Almost all the truly valuable things in life, such as becoming learned, confronting a character flaw, or raising a family, require patience and endurance. Modern technology, with all of its benefits, encourages us to think that problems can disappear with the press of a button. Just consider the absurd frustration we feel when our Internet connection performs two seconds more slowly than usual, and you will realize that modernity challenges us to address this theme.

Protecting Others and Their Identities

> R. Hanina said: "Everyone descends to Gehenom except for three." Do we truly think this about "everyone"? Rather, say that everyone who descends to Gehenom comes up from there except for three who descend but do not come up, and these are the adulterer, the person who publicly embarrasses another, and the person who calls his friend by a nickname.
>
> (*Bava Mezia* 58b)

Tosafot discuss why this list does not include other weighty transgressions. Perhaps the three transgressions it mentions, irrespective of their severity, share a common denominator. Maharal, in his *Hiddushei Aggadot*, suggests that the three sins all challenge the *ezem ha'adam* of the victim. I would define *ezem ha'adam* as meaning the essential identity of a human being. Names are obviously central to identity, and an unwanted nickname threatens identity. Some modicum of social comfort is also crucial to identity, but it is challenged by public humiliation. Finally, the basic family unit enables identity, but the adulterer destroys its fabric. Other crimes, such as theft and violence, seriously hurt others but do not assault their identity.

An idea in contemporary political theory may help convey this point. Minorities and underprivileged groups can raise two separate claims. On the one hand, they want equal rights and opportunities. At the same time, they also want the validation of their identity. Societies can offer one without the other. Charles

Taylor argues in "The Politics of Recognition" that these two goals sometime work at cross-purposes, because the former emphasizes equality, whereas the latter stresses differences.

Taylor writes about large groups, but Maharal reminds us that much the same point applies to individuals. Protecting others from harm includes concern about preserving their identities as well as protecting them against physical or financial harm. (This does not mean, of course, that every identity of a collective or an individual, including identities of an immoral nature, deserves our protection.)

CHAPTER 14

Leadership

Bribery, Popularity, and Integrity

Rava said: "What is the reason for [the prohibition against] bribes? Once a judge accepts a bribe from someone, he feels close to that person as if he himself were the litigant and he will not find himself guilty."

R. Papa said: "A person should not serve as a judge for his friends or for his enemies, because he will not see wrong in his friends or merit in his enemies."

Abbaye said: "If a rabbinic scholar is beloved by all the people in his town, it is not because of his great qualities but because he does not rebuke them in matters of heaven."

Rava said: "Initially, I used to say that all the residents of Mehoza like me. After I became a judge, I said that some of them hate me and some like me. Once I realized that a person declared liable today wins tomorrow, I said that if they like me, all of them like me; and if they hate me, all of them hate me."

(*Ketuvot* 105b)

The first part of this gemara is quite straightforward. Bribery corrupts those in authority and ruins the possibility of just decision-making. The novel ideas in the gemara emerge from a careful analysis of the statements of Abbaye and Rava. Abbaye reminds us that popularity cannot be the barometer of rabbinic success. Without denying that it is good, all things being equal, for rabbis to be liked, too much focus on popularity distorts one's educational vision. A congregational rabbi may achieve popularity by never challenging his congregation. He may win by an overwhelming majority every time renewing his contract comes to a vote, but he fails miserably when it comes to raising the level of his community's learning, davening, kindness, and religious observance. High school educators face a similar challenge. They can achieve easy popularity by telling inappropriate jokes, needlessly criticizing the school administration, or giving in to every whim of their students. If this behavior is to be countered, the educational value of a teacher's work cannot be judged solely by a vote of the students.

The fact that this idea appears in the middle of a discussion of bribery gives it added poignancy. In the case of a normal bribe, the person giving the bribe explicitly offers financial rewards in exchange for a favor. In the case that Abbaye speaks of, a rabbi essentially offers to give his congregants a free pass in exchange for the bribe of popularity. The fact that no money changes hands and that the deal is never explicitly articulated does not alter the parallel to bribery. Thus, the broader talmudic context hammers home the problematic nature of this activity.

Rava adds a different insight. At first he thought that all the townspeople who had won cases before his bench would like him and all those who had lost would dislike him. He soon realized that likes and dislikes based on such matters quickly change with the vicissitudes of time. Rava is teaching us that the rabbi criticized by Abbaye on moral and religious grounds is making a mistake from a practical perspective. It is impossible for anyone in authority to keep everybody happy all the time. Decisions between rival factions and competing visions need to be made, and it is not feasible to find a compromise in every situation. Those who love one of your decisions will hate the next. Thus, the attempt to always make everybody happy by giving them what they want is futile by definition. On an institutional level, an attempt to make everybody happy usually means that the institution will lack a coherent overarching vision. Therefore, the constant search for popularity ultimately results in personal and professional failure.

Rava's final statement envisions the possibility of universal popularity or unpopularity. The path of greater integrity may sometimes lead to communal admiration. Even the less than stellar congregants may develop a grudging respect for a rabbi with courage and conviction. Of course, courage and conviction can also lead to communal hostility. Abbaye reminds us that popularity is the wrong criterion of success, and Rava instructs us that universal popularity simply cannot be achieved.

The First Day of Hillel's Career

Our Rabbis taught: This halakha was forgotten by the sons of Beteira [the family of the patriarchs of the supreme rabbinical court]. One time, the fourteenth of Nissan fell on a Shabbat. They forgot whether or not the service of the Pesah offering overrides the Shabbat. They said: "Does anyone know if Pesah overrides Shabbat?"

They said to them: "A man came up from Babylon by the name of Hillel haBavli. He attended upon the great sages of our generation, Shemaya and Avtalyon, and he knows if Pesah overrides Shabbat."

They sent for him and asked him: "Do you know if Pesah overrides the Shabbat?"

He said to them: "Does only one Pesah offering a year override Shabbat? Is it not the case that more than two hundred Pesah[-like] offerings a year override the Shabbat?"…They immediately sat him at the head and appointed him to be the patriarch. He expounded the laws of Pesah all day. He began to vex them with words. He said to them: "What happened to you, that I came up from Babylon and became the patriarch? Your laziness, that you did not attend upon the great sages of our generation, Shemaya and Avtalyon."

They said to him: "Rebbe, if one forgets to bring the knife [for the paschal offering] on Friday, what is the law?"

He said to them: "This halakha I heard and forgot. Rather, let the Jewish people be. If they are not prophets, they are the children of prophets."

The next day, those whose Pesah offering was a sheep inserted the knife in the wool. Those whose Pesah offering was a kid inserted the knife between the horns. Hillel saw the deed and remembered the law. He said: "This is as I received from Shemaya and Avtalyon."

(*Pesahim* 66a)

R. Yehuda said in the name of Rav: "If a scholar acts arrogantly, his wisdom departs from him...." From where do we know this? From Hillel.

(*Pesahim* 66b)

Let us begin with the relatively minor issue of chronology. Shemaya and Avtalyon taught Torah in Israel, so Hillel could only have been their student if he had moved to Israel from Babylon long before this incident. However, the story implies that he had only recently arrived from Babylon. A number of commentaries therefore suggest that Hillel journeyed from Babylon to Israel twice. The first time he went to Israel to learn from the great teachers of the time, Shemaya and Avtalyon. Later, after years of learning, he returned to his place of birth, perhaps to teach his old community, and then returned to Israel just before this story occurs. Hillel's impressive effort to hear words of Torah from the finest teachers of his time gives added meaning to his harsh admonition of the local population (note Maharsha's understanding that his words of vexation were directed to all the learned local people and not just the sons of Beteira). Hillel left the comforts of his hometown and made the difficult trek to another land to hear Torah at its finest. The local population of rabbinic students, on the other hand, had somehow missed the wonderful opportunity that presented itself in their own backyard.

Hillel's harsh demeanor surprises us. The talmudic paragon of humility here errs in a most arrogant way and immediately receives his comeuppance. This is not the Hillel we are accustomed to learning about. R. Yaakov Reisher, in his *Iyyun Yaakov*, explains that Hillel had very good intentions in administering this reproach. Sometimes a well-placed gibe can spur others on to greater success; for example, a student might remark to his *chavruta*, "Had you come to *seder* on time, maybe you would have understood the material!" Hillel intended such a result, but erred nonetheless. His noble intentions notwithstanding, his comment came across as arrogant and self-aggrandizing, and Hillel temporarily lost his wisdom as a result.

The idea that the arrogant person loses his wisdom can be explained in either metaphysical or naturalistic terms. The metaphysical approach would say, quite simply, that Hashem intervenes, removing the haughty person's wisdom as punishment for his hubris. The naturalistic view states that the boastful fellow will not put in the time and effort needed to arrive at proper conclusions. Assuming that we know everything often stifles our pursuit of knowledge. Hillel stumbled in this regard, and as a result he could not answer a follow-up question.

The oddity of finding Hillel making a mistake in the area of haughtiness may be the point of the story. Hillel eventually becomes the paradigm of humility, able to hear several foolish questions late on a Friday afternoon without feeling that his honor has been affronted (see above, p. 116). The gemara wants us to know that Hillel did not begin his career as a perfectly humble individual. On the contrary, he displayed gratuitous arrogance during his first week on the job. However, the ease with which he admitted his lapse in knowledge and the good-natured way he turned to communal practice for guidance foreshadowed the great strides he would subsequently make in this area.

In an important letter, R. Yizhak Hutner (*Pahad Yizhak Iggerot*, p. 217) faults us for talking about the great sages only at the height of their achievement, ignoring the struggles they endured in arriving at loftier heights. He writes of one of the saintliest men of the twentieth century:

> Everyone talks about, is amazed by, and places on a pedestal the purity of speech of the Hafetz Hayim *zt"l*. But who knows about the battles, struggles, stumbles, losses, and retreats that the Hafetz Hayim experienced along the path of his war with his evil inclination?

R. Hutner explains the educational fallout from our approach. Students who have to struggle to achieve a religious ideal may assume that they have no potential for great achievements, because the models of greatness seem to never have experienced such difficulties. An honest approach, which maintains reverence for the sages but recognized that they were not excellent from birth, would help our students understand that struggle and failure are part of the arduous path to success.

I often think about these ideas when I glance at contemporary rabbinic biographies that rarely mention the difficulties and errors of their heroes, and instead portray them as saintly from the cradle. How different such works are from the portraits of great figures in Tanakh and *Hazal*! These books fail on three levels. On the most basic level, they are simply inaccurate. Second, as R. Hutner argues, they set a standard that gives readers the wrong idea and encourages them to feel excessive negativity about their own shortcomings. Finally, they shortchange the *gedolim* by making greatness a right of birth more than the product of years of arduous work that included the ability to overcome mistakes and failures.

Hillel kicked off his career with great drama, solving a national halakhic problem just before Pesaḥ. The excitement of the moment temporarily bolstered his sense of pride and achievement, and he uttered a condescending remark to those who sought his expertise. However, he soon righted himself and became our enduring model of humility. May we all have similar success in correcting the areas of our religious lives that need improvement.

Do Clothes Make the Halakhic Man?

> R. Ḥiyya Bar Abba and R. Assi were sitting before R. Yoḥanan, and R. Yoḥanan was dozing. R. Ḥiyya said to R. Assi [we now skip the first two questions he raises]: "Why are the *talmidei hakhamim* in Babylonia dressed up? Because they are not *benei Torah*."
>
> (*Shabbat* 145b)

The simplest interpretation of R. Ḥiyya's point is that the scholars in Bavel dress in fine rabbinic garb to cover up their inadequacy as scholars. Rather than doing the arduous work of actually becoming a scholar or a saint, many are tempted to take the easier path to recognition by putting on a long coat or growing a bushy beard. This temptation certainly applies to yeshiva students. It is far easier to feel that we are accomplishing things in yeshiva by putting on a jacket than to actually master the talmudic page or successfully combat our character flaws.

According to this first interpretation, the pronoun "they" in the line "they are not *benei Torah*" refers to the scholars. R. Yisrael Lipshutz, in his *Tiferet Yisrael* (*Avot* 4:6, *Yakhin* 38), points out that if the Babylonian scholars did not know the material, the gemara would not refer to them as *talmidei hakhamim*. He suggests that "they" refers to the general Jewish populace of Bavel. The authentic scholars of Bavel do not receive the recognition that is their due as a result of their scholarship because the people they teach are unable to appreciate the depths of Torah. The scholars are forced to resort to rabbinic garb to obtain respect because this is all that their congregants understand.

If R. Yisrael is correct, R. Hiyya's charge addresses the congregants and not just the scholars. Leaders must exhibit true rabbinic greatness and not just a rabbinic wardrobe. At the same time, the people have a responsibility to learn to appreciate true excellence. While it would be unrealistic to expect every doctor and carpenter in the community to become a scholar, we can ask them to learn enough to differentiate the true man of knowledge and counsel from the phony.

It would be wrong to say that clothes are irrelevant. Dignified clothing can express honor for an endeavor, and certain types of clothing can express identification with a community. At the same time, we must remember that dress pales in comparison with learning and character. We should always prioritize the more difficult attempt to reform the person inside the clothes.

The Ethics of a Monarch

> [A prayer] of David…Guard my soul, for I am virtuous (Tehillim 86:1–2). Levi and R. Yizhak [explained this verse]. One said: "This is what David said before the Holy One, blessed be He: 'Master of the universe, am I not virtuous? All the kings of the East and the West sleep until the third hour of the morning, but I rise at midnight to praise you (Tehillim 119:62).'" The other [sage] says: "This is what David said before the Holy One, blessed be He: 'Master of the universe, am I not virtuous? All the kings of the East and the West have people sitting in groups to honor them, but my hands are dirty with blood, the sac of a fetus and the placenta, to permit a woman to her husband. Not only that, but everything I do is checked with Mefiboshet my master. I say to him: "Mefiboshet, my master, did I judge correctly? Did I condemn correctly? Did I exonerate correctly? Did I purify correctly?" – I was never embarrassed.'"
>
> (Berakhot 4a)

Although David *haMelekh* prides himself on two different accounts in this aggada, it deserves mention that he also showed the capacity to admit when he sinned. His reactions after the sin of the census (*II Shemuel*, chap. 24) and after the sin of Bat Sheva (*Tehillim*, chap. 51) reveal a personality fully capable of admitting fault. Indeed, the very two causes of pride in this story indicate a basic humility often missing in royalty.

What specific virtues does David exhibit in this gemara? His early rising exemplifies great diligence, and his willingness to confront practical halakhic questions shows that he was learned in Torah and employed his knowledge to help others.

Rav Yehiel Yaakov Weinberg (in *LiFrakim*, pp. 394–396) maintains that the entire gemara testifies to David's sterling humility. As Rav Weinberg explains, the other kings, who rise late, might not do so solely out of laziness; indeed, they could argue that the responsibilities of their office place quite a heavy burden upon them, and therefore they need more rest. After a late-night emergency security meeting, who could fault the monarch for rising later than the farmers and shoemakers? Perhaps the delayed start of a monarch's day can be justified. Yet David does not rely upon this reasonable argument, because it divides too sharply between the king and the commoner. He refuses to see his own work as more important than the work of others, and he insists on rising at the normal time. Thus, the first interpretation of David's virtue focuses on his humility.

R. Avraham Yizhak Kook (*Ein Aya*) adds a wrinkle to this idea. He posits that a leader cannot tire himself out with activities that will prevent the fulfillment of his communal responsibilities; therefore, David should not get up early if it would leave him too exhausted to function during the day. However, the degree to which someone finds a given activity tiring often depends upon his attitude toward that activity. If David had not enjoyed his midnight prayers, his schedule would have exhausted him; since David, serving God out of love, found this early endeavor exhilarating, he had enough energy in reserve for a long day of work.

Thus this gemara is also telling us something about the great poet of the Psalms and his enthusiasm for prayer.

According to R. Weinberg, the second interpretation of David's virtue also indicates his humility. Kings must address national issues on a very broad scale. Issues relating to the nation's physical security, economic stability, social cohesiveness, and the like dominate their daily routine. David was no exception. The biblical account has him pursuing military campaigns, and *Hazal* (*Berakhot* 3a) add a focus on economic questions. Our gemara conveys this emphasis on collective national life when it mentions the groups of people who customarily honor a king.

However, those who tackle the big picture are liable to forget the plight of ordinary people and the individuals. They view themselves as dealing only with the most important issues of state. This attitude, while understandable, often leads to a dulling of their moral sensibilities as well as an indifference to the plight of individuals. However, in this aggada, David's humility prevents him from falling into this trap, and he continues to address personal halakhic problems. The same king who preserves the national security is not above taking time to foster family purity. This idea instructs us about humility and reminds the grand visionaries among us not to let their broader focus blind them to the needs of each particular human being.

R. Weinberg adds an insightful note. Apparently Jewish women were not embarrassed to approach the king with their most intimate questions. If the monarch had insisted on always emphasizing the distance between himself and the masses, it is hard to imagine that women would feel comfortable asking him such questions. It must be that David's humility generated an atmosphere in which it seemed normal to ask him for help with the laws of *nidda*.

R. Henokh Zundel of Salant adds two interesting points in *Ez Yosef*. He points out that according to Jewish law, a king is not allowed to remain indifferent to his own honor. The need to demonstrate respect for the office of the monarchy makes it problematic for a king to engage in degrading behavior. What allows David, in this aggada, to get his hands dirty with the messier aspects of Halakha? It must be that our gemara does not consider this behavior degrading. A king should not dirty himself for mundane human purposes, but he certainly can for heavenly reasons. Such efforts honor the monarchy rather than degrade it.

He also notes that David's motivation is "to permit a woman to her husband." It seems, in the aggada, that other rabbinic voices had been content to be stringent in these scenarios, which do not lend themselves to halakhic clarity. David, on the other hand, takes steps to try and see if he can render a lenient verdict. This too reveals his royal compassion and indicates that Halakha is not simply content with stringency every time a difficult question arises.

At this point, the reader might still argue that David shows a bit of haughtiness in his bold halakhic rulings. However, the conclusion of the gemara indicates otherwise. This mighty king feels responsible to check the correctness of each ruling with his teacher. To convey how unusual this is, R. Weinberg tells a story about Emperor Nero (the source of the story is either Suetonius, *Lives of the Caesars*, book 6, or Tacitus, *Annals* 16:4). Nero was a man of diverse talents but had a poor singing voice; nevertheless, precisely for this reason, he wanted to hear lavish praise for his singing. Despite his awareness of the truth, he wanted his courtiers to praise him for the beauty of the vocal music he offered. This made him much happier than the praise for genuine talent.

This tale reflects the norm in royal arrogance. Our gemara, on the other hand, shows us that David is not interested in stressing his greatness and divorcing himself from the common man. In his midnight routine, in his helping ordinary individuals, and in his confirming rulings with his teacher, we see the traits of a truly humble king.

Leadership and Making a Living

> Rabban Gamliel and R. Yehoshua were traveling on a boat. R. Gamliel had brought bread along, while R. Yehoshua had brought both bread and flour along. R. Gamliel's bread ran out, and they relied upon R. Yehoshua's flour.
>
> [R. Gamliel] said to [R. Yehoshua]: "Did you know that the trip would be so delayed, that you brought flour?"
>
> He said to him: "There is one star that rises every seventy years and confuses the sailors. I thought perhaps it would rise and confuse us."
>
> He said to him: "You have so much in your hand [i.e., you know so much], and yet you are sailing on this boat?"
>
> He said to him: "Instead of wondering about me, wonder about your two students on dry land, R. Elazar ben Hisma and R. Yohanan ben Gudgada, who know how to estimate the number of drops in the ocean, and yet they do not have bread to eat or clothes to wear."
>
> [R. Gamliel] decided to appoint them to the top. When he came ashore, he sent for them and they did not come. He sent for them again, and they came.
>
> He said: "You think that I am offering you a position of authority? I am offering you servitude, as it says: *If you will be a servant for this people today* (1 *Melakhim* 12:7)."
>
> (*Horayot* 10a)

What surprises R. Gamliel about R. Yehoshua's presence on the boat? Rashi explains that having seen R. Yehoshua's wide-ranging knowledge, R. Gamliel is surprised that the latter has to struggle to make a living and needs to go on a sea journey. R. Yehoshua points out in response that plenty of intelligent people find it difficult to make a living. He tells R. Gamliel to consider his two outstanding students living in poverty.

On meeting wealthy people, we often find that they do not strike us as brilliant thinkers who would shine in a Talmud or physics class. We are struck by the apparent disparity between their material success and their level of intelligence. Referring to such cases, my grandfather recited an old proverb: "Hashem gave this person a lot of money because he would not otherwise be able to support his family." Of course, the paradox is to some extent resolved when we recall that there are different types of brainpower, and business acumen may be quite different from academic excellence.

Tosafot haRosh cites Ramma, who rejects Rashi's interpretation on the grounds that R. Gamliel surely understands that smart people are not always wealthy. According to Ramma, R. Gamliel wonders how someone who knows so much about the difficulties faced by sailors could undertake a dangerous voyage. As R. Yissakhar Eilenberg points out in his *Be'er Sheva*, Ramma's interpretation makes it hard to understand R. Yehoshua's rejoinder. The two brilliant students had not undertaken a sea voyage, so how are they relevant to R. Gamliel's question? Perhaps R. Yehoshua informs R. Gamliel that making a living is not simple; it forces people to take on certain risks that they might otherwise have avoided. The two excellent students may have chosen to stay safe and secure on dry land, but they are unable to put bread on the table. R. Yehoshua may have undertaken certain risks, but they enable him to support his family.

It is impossible not to link this dialogue with a parallel conversation between the same two figures in *Berakhot* 28a. There, the wealthy patriarch R. Gamliel visits R. Yehoshua's house and is amazed to discover that the walls are blackened (R. Yehoshua was a smith). R. Yehoshua chides R. Gamliel for being a leader who does not understand how ordinary people live. This gemara may also illustrate the need for rich and aristocratic leaders to appreciate the difficulties many face in eking out a living.

Both interpretations assume that the question has to do with R. Yehoshua's wisdom. R. Yizhak of Karlin (in his *Keren Ora*), however, understands it as pertaining to his righteousness. R. Yehoshua's response to the question indicates that material success and *zidkut* do not perfectly overlap in this world. We should not automatically identify the rich with the righteous, and we should not blithely assume that a real *zaddik* would have no trouble making a living.

Various sages in this gemara exhibit broad knowledge of science and mathematics in respect to such matters as the patterns of the stars and the amount of water in the ocean. R. Yisrael Lipshutz (*Tiferet Yisrael, Avot* 3:18) notes that it is the same R. Elazar ben Hisma who says, "Astronomy and geometry are auxiliaries to wisdom" (*Avot* 3:18). These are examples of talmudic sages who value a broad range of intellectual pursuits even as they view Torah as their essential field of study.

Upon hearing about the plight of his two talented students, R. Gamliel decides to offer them a job that would relieve their financial stress. Ramma (cited in Tosafot haRosh) says that he wants to make them *roshei yeshiva*. As an aside, I would call the reader's attention to the discussion of this point in R. Eilenberg's *Be'er Sheva*, where he cites sources that suggest that Rambam was wrong to prohibit taking money for service in a rabbinic position. R. Elazar and R. Yohanan initially do not respond to the summons of R. Gamliel because they do not want the job. R. Gamliel understands, apparently correctly, that they are reluctant to take a job in which they would exercise authority. Perhaps they see themselves as unfit for such an illustrious job, or else they fear the honor that goes with the title.

R. Gamliel assures them that Jewish communal work does not mean a life of power and honor. Rather, it means a life of servitude and responsibility. Therefore, those nervous about the dangers of power and honor can still enter this profession. Presumably, R. Gamliel makes both a descriptive and a prescriptive point. First, rabbinic leaders receive more criticism than honor, and entering this field for the *kavod* seems like a misplaced hope. More important, R. Gamliel instructs them to enter the field for the right reasons; then they will discover that more servitude than authority awaits them.

R. Naftali Zvi Yehuda Berlin (in his *Meromei Sadeh*) states that even idealistic people in leadership positions must sometimes exert their authority to punish rebels or to maintain the honor of their position. It is this occasional need for authority and honor that initially deters R. Elazar and R. Yohanan. R. Gamliel tells them that even these situations can be faced without a focus on personal aggrandizement. Neziv differentiates between leaders interested in personal glory and those trying to preserve the honor of Torah based on the language they employ. I would add that communal leaders must be wary of using the language of *kevod haTorah* even as they actually think about their personal status.

This gemara appears in the appropriate tractate, because *Horayot* deals with scenarios in which Jewish leaders made mistakes. Minimizing such mistakes and having the ability to admit them depends on leaders who appreciate the struggles of average people and serve more out of a sense of duty than a desire for authority and fame.

Leadership, Heroism, and Public Positions

> [Our story begins with R. Yehuda haNassi, known as Rabbi, on his deathbed.] He said to them: "I need the sages of Israel." The sages of Israel entered. He said to them: "Do not eulogize me in the cities, and make a yeshiva after thirty days have passed. Shimon my son will be the *hakham*, Gamliel my son will be the *nasi*, and Hanina bar Hama will sit at the head [of the yeshiva]."
>
> (*Ketuvot* 103a)

> But wasn't there R. Hiyya [who was worthy to become *rosh yeshiva*]? He had already passed away. But didn't R. Hiyya say: "I saw Rabbi's grave and cried upon it"? Reverse the names [it was Rabbi who cried at R. Hiyya's grave]. And didn't R. Hiyya say: "The day that Rabbi died, sanctity was negated"? Reverse the names. And didn't we learn that when Rabbi was [deathly] sick, R. Hiyya came in to visit him and found him crying. He

said: "Rabbi, why are you crying. Did we not learn that if one dies smiling, it is a good sign for him. If one dies crying, it is a bad sign for him."...He [Rabbi] said to him: "I am crying about [the lost opportunity for] Torah and *mizvot*."

If you want, you could reverse the names. If you want, you could say that there is no need to reverse the names. R. Hiyya [who outlived Rabbi] was involved in *mizvot* and Rabbi did not want to stop his work. This as we have learned that when R. Hanina and R. Hiyya were arguing, R. Hanina said: "You are quarreling with me. If, God forbid, Torah was ever forgotten in Israel, I could restore it with my reasoning." R. Hiyya said to him, "I make it so that Torah is not forgotten in Israel because I bring flax and plant it and make nets and trap deer. I feed the meat to orphans, and I make parchment from the deerskin and go to a town that has no teacher of children. I write the five books of *Humash* for five children, and I teach the six orders of Mishna to six children, and I tell each child to teach his part to the others." This is what Rabbi meant when he said: "How great are the deeds of Hiyya."

(*Ketuvot* 103b)

A brief aside before proceeding to the central focus of this gemara. R. Hiyya is surprised that Rabbi would cry while passing away because it is a bad omen. Rabbi tells him that he is crying because his imminent death cancels any opportunity to accomplish more in the realms of Torah and *mizvot*. Rabbi's answer highlights the areas of life that most deserve our attention. Rather than focusing on the possible benefits of *simanim* and *segulot*, we need to devote our energy to acts of intrinsic worth. If our students think that tying a red string around their wrists takes precedence over a good *shiur* or a *hessed* project, we have failed as teachers. Rabbi told R. Hiyya that he was thinking about things that were genuinely important and not about omens.

On his deathbed, Rabbi assigns the various communal leadership positions. Following the path of his ancestors, he himself had acted as both patriarch and *rosh yeshiva*, but he apparently felt that none of his sons was capable or worthy enough to occupy the two posts. R. Yaakov Kamenetsky (*Emet leYaakov* on *Avot*) notes that in *Avot* (2:2), Rabban Gamliel, the son of Rabbi, says: "All those who toil on behalf of the community should toil for the sake of heaven, because the merit of their fathers is aiding them." He explains that this sentiment was particularly crucial in the generation of the speaker. Before this generation, Hillel, R. Gamliel, and the other patriarchs had both directed the learning at the yeshiva and run the political body of the Jewish community. Now that these two jobs had been separated, the danger of the patriarchate turning into a purely secular body, divorced from Torah values, became quite real. R. Gamliel, himself the *nasi*, understood the danger. He reminded himself that his work on behalf of the community demanded the best motives and the humility to realize that only the Torah-excellence of his ancestors had enabled him to become *nasi*.

The gemara apparently thinks that R. Hiyya was the most deserving candidate to head the yeshiva, but Rabbi did not choose him, either because R. Hiyya had already died or because Rabbi did not want to take him away from the important work he was doing. This second answer teaches us that giving official posts to great individuals does not always increase their productivity. Sometimes the weight of office involves them in a world so packed with meetings, fund-raising, and the like that they can no longer teach Torah. I often think that R. Yosef Dov Soloveitchik's refusal of the Israeli Chief Rabbinate in order to remain a *maggid shiur* was a fortunate moment for the Jewish people. Rather than becoming mired in a world of bureaucracy and politics, he continued to teach profound Torah and inspire hundreds of students. While the parallel is imprecise, because the post of *rosh yeshiva* certainly includes teaching Torah, R. Hiyya apparently needed to continue the crucial work he was already engaged in and not be distracted by new titles and responsibilities.

R. Hiyya's crucial work involved teaching children. Clearly, the gemara does not share the common attitude that downplays the significance of elementary school teachers. The denigration of primary school teachers even occurs among educators who teach older students. When I started to have children of elementary school age, I soon discovered that who teaches first grade really does matter. In this story, Rabbi considered R. Hiyya's educating youth more important than his becoming *rosh yeshiva*.

A number of *aharonim* raise a basic question. The closing exchange between R. Hanina and R. Hiyya seems to indicate that R. Hanina was a bigger *talmid hakham* than R. Hiyya. After all, his sheer powers of reasoning could restore the entire Torah. Shouldn't he have been the obvious candidate to head the yeshiva, without any need for special reasons to disqualify R. Hiyya? *Penei Yehoshua* answers that while R. Hanina was superior at analytical reasoning, R. Hiyya knew more material. As a well-known gemara in *Horayot* (14a) states that we prefer the more learned scholar, so, when confronted with a choice of candidates, R. Hiyya became the logical selection. Hatam Sofer offers a different explanation in his commentary on *Ketuvot*. He explains that R. Hiyya was not the best choice because of his erudition, but because of his righteousness. Perhaps R. Hanina knew more and analyzed more deeply than R. Hiyya. At the same time, being an exemplary *rosh yeshiva* depends upon much more than intellectual creativity and stores of knowledge. The *rosh yeshiva* must care greatly about his students and about the rest of Am Yisrael. He must exhibit sterling character and serve as a model of moral refinement. Of course, he must be a fine scholar as well. However, the greatest scholar does not always make the greatest *rosh yeshiva*. Therefore, despite R. Hanina's excellent scholarship, R. Hiyya was the logical choice, except for the fact that Rebbe did not want to take him away from the significant work he was already doing.

To fully appreciate R. Hiyya's work, we should mention another frequently asked question. Why did R. Hiyya feel the need to plant the flax, make the nets, and trap the animals himself? Surely, he could have bought the meat from the butcher and the parchment from the local scribe. Maharsha (commentary on *Bava*

Mezia 85b) explains that he wanted every part of the endeavor to be done for the sake of heaven. In a sense, he wanted to sanctify the nets used for trapping as if they too were ritual objects. We might suggest an alternative explanation. Perhaps the gemara wants to remind us that important work frequently requires more than the actual teaching of Torah. Sometimes, it demands putting major energy into the less glorious task of obtaining food for the students. While a teacher must avoid distractions that might interfere with his teaching of Torah, the teacher must also realize that some aspects of the job require action outside the classroom.

The most powerful note in this *aggada* may emerge from the different conceptions of heroism expressed by R. Hanina and R. Hiyya. The former says that in a crisis of learning, he could save the day and restore the lost Torah. We often think of heroism as books and movies portray it: the hero who enters the fray when everything has fallen apart and proceeds to defuse the crisis. Yet R. Hiyya understands a more profound type of heroism. With laborious effort, clever planning, and an indifference to the limelight, R. Hiyya prevents the crisis from ever occurring. This reflects authentic greatness. A person who persuades others to wear seat belts may save more lives than an emergency medical technician even though the EMT more easily inspires an exciting movie. Lacking the acclaim of public office or the popular recognition that comes from extinguishing a fire, R. Hiyya quietly went from town to town, teaching children and preventing the Torah from becoming lost.

CHAPTER 15

Conclusion

The One Hundred and First Time

Bar He He said to Hillel: "What is the meaning of the verse *And you will return and discern the difference between the righteous and the wicked, between a person who serves God and a person who does not serve Him* (*Malakhi* 3:18)? The *righteous* is the same as those who *serve God*? The *wicked* is the same as those who *do not serve Him*?"

He said to him: "The person who served God and the person who did not serve God are both wholly righteous. One cannot compare the person who studies the material one hundred times with the person who reviews the material one hundred and one times."

He said to him: "And for one time [less], he is referred to as a person who does not serve Him?"

He said to him: "Go and learn from the market of donkey drivers. Hiring a donkey for ten Persian miles costs a *zuz*, while hiring the same for eleven Persian miles costs two *zuz*."

(*Hagiga* 9b)

Reviewing the material one hundred times seems quite responsible. If so, what makes the student who reviews the material one additional time so superior? Some commentators assume that this student is trying to memorize the material, and the extra review session is crucial to fix it in memory.

R. Naftali Zvi Yehuda Berlin (*Meromei Sadeh*) suggests that both students have reviewed the material with sufficient diligence to remember it. One hundred readings would be quite enough for most minds to remember what was read. It is pure love of the material that motivates the one hundred and first reading, not a desire to remember. From this perspective, we can easily understand the significance of the extra reading. We can return to texts we love almost endlessly. *Yeshayahu* 56 inspires me on the afternoon of every fast-day. I enjoy my every reading of Tennyson's *Ulysses* or Yeats's *Easter 1916*. In the same way, the student who studies a section of Torah already committed to memory reveals true love for Torah.

R. Berlin assumes that the student does not study the material one more time for concrete educational gain but only as an expression of love. Earlier, we mentioned an interpretation that the extra time aids memorization. Further study often yields a third benefit as well. Every reading of the richest texts allows for deepening understanding. Perhaps the flash of insight or the illumination of authentic comprehension will only occur on the one hundred and first reading. The dedicated student who finds the time for one more reading comes to truly understand the text in the most nuanced way.

All three themes, but especially the last two, should apply acutely to our learning of the aggadot in this book. Some of the stories, such as R. Shimon bar Yohai in the cave or the prospective converts that come to Hillel, are familiar to us from childhood. Others are less familiar. Either way, all of these stories and maxims merit repeated and serious study. When love of the material inspires us to look them over again and again, the repeated readings will invariably generate new interpretations and fresh insights. The one hundred and first reading beckons.

CHAPTER 16

Rabbinic Biographies

T he following list does not cover every rabbi mentioned in this
work but only those rabbinic figures who devoted intensive
effort to aggadic commentary. The *Encyclopaedia Judaica* was
helpful in compiling the information provided here.

Al-Hakam, R. Yosef Hayyim (1835–1909) was a rav in Baghdad.
He penned the halakhic work *Ben Ish Hai*, a volume of responsa
Rav Pe'alim and a commentary on Aggada entitled *Ben Yehoyada*.

Edels, R. Shemuel (1555–1631), known as Maharsha, was a rabbi in
Chelm, Lublin, and Ostrog. He initially penned separate commentaries on the halakhic and aggadic sections of the Talmud but later,
in his introduction, recommended a more integrated approach.

Ibn Habib, R. Yaakov (ca. 1445–1515/16) was a rabbi in Salonika.
He is most famous for collecting all the Talmud's aggadot with
commentary in his *Ein Yaakov*. His own ideas appear under the
heading *HaKotev*. R. Levi Ibn Habib, his son, completed the work.

R. Hanokh Zundel from Salant (d. 1867) lived in Bialystok. He wrote commentaries on midrash and aggada entitled *Ez Yosef* and *Anaf Yosef*. The commentaries are so named because his father's name was Yosef.

Kook, R. Avraham Yizhak (1865–1935) was the first Ashkenazi chief rabbi of modern Israel and a writer of very wide range. His *Ein Aya* provides aggadic commentary on the tractates *Berakhot* and *Shabbat*. Additional aggadic commentary on the notoriously difficult aggadot in *Bava Batra* appears in his *Ma'amarei haRa'ayah*.

Pinto, R. Yoshiyahu (1565–1648) was a rav in Damascus. His commentary on aggadot entitled *Me'or Eynayim* appears in *Ein Yaakov*.

Loew, R. Yehuda (1525–1609), known as Maharal, was a rav in Prague. A prolific writer, he authored two works of particular significance for aggadic study. His *Hiddushei Aggadot* is a running commentary on the nonlegal sections of the Talmud. His *Be'er haGolah* defends *Hazal* against various critiques and addresses many aggadot.

Reisher, R. Yaakov (ca. 1670–1733) was a rav in Prague, Ansbach, and Worms. His responsa are entitled *Shvut Yaakov*, and his commentary on aggadot, *Iyyun Yaakov*, appears in the *Ein Yaakov*.

Weinberg, R. Yehiel Yaakov (1885–1966) was the rector of the rabbinical seminary in Berlin before World War II and a rav in Montreux after the war. His responsa are entitled *Seridei Eish*; his work on Jewish thought, *LiFrakim*, contains a significant section of aggadic commentary.

BIBLIOGRAPHY

T his bibliography only lists works referenced by page number in this volume. It does not include commentaries on the Tanakh or Talmud, as these can be located in any edition by looking at the biblical verse or talmudic page in question. The page number citations for *Derashot haRan* are to Leon Feldman's edition (Jerusalem: Shalem Institute, 1973). The citations of Ramban's *Sha'ar haGemul* are to page numbers in Hayyim Chavel's edition of *Kitvei haRamban* (Jerusalem: Mossad Harav Kook, 5764). Citations of Abravanel's *Perush al haTorah* refer to the Jerusalem 5744 edition published by Hapoel Hamizrachi.

Agus, Aharon. *The Binding of Isaac and Messiah: Law, Martyrdom and Deliverance in Early Rabbinic Religiosity*. Albany, N.Y.: SUNY Press, 1988.

Berkovits, Eliezer. *Crisis and Faith*. New York: Sanhedrin Press, 1976.

Berlin, Isaiah. *Four Essays on Liberty*. Oxford: Oxford University Press, 1969.

Blau, Yitzchak. "Aggada and *Aharonim*." *Hamevaser* 1:3 (Nov. 6, 2007).

———. "Redeeming the *Aggadah* in *Yeshivah* Education." In *Wisdom From All My Teachers*, ed. Jeffrey Saks and Susan Handelman. Jerusalem: Urim Publications, 2003.

Blum, Lawrence. *Friendship, Altruism and Morality*. London: Routledge & Kegan Paul, 1980.

Butler, Samuel. *Erewhon*. Middlesex: Penguin Books, 1970.

Carlyle, Thomas. *Sartor Resartus*. Oxford: Oxford University Press, 1987.

Carmy, Shalom. "Rejoinder: Synthesis and the Unification of Human Existence." *Tradition* 21:4 (Fall 1985).

Chesterton, G.K. *Orthodoxy*. New York: Doubleday, 1990.

Elman, Yaakov. "The Contribution of Rabbinic Thought to a Theology of Misfortune." In *Jewish Perspectives on the Experience of Suffering*, ed. Shalom Carmy. Northvale, N.J.: Jason Aronson, 1999.

Frankel, Yonah. *Iyyunim beOlamo haRuhani shel Sippur haTalmudi*. Tel Aviv: Hakibbutz Hameuchad, 1981.

———. *Sippur haAggada – Ahdut Shel Tohen veZurah*. Tel Aviv: Hakibbutz Hameuchad, 2001.

Gide, André. In *The God That Failed*, ed. Richard Crossman. New York: Bantam Books, 1952.

Hick, John. *Evil and the God of Love*. San Francisco: HarperCollins, 1977.

Hutner, R. Yizhak. *Iggerot uKetavim*. New York: Gur Aryeh Institute, 1998.

Kaufmann, Walter. *Critique of Philosophy and Religion*. Garden City, N.Y.: Doubleday, 1961.

Kierkegaard, Søren. *The Attack Upon Christendom*. Princeton: Princeton University Press, 1944.

———. *Concluding Unscientific Postscript*. Trans. David Swenson and Walter Lowrie. Princeton: Princeton University Press, 1974.

————. *Either/Or*, vol. 1. Trans. David F. Swenson and Lillian Marvin Swenson. Princeton: Princeton University Press, 1944.

Kook, R. Avraham Yizhak haKohen. *Arpilei Tohar*. Jerusalem: HaMahon al Shem Harav Zvi Yehuda haKohen Kook, 5743.

————. *Orot haKodesh*. Jerusalem: Mossad Harav Kook, 1985.

Lamm, Norman. *Faith and Doubt: Studies in Traditional Jewish Thought*. Jersey City, N.J.: Ktav Publishing House, 2006.

Lewis, C.S. *The Four Loves*. San Diego: Harcourt, Brace, 1960.

Mill, John Stuart. *Mill on Bentham and Coleridge*. With an introduction by F.R. Leavis. London: Chatto & Windus, 1959.

Rakeffet-Rothkoff, Aaron. *The Rav: The World of Rabbi Joseph B. Soloveitchik*. Hoboken, N.J.: Ktav, 1999.

Rubenstein, Jeffrey. *Talmudic Stories: Narrative Art and Composition*. Baltimore: Johns Hopkins University Press, 1999.

Shatz, David. "The Integration of Torah and Culture: Its Scope and Limits in the Thought of Rav Kook." In *Hazon Nahum: Studies in Jewish Law, Thought, and History Presented to Dr. Norman Lamm on the Occasion of His Seventieth Birthday*, ed. Yaakov Elman and Jeffrey Gurock. New York: Yeshiva University Press, 1997.

————. "Rav Kook and Modern Orthodoxy: The Ambiguities of 'Openness.'" In *Engaging Modernity: Rabbinic Leaders and the Challenge of the Twentieth Century*, ed. Moshe Z. Sokol. Northvale, N.J.: Jason Aronson, 1997.

Soloveitchik, R. Joseph B. *The Lonely Man of Faith*. New York: Doubleday, 1992.

————. "Majesty and Humility." *Tradition* 17:2 (Spring 1978).

————. *Shiurei HaRav: A Conspectus of the Public Lectures of Rabbi Joseph B. Soloveitchik*. ed. Joseph Epstein. Hoboken, N.J.: Ktav, 1994.

Taylor, Charles. "The Politics of Recognition." In *Multiculturalism and the Politics of Recognition*, ed. Amy Gutman. Princeton: Princeton University Press, 1992.

Weinberg, R. Yehiel Yaakov. *LiFrakim*. Jerusalem, 2002.

Index of Biblical and Rabbinic Sources

Index of Names

Subject Index